Azure Data Factory by Example

Practical Implementation for Data Engineers

Second Edition

Richard Swinbank

Apress®

Azure Data Factory by Example: Practical Implementation for Data Engineers, Second Edition

Richard Swinbank
Tewkesbury, UK

ISBN-13 (pbk): 979-8-8688-0217-1   ISBN-13 (electronic): 979-8-8688-0218-8
https://doi.org/10.1007/979-8-8688-0218-8

Managing Director, Apress Media LLC: Welmoed Spahr
Acquisitions Editor: Smriti Srivastava
Development Editor: Laura Berendson
Coordinating Editor: Jessica Vakili

Cover designed by eStudioCalamar

Cover image by Freepik (www.freepik.com)

Distributed to the book trade worldwide by Apress Media, LLC, 1 New York Plaza, New York, NY 10004, U.S.A. Phone 1-800-SPRINGER, fax (201) 348-4505, e-mail orders-ny@springer-sbm.com, or visit www.springeronline.com. Apress Media, LLC is a California LLC and the sole member (owner) is Springer Science + Business Media Finance Inc (SSBM Finance Inc). SSBM Finance Inc is a **Delaware** corporation.

For information on translations, please e-mail booktranslations@springernature.com; for reprint, paperback, or audio rights, please e-mail bookpermissions@springernature.com.

Apress titles may be purchased in bulk for academic, corporate, or promotional use. eBook versions and licenses are also available for most titles. For more information, reference our Print and eBook Bulk Sales web page at http://www.apress.com/bulk-sales.

Any source code or other supplementary material referenced by the author in this book is available to readers on GitHub (https://github.com/Apress/Azure-Data-Factory-by-Example-Second-Edition). For more detailed information, please visit https://www.apress.com/gp/services/source-code.

Paper in this product is recyclable

To Catherine, thank you for everything.

Table of Contents

About the Author

Richard Swinbank is a data engineer and Microsoft Data Platform MVP. He specializes in building and automating analytics platforms using Microsoft technologies from the SQL Server stack to the Azure cloud. He is a fervent advocate of DataOps, with a technical focus on bringing automation to both analytics development and operations. An active member of the data community and keen knowledge-sharer, Richard is a volunteer, organizer, speaker, blogger, open source contributor, and author. He holds a PhD in computer science from the University of Birmingham, UK.

About the Technical Reviewer

Kasam Shaikh is a prominent figure in India's artificial intelligence landscape, holding the distinction of being one of India's first four Microsoft Most Valuable Professionals (MVPs) in AI. Currently serving as a Senior Architect at Capgemini, Kasam boasts an impressive track record as an author, having authored five best-selling books dedicated to Azure and AI technologies. Beyond his writing endeavors, Kasam is recognized as a Microsoft Certified Trainer (MCT) and influential tech YouTuber (@mekasamshaikh). He also leads the largest online Azure AI community, known as DearAzure | Azure INDIA, and is a globally renowned AI speaker. His commitment to knowledge sharing extends to contributions to Microsoft Learn, where he plays a pivotal role.

Within the realm of AI, Kasam is a respected subject matter expert (SME) in generative AI for the cloud, complementing his role as a senior cloud architect. He actively promotes the adoption of No Code and Azure OpenAI solutions and possesses a strong foundation in hybrid and cross-cloud practices. Kasam's versatility and expertise make him an invaluable asset in the rapidly evolving landscape of technology, contributing significantly to the advancement of Azure and AI.

Kasam was recently awarded as top voice in AI by LinkedIn, making him the sole exclusive Indian professional acknowledged by both Microsoft and LinkedIn for his contributions to the world of artificial intelligence.

Kasam Shaikh is a multifaceted professional who excels in both technical expertise and knowledge dissemination. His contributions span writing, training, community leadership, public speaking, and architecture, establishing him as a true luminary in the world of Azure and AI.

Acknowledgments

While this book is about one specific service – Azure Data Factory – it is the product of years of experience working as a data engineer. I am enormously grateful to the many colleagues, past and present, from whom I continue to learn every day. I'm indebted to the wider Microsoft data platform community, a group of engaged, generous people who are unstinting in their advice and support for others working in this space.

Innumerable technical conversations with Paul Andrew made the first edition of this book many times better than it could otherwise have been, and his influence pervades this updated version. Paul is a real expert in this technology, and I continue to be fortunate to have benefited from his advice. I'm grateful to Kasam Shaikh, technical reviewer for this edition, for providing an indispensable second pair of eyes over the text. Thanks also to the editorial team at Apress – Smriti Srivastava, Nirmal Selvaraj, Mark Powers, and others, without whom this book would not have been possible.

Finally, to Catherine, whose patient encouragement accompanies my every endeavor – thank you so very much.

Introduction

Azure Data Factory (ADF) is Microsoft's cloud-based ETL service for scale-out serverless data movement, integration, and transformation. The earliest version of the service went into public preview in 2014 and was superseded by version 2 in 2018. After support for version 1 of ADF was discontinued at the end of August 2023, ADF V2 remains the only version of the service available – it is on that version that this book is exclusively focused.

From the outset, a major strength of ADF has been its ability to interface with many types of data source and to orchestrate data movement between them. Data transformation was at first delegated to external compute services such as HDInsight and Stream Analytics, but with the introduction of Mapping Data Flows in 2019 (now simply "Data Flows"), it became possible to implement advanced data transformation activities natively in ADF.

ADF can interact with 100 or more types of external service. The majority of these are data storage services – databases, file systems, and so on – but the list of supported compute environments has also grown over time and now includes Azure Databricks, Azure Synapse Analytics, and Azure Machine Learning, among others. The object of this book is not to give you the grand tour of all of these services, each of which has its own complexities and many of which you may never use. Instead, it focuses on the rich capabilities that ADF offers to integrate data from these many sources and to transform it natively.

Services in Microsoft Azure evolve rapidly, with new features emerging with every month that passes. Inevitably, you will find places in which user experiences – such as Azure Data Factory Studio or the Azure portal – differ from the screenshots and descriptions presented here, but the core concepts remain the same. The conceptual understanding that you gain from this book will enable you confidently to expand your knowledge of ADF, in step with the evolution of the service.

Since the first edition of this book, pipelines in the style introduced by ADF have appeared in two newer Microsoft products – first in Azure Synapse Analytics, then in Microsoft Fabric. Many of the concepts and tools described in this book are transferable to Synapse, Fabric, or both. At the time of writing, ADF remains the most mature implementation of data integration pipelines, and a firm background in ADF will provide you with a solid foundation for pipeline creation in either of the two newer services. Chapter 13 provides a brief comparison of pipeline implementation in ADF compared to that in Azure Synapse Analytics or Microsoft Fabric.

About You

The book is designed with the working data engineer in mind. It assumes no prior knowledge of Azure Data Factory so is suited to both new data engineers and seasoned professionals new to the ADF service. A basic working knowledge of T-SQL is expected.

If you have a background in SQL Server Integration Services (SSIS), you will find that ADF contains many familiar concepts. The "For SSIS developers" notes inserted at various points in the text are to help you to leverage your existing knowledge, or to indicate where you should be aware of differences from SSIS.

How to Use This Book

The book uses a series of tutorials to get you using ADF right away, introducing and reinforcing concepts naturally as you encounter them. To undertake exercises, you will need access to an Azure subscription and a web browser supported by ADF Studio – browsers supported currently are Microsoft Edge and Google Chrome. Choose a subscription in which you have sufficient permissions to create and manage the various Azure resources you will be using. Chapter 1 includes the creation of a free Azure trial subscription, ensuring that you have the necessary access. A Windows computer is necessary for certain parts of Chapter 8.

Work through the chapters in order, as later chapters rely on both knowledge and ADF resources developed in earlier chapters. When directed to give a resource a specific name, do so, because that name may later be used to refer back to the resource. References to labels in user interface components, for example, field names or page titles, are given in italics. Input values, for example, for text box input or radio button selection, are given in quotes – when you are asked to enter a value given in quotes, do not include the quote characters unless you are directed to do so.

CHAPTER 1

Creating an Azure Data Factory Instance

A major responsibility of the data engineer is the development and management of *extract, transform, and load* (ETL) and other data integration workloads. Real-time integration workloads process data as it is generated – for example, a transaction being recorded at a point-of-sale terminal or a sensor measuring the temperature in a data center. In contrast, *batch* integration workloads run at intervals, usually processing data produced since the previous batch run.

Azure Data Factory (ADF) is Microsoft's cloud-native service for managing batch data integration workloads. ADF is an example of a *serverless* cloud service – you use it to create your own ETL applications, but you don't have to worry about infrastructure like operating systems or servers or how to manage changes in demand. Access to the service is achieved by means of a data factory *instance* (often simply called "a data factory"). The majority of this book is concerned with the authoring and management of ADF *pipelines* – data integration workload units written and executed in an ADF instance.

In order to create pipelines, you need first to have access to an ADF instance. In this chapter, you will create a new ADF instance, ready to start building pipelines in Chapter 2. To get started, you will need nothing more than an Internet connection and either the Microsoft Edge or Google Chrome web browser.

Note You may be using variations on ETL like *extract, load, and transform* (ELT) or *extract, load, transform, and load* (ELTL). ADF can be used in any of these data integration scenarios, and I use the term "ETL" loosely to describe any of them.

© Richard Swinbank 2024
R. Swinbank, *Azure Data Factory by Example*, https://doi.org/10.1007/979-8-8688-0218-8_1

Get Started in Azure

To access cloud services in Microsoft Azure, you need a Microsoft account and an Azure *subscription*. My goal is to get you up and running at zero cost – in the following sections, I step through the creation of a free Azure trial subscription that you will be able to use throughout this book, then introduce the Azure portal to interact with it. Azure Data Factory Studio (introduced later in the chapter) is only supported in Microsoft Edge or Google Chrome, so you will need to use one of those two web browsers. If you don't already have a Microsoft account, you can create one at `https://signup.live.com/`.

Create a Free Azure Account

Many of the exercises in the book require elevated access permissions in Azure. You may choose to skip this section if you already have an Azure subscription that you would prefer to use, but make sure that it grants you sufficient access to create and modify resources.

1. In your chosen web browser, go to `https://azure.microsoft.com`. Click the *Free account* button in the top right.

2. On the following page, click *Start free*. If you aren't already logged in, you will be prompted to sign into a Microsoft acount.

3. Follow the two-page process to set up your account. During the account setup, you will be required to provide billing information, but your credit card will not be charged unless you upgrade to a paying subscription.

After successful account creation, a *Go to Azure portal* button is displayed – click it. If you don't see the button, you can browse to the portal directly using its URL: `https://portal.azure.com`. You may be directed to the portal's "Quickstart Center" – if so, select *Home* from the hamburger menu in the top left.

Explore the Azure Portal

The Azure portal is where you manage all your Azure resources. You'll use the portal regularly, so it's a good idea to bookmark this page. The portal home page looks something like Figure 1-1. I say "something like" because you may see different tools, recommendations, links, or other messages from time to time. Three features are always present:

1. In the top left of the home page, you will find a *Create a resource* button ("plus" icon). This option is also available from the portal menu, accessed using the hamburger button in the top left.

2. In the top right, the email address you used to sign in is displayed.

3. Immediately below your email address is your current directory. If you are using a free trial subscription, this will say *DEFAULT DIRECTORY*.

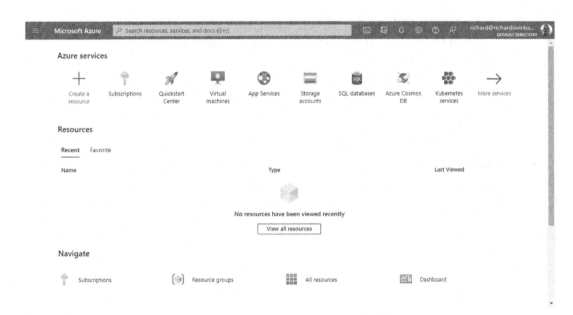

Figure 1-1. *Azure portal home page*

Your directory, commonly called a *tenant*, is an instance of Microsoft Entra ID, formerly known as Azure Active Directory (AAD). "Default Directory" is the default name of a new tenant. If you are already using Azure in your job, you will probably be using a tenant that represents your company or organization – often, all of an organization's Azure resources and users are defined in the same single tenant.

Note   The Azure Active Directory service was renamed Microsoft Entra ID during 2023. You may occasionally find Microsoft services or documentation which make reference to Azure Active Directory, or to AAD – these should be understood to refer to Microsoft Entra ID and will be updated over time.

A tenant contains one or more *subscriptions*. A subscription identifies a means of payment for Azure services – the cost of using any Azure resource is billed to the subscription with which it is associated. An Azure trial subscription includes an amount of time-limited free credit, and if you want to spend more, you can do so by upgrading to a paying subscription. Your organization might have multiple subscriptions, perhaps identifying separate budget holders responsible for paying for different resources.

If you have created a free trial subscription, you can see the amount of credit remaining as follows:

1. Click the *Subscriptions* icon (to the right of the *Create a resource* button in Figure 1-1). If you can't see the icon, use the search bar at the top of the portal.

2. The *Subscriptions* blade is displayed, showing the free trial subscription. Click the link to the subscription (in the *Subscription name* column) to access more detail.

3. After a few moments, a pop-up banner is displayed, indicating the amount of credit remaining. Figure 1-2 shows a newly created subscription in which $200 of credit is available.

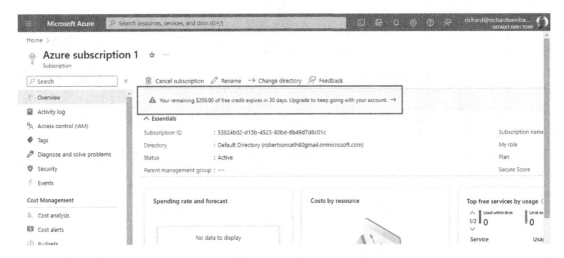

Figure 1-2. *Remaining credit in Azure subscription*

Signing up for a trial Azure subscription creates a number of things, including

- An Azure tenant

- An Azure subscription in the tenant with some time-limited free credit for you to use

- Your Azure user account, with administrator-level Microsoft Entra ID permissions inside the tenant

Create a Resource Group

Instances of Azure services are referred to generally as *resources*. An instance of Azure Data Factory is an example of a resource. Resources belonging to a subscription are organized further into *resource groups*. A resource group is a logical container used to collect together related resources – for example, all the resources that belong to a data warehousing or analytics platform.

Figure 1-3 illustrates the logical grouping of resources in Azure. In this section, you will create a resource group to contain an ADF instance and other resources that will be required in later chapters.

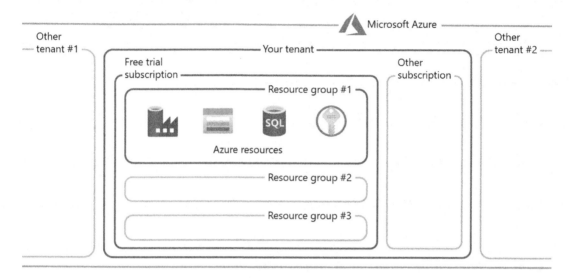

Figure 1-3. *Logical resource grouping in Azure*

1. Click *Create a resource*, using either the button on the portal home page or the menu button in the top left.

2. Resource management pages in the Azure portal are referred to as *blades* – the new resource blade is shown in Figure 1-4. You can browse available services using the *Popular Azure services* icons (filtered using the *Categories* sidebar), or you can use the *Search services and marketplace* function. In the search box, enter "resource group" (without the quotes).

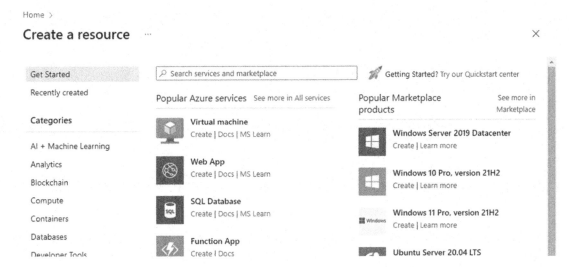

Figure 1-4. *New resource blade*

3. As you type, a filtered dropdown menu will appear. When you see the "resource group" menu item, click it. This takes you to a list of matching resource types available in the Azure marketplace, as shown in Figure 1-5.

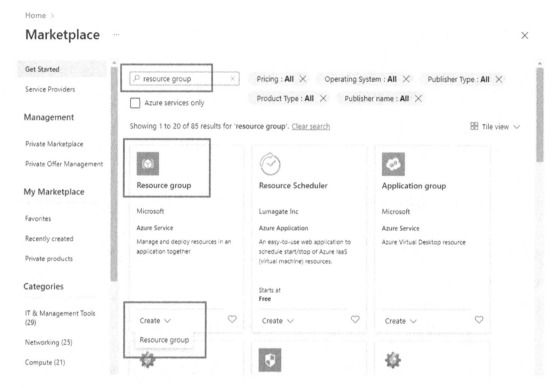

Figure 1-5. *Marketplace search results*

4. Marketplace search results are presented as tiles – click the
    Create dropdown on the *Resource group* tile (also shown in
    Figure 1-5) and select *Resource group* to begin creation of a new
    resource group.

5. Complete the fields on the *Create a resource group* blade, shown
    in Figure 1-6. Ensure that your trial subscription is selected in
    the *Subscription* field, and provide a name for the new resource
    group. I use resource group names ending in "-rg" to make it
    easy to see what kind of Azure resource this is. Choose a *Region*
    geographically close to you – mine is "(Europe) UK South," but
    yours may differ. When you are ready, click *Review + create*.

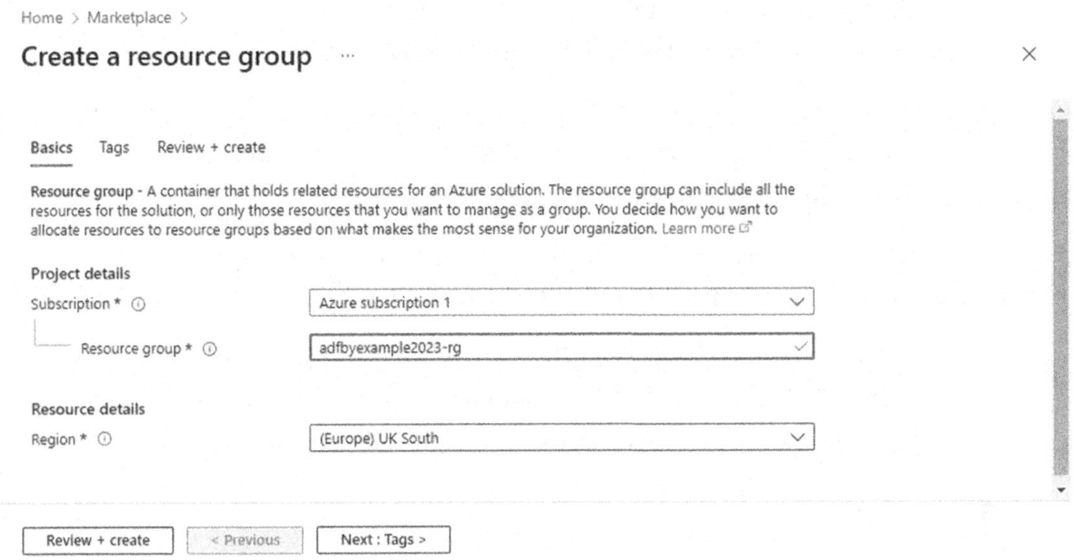

Home > Marketplace >

Create a resource group   ...   ✕

Basics   Tags   Review + create

Resource group - A container that holds related resources for an Azure solution. The resource group can include all the
resources for the solution, or only those resources that you want to manage as a group. You decide how you want to
allocate resources to resource groups based on what makes the most sense for your organization. Learn more ☐

Project details

Subscription * ⓘ | Azure subscription 1   ⌄ |

       ┌── Resource group * ⓘ | adfbyexample2023-rg   ⌄ |

Resource details

Region * ⓘ | (Europe) UK South   ⌄ |

[Review + create]   [< Previous]   [Next : Tags >]

Figure 1-6. *Create a resource group blade*

6. On the *Review + create* tab which follows, check the details you
    have entered, then click *Create*.

Note   You will notice that I have skipped the *Tags* tab. In an enterprise
environment, tags are useful for labeling resources in different ways – for
example, allocating resources to cost centers within a subscription or flagging
development-only resources to enable them to be stopped automatically overnight
and at weekends. I won't be using tags in this book, but your company may use a
resource tagging policy to meet requirements like these.

Create an Azure Data Factory

The resource group you created in the previous section is a container for Azure resources
of any kind. In this section, you will create the group's first new resource – an instance of
Azure Data Factory.

1. Go back to the Azure portal home page and click *Create a resource*, in the same way you did when creating your resource group.

2. In the *Search services and marketplace* box on the *Create a resource* blade, enter "data factory". When "data factory" appears as an item in the dropdown menu, select it.

3. Find the *Data Factory* tile in the marketplace search results, then select *Data Factory* from the tile's *Create* dropdown.

4. The *Basics* tab of the *Create Data Factory* blade is displayed, as shown in Figure 1-7. Select the *Subscription* and *Resource group* you created earlier, then choose the *Region* that is geographically closest to you.

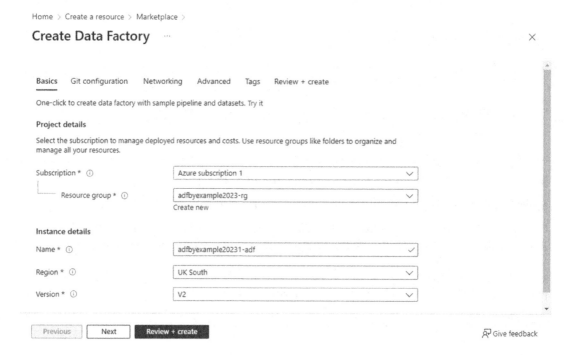

Figure 1-7. *Create Data Factory blade*

5. Choose a *Name* for your ADF instance. Data factory names can only contain alphanumeric characters and hyphens and must be *globally* unique across Azure – your choice of name will not be available if someone else is already using it. I use data factory names ending in "-adf" to make it easy to see what kind of Azure resource this is.

6. *Version* is set automatically to "V2." (It is no longer possible to create instances of ADF V1, and this book is concerned exclusively with Azure Data Factory V2).

7. Click the *Next* button, then on the *Git configuration* tab, ensure that the *Configure Git later* check box is ticked.

8. Finally, click *Review + create*, check the factory settings you provided in steps 4 to 7, then click *Create* to start deployment. (I am purposely bypassing the three remaining tabs – *Networking, Advanced,* and *Tags* – and accepting their default values).

When deployment starts, a new blade containing the message *Deployment is in progress* is displayed. Creation of a new ADF instance usually takes no more than 30 seconds, after which the message *Your deployment is complete* will be displayed, as shown in Figure 1-8. Click *Go to resource* (indicated in the figure) to inspect your new data factory.

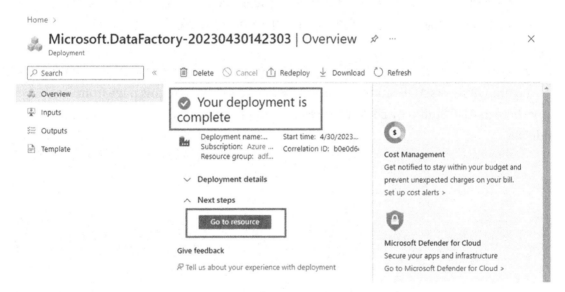

Figure 1-8. *ADF deployment blade*

The portal blade displayed when you click *Go to resource* provides an overview of your data factory instance. It contains access controls and other standard Azure resource tools, along with monitoring information and basic details about the factory – for example, its subscription, resource group, and location.

Beneath the factory's basic details, you will find an *Azure Data Factory Studio* tile. Azure Data Factory Studio (ADF Studio) is a separate development and management tool for data factory resources and is where you will spend most of your time when working with ADF. Click on the tile to launch ADF Studio.

Explore Azure Data Factory Studio

Azure Data Factory Studio provides a low-code *integrated development environment* (IDE) for authoring ADF pipelines, publishing them, then scheduling and monitoring their execution. You'll use ADF Studio frequently, so it's a good idea to bookmark this page.

Note   Azure Data Factory Studio is referred to variously in Microsoft's online documentation as the Azure Data Factory User Experience (ADF UX), Azure Data Factory User Interface (ADF UI), or in more recent documentation as ADF Studio. Each of these names refers to the same tool – nowadays ADF Studio is its preferred name.

Figure 1-9 shows ADF Studio's Home page. You can return to this page from anywhere in ADF Studio by clicking the *Home* button (house icon) in the navigation sidebar.

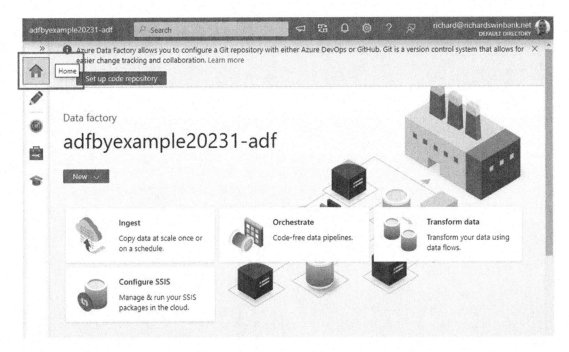

Figure 1-9. *ADF Studio Home page*

An ADF Studio page has three regions:

- A navigation header bar

- An expandable navigation sidebar

- A content pane

The navigation header bar and sidebar are visible at all times, wherever you are in ADF Studio. The content pane displays different things, depending on which part of the IDE you are using – in Figure 1-9, the content pane displays ADF Studio's Home page.

Navigation Header Bar

Figure 1-10 shows ADF Studio with the navigation sidebar expanded and the navigation header bar functions labeled. For clarity, the content pane has been removed from the screenshot.

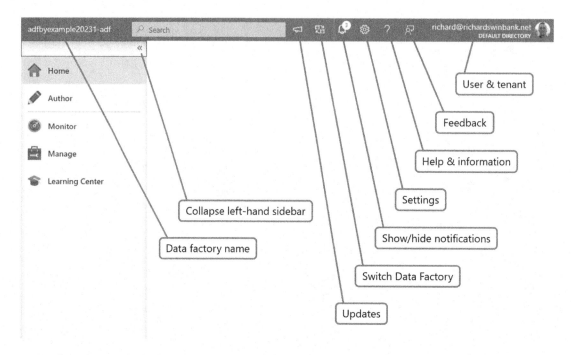

Figure 1-10. *Labeled ADF Studio navigation header bar*

Toward its left-hand end, the navigation header bar indicates the name of the data factory instance to which ADF Studio is connected. At its other end, it identifies the current user and tenant, in the same way as in the Azure portal. Between the two is a row of six buttons:

- **Updates:** Displays recent updates to the Azure Data Factory service. ADF is in constant development and evolution – announcements about changes to the service are made here as they happen.

- **Switch Data Factory:** Enables you to disconnect from the current ADF instance and connect to a different one.

Note   When you opened ADF Studio from the Azure portal data factory blade, it connected automatically to the new factory. In fact, ADF Studio is *always* connected to an ADF instance. If you access it directly (using the URL `https://adf.azure.com/`), you are required to select a data factory before ADF Studio opens.

- **Show notifications:** ADF Studio automatically notifies you of events that occur during your session – this button toggles display of those notifications. The circled "3" in the screenshot indicates that there are currently three unread notifications.

- **Settings:** Allows you to configure preferences for working in ADF Studio, such as the display theme, language, and internationalization. You may also choose to enable *Azure Data Factory Studio preview update*, which gives you preview access to new ADF Studio features as they are developed.

- **Help/information:** Provides links to additional ADF support and information.

- **Feedback:** If you wish to provide Microsoft with feedback about your experience of Azure Data Factory, you can do so here.

Navigation Sidebar

The navigation sidebar provides access to different parts of ADF Studio, changing what is displayed in the content pane. The chevron icon at the top of the sidebar toggles its state between collapsed and expanded – in Figure 1-9, the sidebar is collapsed, while Figure 1-10 shows it expanded.

- The *Home* button (house icon) returns you to the home page. This page contains quick links to common ADF tools and features, along with links to libraries of templates for common ADF tasks. You will use one of the tools here in Chapter 2.

- The *Author* button (pencil icon) loads ADF Studio's authoring canvas. The authoring canvas provides a visual editor for building ADF pipelines. As this book is primarily about authoring pipelines, you will be spending a lot of time here.

- The *Monitor* button (gauge icon) provides access to visual monitoring tools. Here, you are able to see ADF pipeline runs executed in the factory instance and can drill down into execution details. Chapter 12 looks at the monitoring experience in more detail.

- The *Manage* button (toolbox icon) loads the ADF management hub. This includes a variety of features such as connections to external data storage and compute resources, along with the ADF instance's Git configuration, introduced in the next section. You will return to the management hub at various times throughout this book.

- The *Learning Center* button (academic cap icon) links to a collection of learning resources: quick start guides, tutorials, videos, templates, and more.

Link to a Git Repository

A data factory instance can be brought under source control by linking it to a cloud-based Git repository. While it is possible to undertake development work in ADF without linking your data factory to a Git repository, there are many disadvantages of doing so – without a linked repository, even saving work in progress is difficult. Before beginning work in your new ADF instance, you will link it to a Git repository.

Tip   It is easier to configure a data factory's Git repository from ADF Studio than from the Azure portal – this is why you chose the *Configure Git later* option when you created your data factory.

Create a Git Repository in Azure Repos

Before linking a data factory to a Git repository, you need a repository to which the factory can be linked. Support for different Git service providers varies between different Azure services – currently, an ADF instance can be linked to a Git repository provided by either *Azure Repos* or GitHub. Azure Repos is one of a number of cloud-native developer tools provided by *Azure DevOps Services*.

Git repositories (and other service instances) provided by Azure DevOps are grouped into *projects* – in this section, you will create a free Azure DevOps *organization* to host a project and then initialize a Git repository in the new project.

1. Browse to `https://microsoft.com/devops` and click *Start free*. If you are prompted to sign in, do so with the same account you used to create your Azure tenant.

2. The *Get started with Azure DevOps* dialog appears. Near the top of the dialog is displayed the email address you signed in with and a *Switch directory* link. Use the link to ensure that the Azure tenant containing your ADF instance is selected (called "Default Directory" if you have created a free trial subscription) then click *Continue*.

Caution   If "Microsoft account" appears in the list of directories, do not select it. The simplest way to allow ADF to connect to your Git repository is to create your Azure DevOps organization in the same tenant as your Azure Data Factory.

3. Provide a name for your Azure DevOps organization and choose where your projects will be hosted. Complete the CAPTCHA is required, then click *Continue*.

4. After creating your organization, Azure DevOps prompts you to create a project – name your project "AdfByExample" as shown in Figure 1-11, set its visibility to "Private", then click *Create project*.

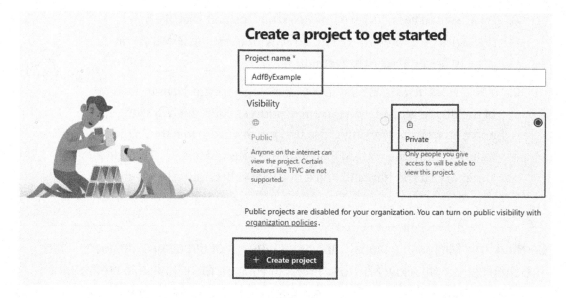

Figure 1-11. *Azure DevOps project creation*

5. The new project's welcome page is displayed, as shown in
    Figure 1-12. Choose to start with the *Azure Repos* service, either
    by clicking the welcome page's *Repos* button or by selecting *Repos*
    (red button with branch icon) from the navigation sidebar.

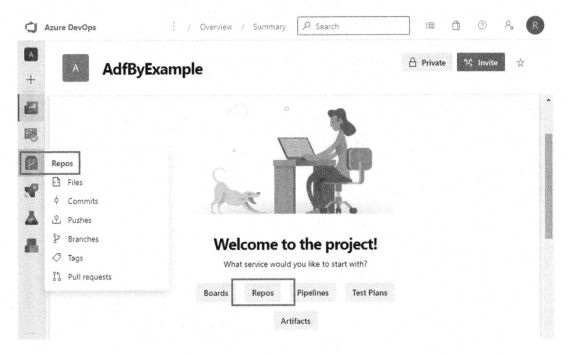

Figure 1-12. *Azure DevOps project welcome page*

6. Because no repositories exist yet, Azure DevOps prompts that your project is empty. Scroll down to the heading *Initialize main branch with a README or gitignore*, then click *Initialize* to create a new repository with the same name as your project.

You can choose to link a data factory to a Git repository provided either by Azure Repos or by GitHub. I have chosen an Azure Repos repository because doing so makes integration with other Microsoft services slightly simpler and because you will be using another service provided by Azure DevOps later in the book.

Link the Data Factory to the Git Repository

In this section, you will link your ADF instance to your new Git repository.

1. Return to ADF Studio and open the management hub by clicking *Manage* (toolbox icon) in the navigation sidebar.

2. In the *Source control* section of the management hub menu, click *Git configuration*.

3. The content pane indicates that no repository is configured, as shown in Figure 1-13. Click the central *Configure* button to connect the factory instance to your Git repository.

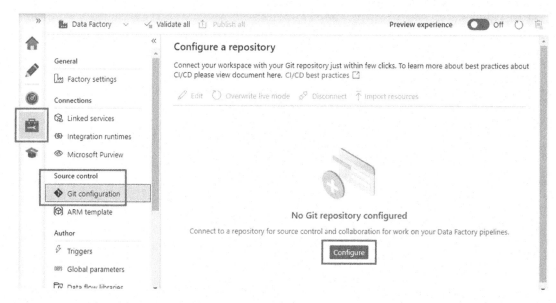

Figure 1-13. *Configure a Git repository in ADF Studio's management hub*

4. The *Configure a repository* flyout appears. Choose "Azure DevOps Git" from the *Repository type* dropdown. As you do so, a *Microsoft Entra ID* list appears – select your tenant from the list and click *Continue*.

5. On the following page, ensure that the "Select repository" radio button is selected. Select your Azure DevOps organization from the *Azure DevOps organization name* dropdown.

Tip   If your Azure DevOps organization name does not appear in the dropdown, check that your Azure DevOps organization is correctly connected to your tenant. You can use the *Organization Settings* page in Azure DevOps to inspect and edit the organization's *Microsoft Entra* connection.

---

6. As more options appear, select the "AdfByExample" Azure
   DevOps project you created in the previous section from the
   Project name dropdown, then under *Repository name,* select
   "AdfByExample" again.

7. Set the factory's *Collaboration branch* to "main" and accept the
   default value of "adf_publish" for *Publish branch.* Set the value
   of *Root folder* to "/data-factory-resources" (without quotes). It
   is good practice to store your factory resources in a repository
   subfolder (rather than in the repository's own root), because it
   enables you to segregate files managed by ADF from any other
   files stored in the same Git repository.

8. Untick the *Custom comment* check box but ensure that the *Import
   existing resources* box remains ticked. The correctly completed
   form, including default values for the remaining settings, is shown
   in Figure 1-14 (your form should refer to your own Azure DevOps
   organization and project). Click *Apply* to link the data factory to
   the Git repository.

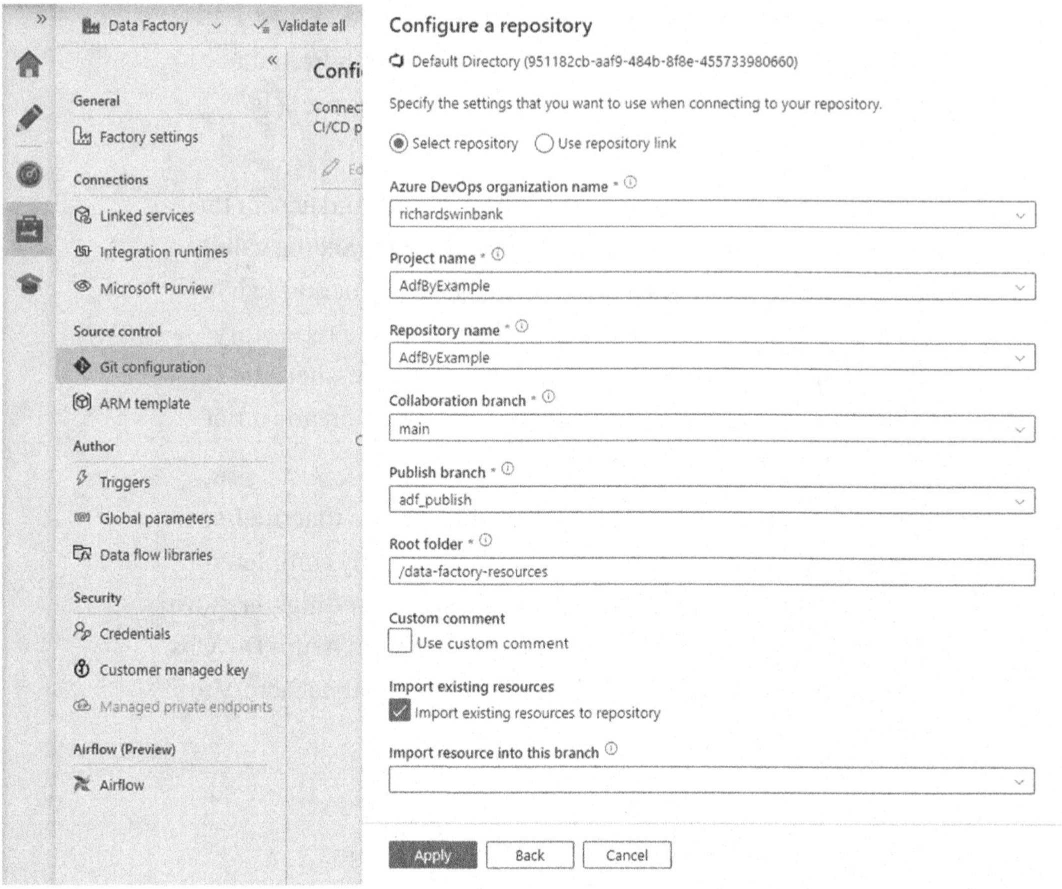

Figure 1-14. *Linking a data factory to an Azure DevOps Git repository*

When an ADF instance is linked to a Git repository, the "Data Factory" logo and label in the top left of ADF Studio (visible in Figure 1-14) are replaced by the logo of the selected Git repository service. Immediately to its right, the name of your working branch – which defaults to "main" for new repositories – is displayed.

ADF Studio As a Web-Based IDE

If you have experience with almost any other kind of development work, then the relationship between a data factory instance, Git, and ADF Studio may seem strange. In a "traditional" development model, you use a locally installed tool like Visual Studio to author developments on your own computer. An IDE such as Visual Studio enables you to debug your work using the local compute power of your own machine and supports source control using a local clone of a remote shared Git repository.

In this scenario, when a piece of development work is complete, changes are deployed to target servers or services. Additional tools may be available to monitor the performance of the *published environment* – the Azure portal offers functionality like this for many Azure services. Figure 1-15 shows the high-level arrangement of components in this model. It shows two possible routes for publishing changes to a service – either directly from the development environment or, as is becoming more common, through automated deployments from the source control repository.

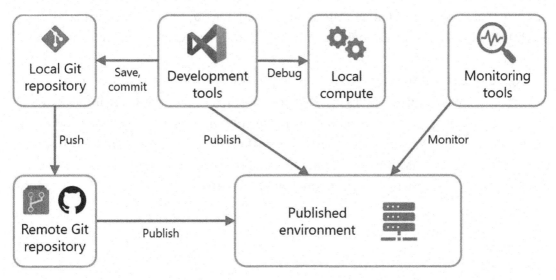

Figure 1-15. *High-level components in a "traditional" development model*

For SSIS developers   This arrangement of components will be familiar to users of SQL Server Integration Services (SSIS). Typically, SSIS packages are authored in Visual Studio SSIS projects and committed to source control using an installed extension. When ready, SSIS projects are published to an SSIS catalog, where reporting tools provided by SQL Server Management Studio (SSMS) enable you to monitor package behavior and performance.

When developing for Azure Data Factory, a significant difference is that its IDE – Azure Data Factory Studio – is web based. This means that the development environment has no local compute of its own. To be able to debug pipelines, ADF Studio must be attached to cloud-based compute, which is why it is always connected to a data factory instance. ADF Studio also has no storage of its own – all its configuration information comes from the connected data factory – so the connected instance is the only place available to store Git repository settings. Although it is the data factory instance that is linked to a Git repository, the underlying objective is actually to link the ADF Studio development environment to source control via the connected factory instance.

Figure 1-16 shows the equivalent arrangement of components for Azure Data Factory. The computing resources of the factory instance – described here informally as "factory compute" – are used in both the *debugging environment* (while developing in ADF Studio) and the published environment (after pipelines have been published). Development and management tools, frequently separated in the traditional development model, are unified for Azure Data Factory by ADF Studio.

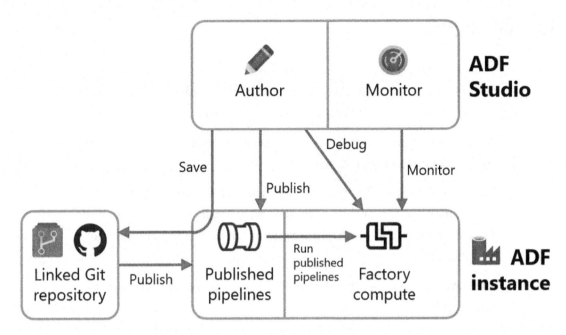

Figure 1-16. *High-level components in the ADF development model*

Note   Although Figure 1-16 shows no local Git repository, ADF manages one for you as part of your ADF Studio session. Internally, ADF Studio's "Save" action consists of a Git commit to the ADF session's repository clone, followed by a push to the factory's linked repository.

Chapter Review

In this chapter, you created an Azure subscription and a resource group inside it. You then created a Git-enabled instance of Azure Data Factory, using a repository hosted by Azure DevOps Repos. In the next chapter, you will start to use your new data factory by creating your first ADF pipeline.

Key Concepts

- **Azure tenant:** A tenant (or directory) is an instance of Microsoft Entra ID (formerly Azure Active Directory). It identifies Azure users and enables them to gain access to Azure services.

- **Resource:** An instance of an Azure service, enabling the service to be accessed by a tenant's users.

- **Subscription:** Specifies a means of payment for Azure services. A tenant may contain one or more subscriptions. Every Azure resource is associated with a subscription to which consumption charges can be billed.

- **Resource group:** A logical subgrouping of Azure resources inside a subscription.

- **Azure portal:** Browser-based console for creating, monitoring, and managing Azure resources.

- **Blade:** Pages in the web-based Azure portal are referred to as blades.

- **Software as a service (SaaS):** Delivery model in which end-user applications are delivered as cloud services. Microsoft Office 365 applications are examples of SaaS services.

- **Platform as a service (PaaS):** Delivery model in which application services and developer tools are delivered as cloud services. Database management systems that do not require you to manage the underlying server infrastructure – for example, Azure SQL Database – are examples of PaaS services.

- **Serverless service:** Like PaaS, serverless cloud services provide applications typically not used directly except by IT specialists, but with additional automated management features – for example, the ability to auto-scale in response to changes in demand. Azure Data Factory is an example of a serverless service.

- **Infrastructure as a service (IaaS):** Cloud service delivery model in which computing infrastructure components – for example, virtual servers and networks – are provided without requiring you to manage the physical hardware involved. Virtual machines give you the freedom to choose your own operating system and application software, but at the cost of managing installation and updates yourself.

- **Azure Data Factory (ADF):** Microsoft's cloud-native, serverless service for managing batch ETL and other data integration workloads.

- **Data factory instance:** An instance of the Azure Data Factory service, often referred to simply as "a data factory." An ADF instance is an example of an Azure resource.

- **ADF V2:** Version 2 of the ADF service is the latest and preferred choice for Azure Data Factory instances. New instances of ADF Version 1 can no longer be created.

- **Integrated development environment (IDE):** Application used for software development that includes supporting features such as editing, debugging, and breakpoint capabilities. Visual Studio and VS Code are examples of IDEs that can be used with many Microsoft technologies.

- **Azure Data Factory Studio (ADF Studio):** Low-code IDE enabling visual authoring, debugging, and publishing of ADF pipelines. Additionally, ADF Studio includes tools for scheduling published pipelines and monitoring their execution.

- **Azure Data Factory User Interface, User Experience, or User Interface Experience (ADF UX):** Other, older names for Azure Data Factory Studio.

- **Authoring canvas:** Visual editor in ADF Studio where you create, modify, and debug ADF pipelines. Use the *Author* button (pencil icon) in the navigation sidebar to access the canvas.

- **Monitoring experience:** ADF Studio feature allowing you to inspect pipeline execution history. Use the *Monitor* button (gauge icon) in the navigation sidebar to access this tool.

- **Management hub:** Area of ADF Studio used to manage various factory features. In this chapter, you used the management hub to edit the ADF instance's Git configuration, and you will return to it in later chapters. Use the *Manage* button (toolbox icon) in the navigation sidebar to open the management hub.

- **Learning center:** Area of ADF Studio containing learning resources: quick start guides, tutorials, videos, templates, and more.

- **Git-enabled:** An ADF instance linked to a Git repository is said to be "Git-enabled." Linking a data factory to a Git repository allows you to commit development work into source control directly from ADF Studio.

- **Collaboration branch:** Git branch, usually the repository's default branch, where changes intended for publishing to ADF are made.

- **Publish branch:** Reserved branch used by ADF to support pipeline publishing processes. Publishing to ADF is the subject of Chapter 10.

- **Root folder:** Path in a Git repository where a linked ADF instance saves its files. Choosing an ADF root folder below the level of the repository root is good practice, because it enables other data platform resources to be managed in the same Git repository.

- **Published environment:** Refers to the environment into which ADF pipelines are published after development; the environment in which real data integration work is done.

- **Debugging environment:** Refers to the use of factory resources by ADF Studio to run pipelines under development interactively for debugging purposes.

For SSIS Developers

ADF Studio provides a collection of tools with purposes familiar to users of SQL Server Integration Services, but linked together in a new way:

- The authoring canvas provides a visual IDE for pipeline development, equivalent to using Visual Studio to develop an SSIS project.

- The monitoring experience enables you to inspect the outcome of published ADF pipelines, in a similar way to using SSIS catalog reports in SSMS to view package execution history.

Using ADF Studio is like editing an SSIS project paired permanently with a single Integration Services server. Connecting ADF Studio to a data factory is necessary because the web-based ADF IDE has no compute power or storage of its own.

Looking Ahead

Earlier in this chapter I observed that you will be using another service provided by Azure DevOps later in the book – in Chapter 10 you will be using the *Azure Pipelines* service to deploy Azure Data Factory resources into a production environment. Deployment activities are performed by *agents*, computers equipped with agent software to run deployment jobs.

You can provide your own *self-hosted* agents or can use *Microsoft-hosted* agents – virtual machines created for you automatically at deployment time. At the time of writing, zero-cost access to Microsoft-hosted agents is provided in response to a *parallelism request* made for your Azure DevOps organization.

Granting a parallelism request may take a few days. If you are not already using deployment pipelines in your Azure DevOps organization – certainly the case if you created your own organization following the instructions in this chapter – you may wish to make a parallelism request now, in readiness for Chapter 10. Instructions for making a parallelism request are available at `https://learn.microsoft.com/en-us/azure/devops/pipelines/licensing/concurrent-jobs`.

CHAPTER 2

Your First Pipeline

ETL workloads are implemented in Azure Data Factory in units called *pipelines*. Using the data factory instance you created in Chapter 1, in this chapter, you will create a pipeline using the *Copy Data tool* – a pipeline creation wizard that steps through creating the various components that make up a pipeline. Afterward, you'll be able to examine the pipeline in detail to gain an understanding of how it is constructed.

The Copy Data tool guides you through building pipelines with the purpose of copying data from one place to another. Before you can do that, you need some data to copy. In the first section of this chapter, you will create an Azure Storage account and upload some sample data to work with.

Work with Azure Storage

Azure Storage is Microsoft's managed cloud storage platform. Data stored using Azure Storage services is encrypted, replicated, and can be accessed securely from anywhere in the world. The scalability of the service's capacity and speed makes it a good choice for many data storage and processing scenarios.

Create an Azure Storage Account

To use Azure Storage services, you must first create an *Azure Storage account*. Create your storage account as follows:

1. In the Azure portal, create a new resource of type *Storage account*.

2. Complete the *Basics* tab of the *Create a storage account* form (Figure 2-1). Under *Project details*, select the *Subscription* and *Resource group* you used to create your data factory in Chapter 1.

© Richard Swinbank 2024
R. Swinbank, *Azure Data Factory by Example*, https://doi.org/10.1007/979-8-8688-0218-8_2

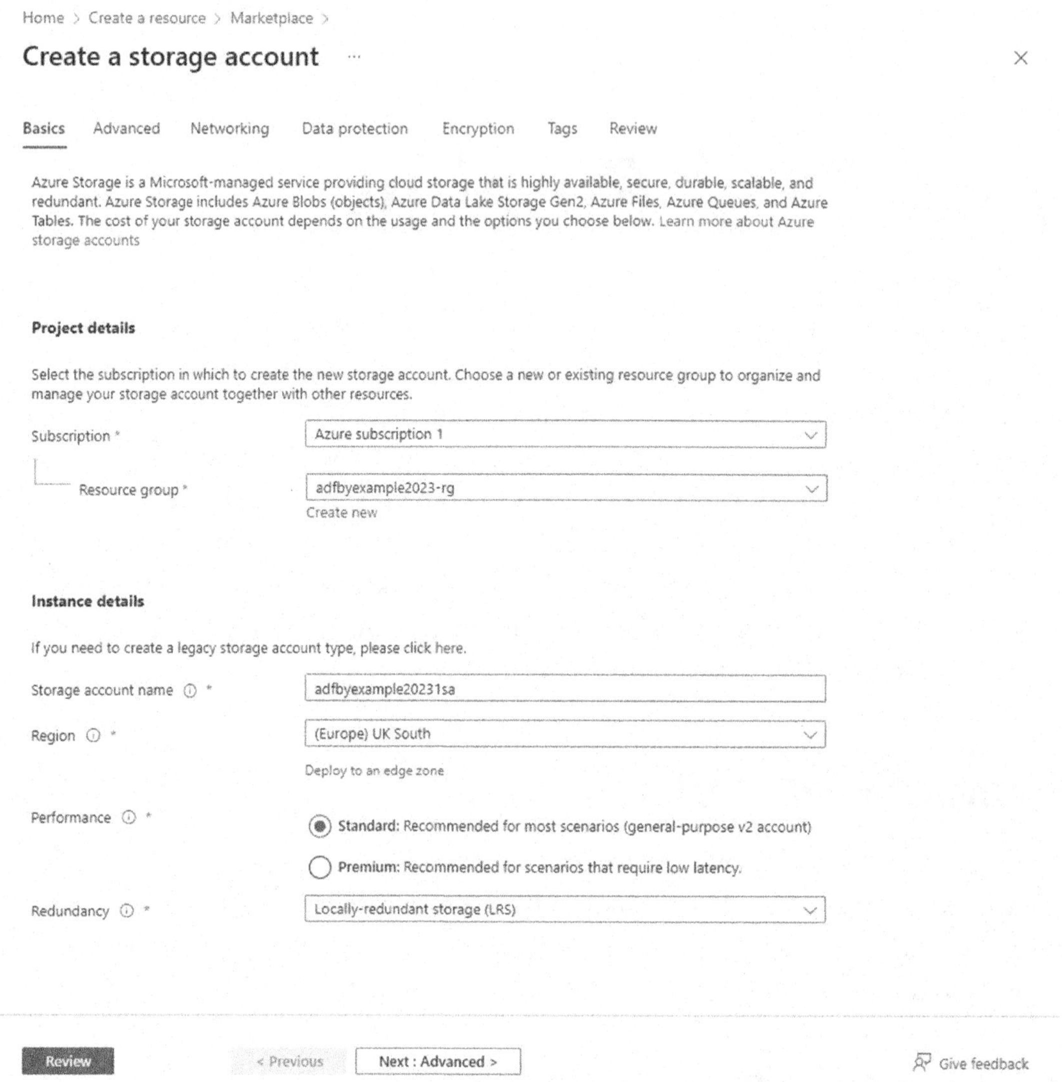

Home > Create a resource > Marketplace >

Create a storage account   ...   ×

Basics   Advanced   Networking   Data protection   Encryption   Tags   Review

Azure Storage is a Microsoft-managed service providing cloud storage that is highly available, secure, durable, scalable, and
redundant. Azure Storage includes Azure Blobs (objects), Azure Data Lake Storage Gen2, Azure Files, Azure Queues, and Azure
Tables. The cost of your storage account depends on the usage and the options you choose below. Learn more about Azure
storage accounts

Project details

Select the subscription in which to create the new storage account. Choose a new or existing resource group to organize and
manage your storage account together with other resources.

Subscription * | Azure subscription 1   ⌄ |

    Resource group * | adfbyexample2023-rg   ⌄ |
                                Create new

Instance details

If you need to create a legacy storage account type, please click here.

Storage account name ⓘ * | adfbyexample20231sa |

Region ⓘ * | (Europe) UK South   ⌄ |
                               Deploy to an edge zone

Performance ⓘ *   ◉ Standard: Recommended for most scenarios (general-purpose v2 account)

                                ○ Premium: Recommended for scenarios that require low latency.

Redundancy ⓘ * | Locally-redundant storage (LRS)   ⌄ |

[Review]   < Previous   [Next : Advanced >]   ⅋ Give feedback

Figure 2-1.   Basics tab of the Create a storage account blade

Note   I suggest you use the same resource group because it will help you keep track of resources you create while using this book. It certainly isn't a requirement for Azure Data Factory – your ADF instance can connect to resources pretty much anywhere! These might be resources in other resource groups, subscriptions, or Azure tenants; or your own on-premises systems; or even resources in competitor cloud platforms such as Amazon Web Services (AWS) or Google Cloud Platform (GCP).

3. Specify a globally unique *Storage account name*. I use names ending in "sa" (storage account names may only contain lowercase alphanumeric characters).

4. Choose the *Location* closest to you geographically – the one where you created your data factory.

Tip   Choosing a location close to you reduces data retrieval latency. Choosing the same location as your data factory reduces cost, because moving data out of one Azure region and into another incurs a *bandwidth* charge (sometimes referred to as an *egress* charge).

5. For *Performance*, select "Standard." Performance tiers for storage are linked to the underlying hardware type. Premium storage uses solid-state disks and is more expensive.

6. Select *Redundancy* option "Locally-redundant storage (LRS)." This is the cheapest of the available options because data is only replicated within the same data center. LRS protects you against hardware failure but not against data center outage or loss – this is sufficient for learning or development purposes, but in production environments, a higher level of resilience is likely to be required.

7. The final step on the *Basics* tab is to click *Review*, then after validation, click *Create*. (I am purposely bypassing the five remaining tabs – *Advanced, Networking, Data protection, Encryption*, and *Tags* – and accepting their default values.)

8. A notification message is displayed when deployment is complete, including a *Go to resource* button. Click it to open the portal's storage account blade (shown in Figure 2-2).

Tip   You can navigate to any resource from the portal menu (top left) or home page. Use the *Resource groups* option to display all your resource groups, then select one from the list to explore the resources it contains.

Explore Azure Storage

A variety of tools are available for interaction with storage accounts. One readily available option is *Storage browser*, hosted inside the Azure portal. Alternatively, you may choose to install *Azure Storage Explorer*, a free downloadable app available for Windows and other operating systems. You can launch either of these tools directly from the portal – to launch the online app, click *Storage browser* in the portal's storage account blade (Figure 2-2).

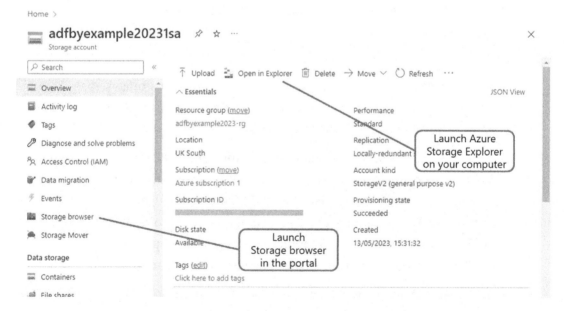

Figure 2-2. *Azure portal storage account blade*

Figure 2-3 shows the online Storage browser in the Azure portal. Its own sidebar shows the four types of storage supported by the storage account: *blob containers* (blob storage), *file shares*, *queues*, and *tables*. Select a storage type from the sidebar to display its contents.

Note   The term *blob* is used to refer to a file without considering its internal data structure. This doesn't imply that files described as blobs have no structure – it simply means that the structure isn't important for the task at hand. The name "blob storage" reflects the fact that the service provides a general-purpose file store, with no restrictions on the types of files it can contain.

Blob storage is divided into a single level of blob *containers* – containers cannot be nested. A container named "$logs" is created automatically to store log data generated by the storage account itself. Use the + *Add container* button to create two additional private blob containers called "landing" and "sampledata," as shown in Figure 2-3.

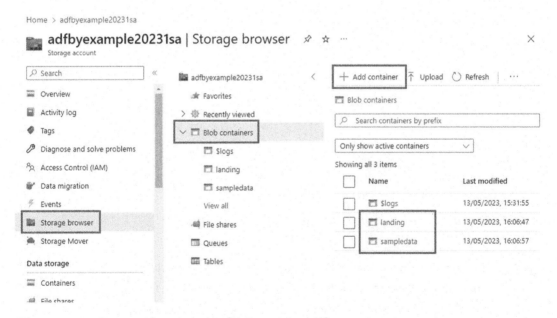

Figure 2-3.   *Storage browser in the Azure portal*

Upload Sample Data

Sample data files used in this book are available from the book's GitHub repository, located at https://github.com/Apress/Azure-Data-Factory-by-Example-Second-Edition.

1. Download the repository as a zip file so that you can transfer sample data into your storage account. This option is available from the green *Code* menu button on the repository home page (shown in Figure 2-4).

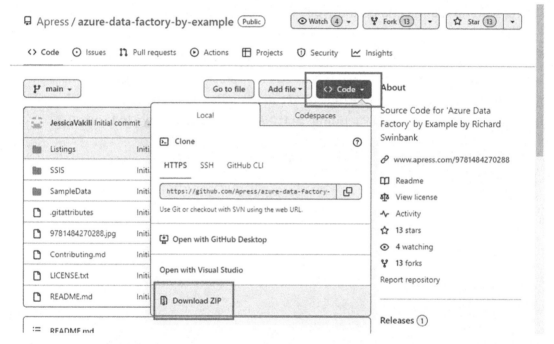

Figure 2-4. *Download sample code zip file from GitHub*

2. Return to Storage browser in the Azure portal and select the "landing" container. Click *Upload* on the toolbar above the container contents list, shown in Figure 2-5. The *Upload blob* flyout is displayed.

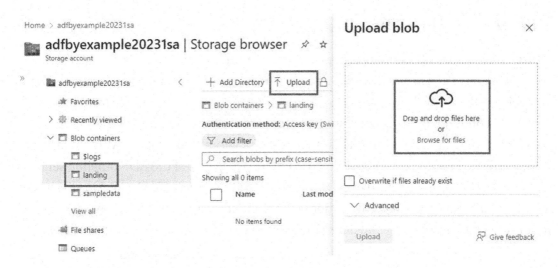

Figure 2-5. *Use Storage browser to upload files into blob storage*

3. Use the file selection tools on the *Upload blob* flyout to locate and select azure-data-factory-by-example-main.zip, the zip file you downloaded.

4. Back in the *Upload blob* flyout, click *Upload*, then close the flyout.

5. An entry for the zip file now appears in the "landing" container contents list. (If you don't see it, try clicking *Refresh* in the toolbar above the container contents list.)

The sample data files contain sales data for products made by a fictional multinational confectionery manufacturer, Acme Boxed Confectionery (ABC). The manufacturer does not sell directly to consumers, but to a variety of retailers that report monthly sales activity back to ABC. Sales reports are typically produced using retailers' own data management systems and are supplied in a wide variety of file formats. Handling these formats will expose you to many of ADF's data transformation features in the coming chapters.

Use the Copy Data Tool

Azure Data Factory's Copy Data tool provides a wizard-style experience for creating a pipeline with a specific purpose: copying data from one place to another. In this section, you will use the Copy Data tool to create a pipeline that copies the zip file from the "landing" container in your Azure storage account, unzips it, and then writes its contents into the "sampledata" container. This is purposely a very simple data movement task – implementing a simple task allows you to focus on the detail of the ADF pipeline setup.

The Copy Data tool is found on ADF Studio's home page, accessed by clicking the house icon in the navigation sidebar. On the home page, click the *Ingest* tile to launch a guided multi-step process to create a pipeline – the page for the first step appears in Figure 2-6.

Tip   If the process shown in Figure 2-6 fails to launch, click the pencil icon to access the authoring canvas, then locate the search field below the *Factory Resources* explorer heading. Click the plus symbol button to the right of the search box, then select *Copy Data tool* from the pop-up menu.

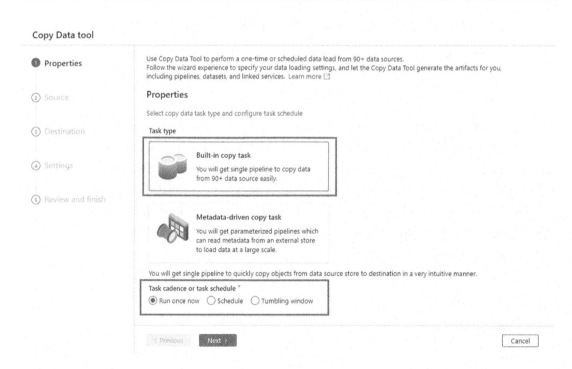

Figure 2-6. *First step of the Copy Data tool*

Complete the process as follows:

1. On the *Properties* page, select the *Task type* "Built-in copy task" and set *Task cadence or task schedule* to "Run once now". Click *Next*.

2. On the *Source data store* page, click + *New connection*. Choose the linked service type *Azure Blob Storage* and click *Continue*.

3. Use the *New connection* flyout (Figure 2-7) to create a connection to your Azure Storage account. Provide a name and description – I have reused the name of the underlying storage account – then under *Account selection method*, ensure that "From Azure subscription" is selected. Choose the relevant subscription and storage account you created earlier. At the bottom of the flyout, click *Test connection* to check that it's working, then click *Create*.

Note   ADF Studio uses a *storage key* (part of your storage account's configuration) to authorize connection to your storage account. The reason you don't need to specify a key explicitly is that the IDE uses your logged-in identity to retrieve its value.

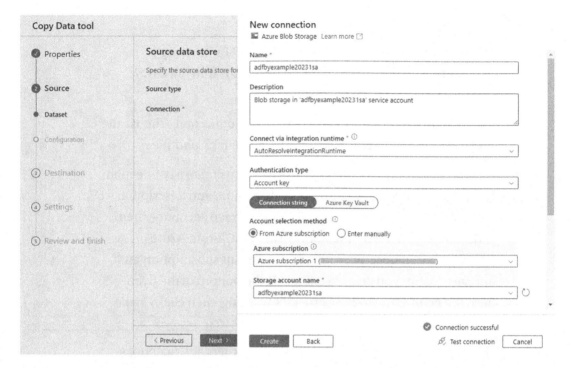

Figure 2-7. *New connection flyout*

4. Back on the *Source data store* page, click the *Browse* button to
    the right of the *File or folder* text box. Browse into the "landing"
    container, select the uploaded zip file, and click *OK*.

5. As indicated in Figure 2-8, tick the *Binary copy* check box, select
    Compression type "ZipDeflate", and uncheck *Preserve zip file name
    as folder*. Click *Next*.

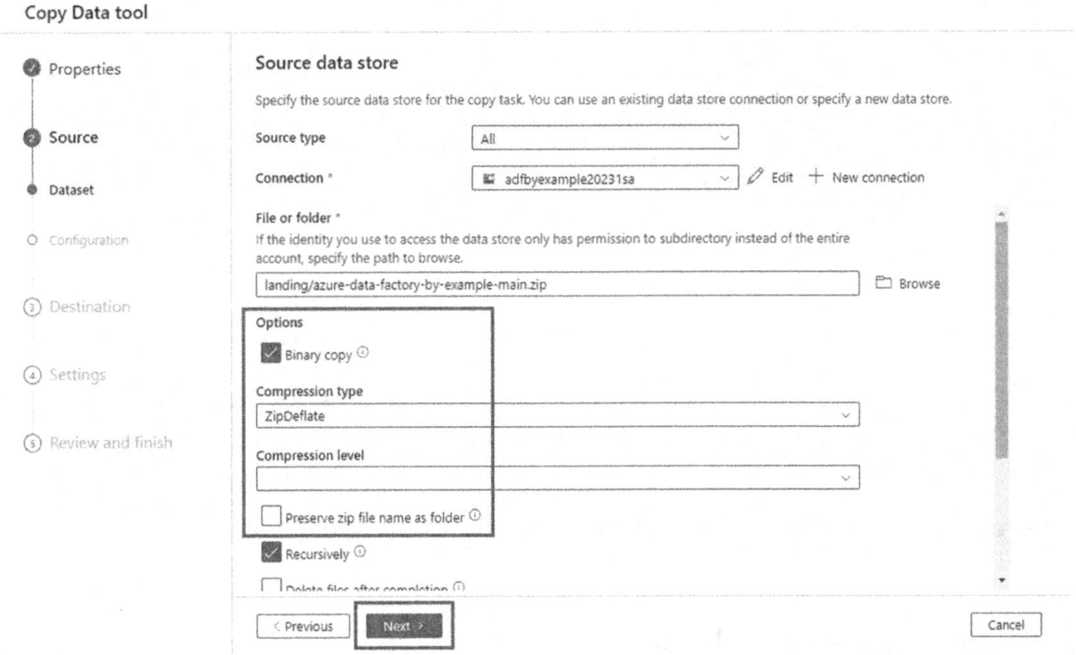

Copy Data tool

Figure 2-8. *Source data store options in the Copy Data tool*

6. On the *Destination data store* page, you will find that the *Connection* dropdown now contains an entry for the linked service you created in step 3. Select it and notice that a number of related fields now appear.

7. Use the *Browse* button to the right of the *Folder path* field to choose a copy destination. Select your "sampledata" container and click *OK*, then click *Next*.

8. Accept the default options presented on the *Settings* page by clicking *Next*, then review your inputs on the *Summary* page. When you are ready, click *Next* to start pipeline creation.

The last stage in the Copy Data tool process is the *Deployment* page. This will quickly run through resource creation before a *Finish* button appears, as in Figure 2-9, indicating that you have successfully created your pipeline. Click *Finish* to close the tool.

Figure 2-9. *Copy Data tool's Deployment page*

Explore Your Pipeline

In the previous section, you used the Copy Data tool to create your first ADF pipeline. To achieve this, ADF Studio took the following actions on your behalf:

- Created a linked service connection to your storage account

- Published the linked service connection

- Created datasets representing the inputs and outputs of the copy process

- Created an ADF pipeline to perform the copy process

- Committed and pushed the linked service, datasets, and pipeline to your Git repository

---

Note   To prevent exposure, the storage key used to authorize ADF's connection to your storage account is not committed to Git. Instead, the key is saved directly to ADF by publishing the linked service connection immediately.

In this section, you will examine the various resources created by the Copy Data tool.

Linked Services

A common way to define resources for any data operation is in terms of *storage* and *compute*:

- **Storage** refers to the holding of data, without any additional processing or movement being performed (except, e.g., movement occurring within the storage system for storage replication).

- **Compute** describes computational power used to move stored data around, to transform it, and to analyze it.

The separation of storage and compute services in cloud platforms like Azure is very common. It adds flexibility by allowing the two to be scaled up and down independently of one another as demand rises and falls.

Azure Data Factory has no storage resources of its own, but factory instances can access and use external storage and compute resources via *linked services*. A linked service may provide a connection to a storage system – for example, an Azure storage account or a database – or may enable access to external compute resources like an Azure Function App or an Azure Databricks cluster.

Using the Copy Data tool, you created an Azure Blob Storage linked service to connect to your Azure storage account. Linked services can be configured in ADF Studio's management hub, accessed by clicking the toolbox icon in the navigation sidebar. Figure 2-10 shows the *Linked services* page of the management hub, containing the Azure Blob Storage connection created earlier.

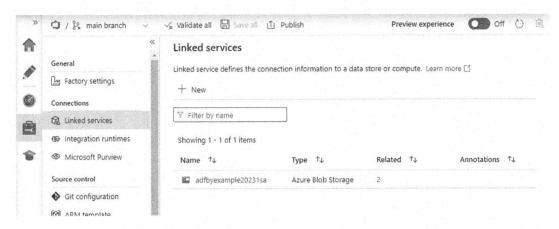

Figure 2-10. *Linked services in the ADF Studio management hub*

Datasets

A linked service storage connection provides information necessary to connect to an external data store, but nothing more. For a database system, this might consist of a database connection string, including server, database, and credential details, but with no information about database tables. Similarly, the linked service you created in the previous section contains metadata to locate the relevant Azure Blob Storage account but has no information about files stored there. Azure Data Factory stores metadata to represent objects inside external storage systems as *datasets*.

Datasets are defined in ADF Studio's authoring canvas (accessed by clicking the pencil icon in the navigation sidebar). In here, you will find two datasets created by the Copy Data tool – one representing the source zip file of the copy activity and the other the destination container. The canvas has three regions, as shown in Figure 2-11:

- A factory header bar (beneath the main navigation header bar), containing various controls and indicating that the factory is linked to an Azure DevOps Git repository. The figure indicates that the current working branch is "main".

- The *Factory Resources* explorer, listing pipelines, datasets, and other factory resources.

- A tabbed design surface, displaying details of selected factory resources.

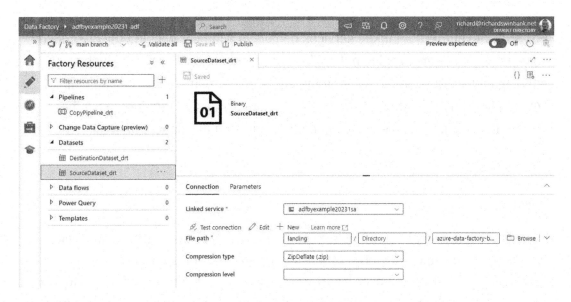

Figure 2-11. *Dataset configuration in the ADF Studio authoring canvas*

Tip   The term *resource* is used in the Azure portal to describe different instances of Azure services (e.g., a storage account or a data factory) and is used within ADF to describe various factory components such as pipelines and datasets. The reuse of terminology can be confusing, but it should be clear from the context whether I'm referring to Azure resources or ADF resources.

Notice also that in the authoring canvas, the navigation header bar features a *Search* box. This allows you to search factory resource definitions, including text descriptions like the one you created for your storage account linked service.

The design surface in Figure 2-11 shows the source dataset "SourceDataset_drt". (The dataset name was generated automatically by the Copy Data tool – yours will likely differ.) The *Connection* tab on the tabbed configuration pane below the design surface displays details of the selected file path: the "landing" container, file "azure-data-factory-by-example-main.zip", and compression type "ZipDeflate".

For SSIS developers   Linked services behave in a similar way to project-scoped connection managers in SSIS, but unlike some connection managers (such as flat file), they do not contain schema metadata. Schema metadata can be defined separately in an ADF dataset, although it may not always be required (as in the case of the schemaless file copy you performed using the Copy Data tool).

Pipelines

Pipelines are at the very heart of Azure Data Factory. A *pipeline* is a collection of data movement, transformation, and control *activities*, grouped together to achieve a higher-level data integration task. Figure 2-12 shows the ADF Studio authoring canvas with the "CopyPipeline_drt" pipeline displayed. When authoring pipelines, the canvas additionally contains an *Activities* toolbox, a menu of available pipeline activities. Activities can be dragged from the Activities toolbox and dropped onto the design surface.

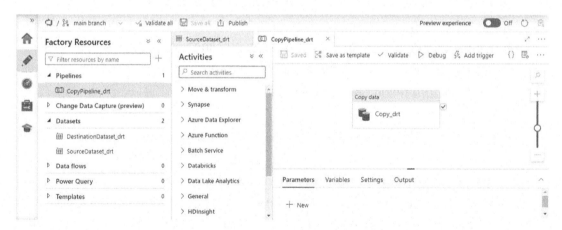

Figure 2-12. *Pipeline configuration in the ADF Studio authoring canvas*

On the design surface in Figure 2-12, you can see that the pipeline contains a single *Copy activity*, named "Copy_drt". (The pipeline and activity names were also generated automatically by the Copy Data tool.)

For SSIS developers   A data factory pipeline is equivalent to an SSIS package, and the design surface shown in Figure 2-12 provides functionality comparable to the SSIS control flow surface. This simple pipeline is like an SSIS package that contains a single File System Task to copy files from one location to another – but with the additional ability to unzip files on the fly.

Activities

The Activities toolbox provides a variety of activity types available for use in ADF pipelines. Activities are available for the native movement and transformation of data inside ADF, as well as to orchestrate work performed by external resources such as Azure Databricks and Machine Learning services.

This simple pipeline contains only one activity, but in Chapter 4, you will start to see how multiple activities can be linked together inside a pipeline to orchestrate progressively more complex ETL workflows. ADF defines a library of nearly 40 activity types, including the ability to write your own custom activities, making the scope of tasks that a pipeline can accomplish virtually limitless.

Integration Runtimes

Azure Data Factory accesses compute in one of two ways:

- Externally, by creating a linked service connection to a separate compute service like Azure Databricks or an Azure Synapse Analytics Spark pool

- Internally, using an ADF-managed compute service called an *integration runtime*

Native data transformations and movements – such as the Copy activity – use compute resources provided by an integration runtime. This is what I described in Chapter 1 as "factory compute."

Integration runtimes are listed in ADF Studio's management hub, immediately below *Linked services* on the hub menu. Every ADF instance automatically includes one integration runtime, called the *AutoResolveIntegrationRuntime*. This provides access to Azure compute resources in a geographic location that is chosen automatically, depending on the task being performed. Under certain circumstances, you may wish to create integration runtimes of your own – Chapter 8 returns to this question in greater detail.

The compute required for your pipeline's Copy activity is provided by the AutoResolveIntegrationRuntime. This is not specified as part of the activity itself, but as part of the storage account linked service(s) it uses. If you review Figure 2-7, you will notice that the option *Connect via integration runtime* has the value "AutoResolveIntegrationRuntime".

For SSIS developers   The closest parallel to an integration runtime in SSIS is the Integration Services Windows service – it provides access to server compute resources for data movement and transformation. The concept is less visible in SSIS, simply because there is only one runtime, used by all tasks in all packages.

Figure 2-13 illustrates the relationship between linked services, datasets, activities, integration runtimes, and your pipeline. The arrows indicate the direction of data flow from the "landing" to the "sampledata" container.

In the figure, you can see that

- The dataset "SourceDataset_drt" uses the "adfbyexample20231sa" linked service to connect to the "landing" container in the storage account of the same name.

- The dataset "DestinationDataset_drt" uses the "adfbyexample20231sa" linked service to connect to the "sampledata" container in the same storage account.

- The "CopyPipeline_drt" pipeline contains a single Copy activity, "Copy_drt", which uses the AutoResolveIntegrationRuntime to copy data from "SourceDataset_drt" to "DestinationDataset_drt".

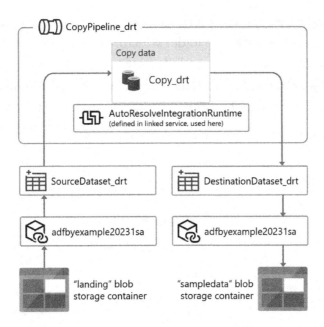

Figure 2-13. *Relationship between Azure Data Factory resources*

The features of pipeline implementation illustrated by Figure 2-13 are very common:

- Access to identified data in external storage is provided by a dataset via a linked service connection.

- Pipeline activities use an ADF integration runtime to move and transform data between datasets.

Factory Resources in Git

Linked services, datasets, and pipelines are all examples of factory resources, created for you here by the Copy Data tool. In addition to creating resource definitions in ADF Studio, the tool also saved them, by committing and pushing them to your Git repository. Changes in ADF Studio are committed to its working branch, shown at the left-hand end of the factory header bar – in this case, the collaboration branch you selected for your ADF instance when linking it to Git.

Look at your Azure DevOps repository again, and you will see a structure similar to Figure 2-14. The screenshot shows the folder structure of my "AdfByExample" repository, which now contains four folders: "dataset," "factory," "linkedService," and "pipeline." Each folder contains definitions for resources of the corresponding type, stored as JSON files – the content pane on the right shows the JSON definition of my "SourceDataset_drt" dataset.

Figure 2-14. *Git repository contents after creating factory resources*

Working with – and committing directly to – your collaboration branch is characteristic of a centralized Git workflow. More sophisticated development workflows using Git feature branches are also supported by ADF Studio. The branch dropdown, indicated in Figure 2-15, enables you to switch between Git branches, create new ones, and open pull requests. Development workflows are outside the scope of this book – during the following chapters, you should continue to commit changes directly to the factory's collaboration branch, main.

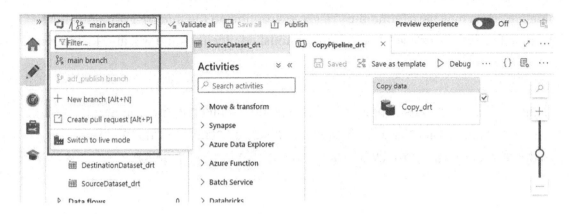

Figure 2-15. *Git branch dropdown in ADF Studio*

Debug Your Pipeline

With the work you've done using the Copy Data tool, you now have factory resource definitions in a number of different places:

- Your Git repository contains saved linked service, dataset, and pipeline definitions.

- Those definitions are loaded into your ADF Studio session, where you can edit them.

- The ADF published environment contains the linked service definition (because the Copy Data tool published it in order to save the storage account key securely).

You can connect ADF Studio directly to the factory's published environment using the *Switch to live mode* option on the branch selection dropdown, shown in Figure 2-15. Use this to verify that the linked service resource has been published but that the pipeline and datasets have not. In live mode, the branch selection dropdown is replaced by a *Data Factory* dropdown – use the *Azure DevOps Git* option on that menu to return ADF Studio to development mode.

To run the pipeline in the published environment, you would need first to publish *all* its related resources. Publishing factory resources is the subject of Chapter 10. Until then, you will be running pipelines interactively in ADF Studio, using its *Debug* mode – whenever I say "run the pipeline" from now on, I mean "Click *Debug* to run the pipeline." (You may have found the *Trigger now* option on the *Add trigger* menu above the pipeline design surface – this executes published pipelines and will also be examined in Chapter 10.)

Note   "Debug" means simply "run the pipeline definition in my ADF Studio session, without publishing it." A pipeline debug run accesses and modifies external resources in exactly the same way as a published pipeline.

Run the Pipeline in Debug Mode

To run the pipeline created by the Copy Data tool in debug mode, open the authoring canvas and select the pipeline from the *Factory Resources* explorer. The toolbar immediately above the design surface contains a *Debug* button, as shown in Figure 2-16 – click it to run the pipeline.

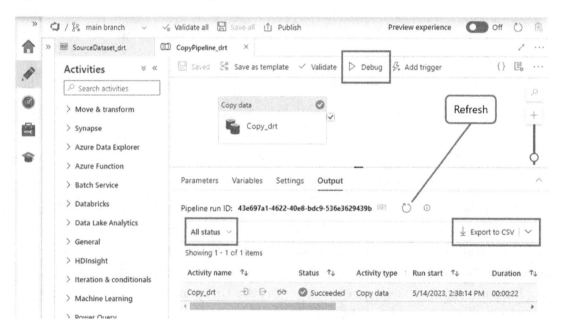

Figure 2-16. *Debug controls on the pipeline design surface*

As soon as you click *Debug*, the tabbed configuration pane below the design surface automatically expands, with the *Output* tab selected. Figure 2-16 shows the tab after the debug run has completed successfully – while the pipeline is still running, you can click the *Refresh* button to update the tab with the latest status information.

At the bottom of the tab is a list of activity runs performed during the pipeline's execution. In this case, there is only one – the Copy activity. You can use the icons to the right of an activity's name to view its inputs, outputs, and performance information. Larger pipelines may report many activity runs that can be navigated by paging through the list or by using the activity run status filter (indicated in the figure, currently displaying "All status"). If you wish to perform more detailed analysis of a pipeline's activity runs, you can export them in CSV format using the *Export to CSV* dropdown, also indicated in the figure.

Inspect Execution Results

An unpublished pipeline is still connected to all the same external resources as its published equivalent, and running the pipeline accesses and modifies those same resources. Running your pipeline in debug mode has performed a real data copy from the "landing" container to the "sampledata" container.

Return to Storage browser in the Azure portal to inspect the "sampledata" container and verify that it now contains a nested folder structure, extracted from the zip file in the "landing" container. You will make use of the data unzipped to this container in the following chapters.

Chapter Review

In this chapter, you created an Azure Storage account and used an ADF pipeline to unzip and copy files from one container into another.

The Copy activity used by the pipeline is the workhorse of data movement in ADF. In your pipeline, the activity treats files as unstructured blobs, but in Chapter 3, you will explore its handling of structured and semi-structured text file formats, along with other structured datasets.

Key Concepts

This chapter introduced five core concepts for Azure Data Factory:

- **Pipeline:** A data integration workload unit in Azure Data Factory. A logical grouping of activities assembled to execute a particular data integration process.

- **Activity:** Performs a task inside a pipeline, for example, copying data from one place to another.

- **Dataset:** Contains metadata describing a specific set of data held in an external storage system. Pipeline activities use datasets to interact with external data.

- **Linked service:** Represents a connection to an external storage system or external compute resource.

- **Integration runtime:** Provides access to internal compute resource inside Azure Data Factory. ADF has no internal storage resources.

Figure 2-13 illustrates the interaction between these components. Other concepts encountered in this chapter include the following:

- **Debug:** You can run a pipeline interactively in ADF Studio using "Debug" mode. This means that the pipeline definition present in the ADF Studio session is executed – it does not need to be published to the connected factory instance, or even saved. During a debugging run, a pipeline treats external resources in exactly the same way as in published pipeline runs.

- **Copy Data tool:** A wizard-style experience in ADF Studio that creates a pipeline to copy data from one place to another. I have presented it in this chapter as a quick way to start exploring the pipeline structure, but in practice, you are unlikely to use the tool very often.

- **Azure Storage:** Microsoft's cloud-based managed storage platform.

- **Storage account:** A storage account is created in order to use Azure Storage services.

- **Storage key:** Storage keys are tokens used to authorize access to a storage account. You can manage an account's keys in the Azure portal.

- **Blob storage:** General-purpose file (blob) storage, one of the types of storage offered by Azure Storage. Other supported storage types (not described here) include file shares, queues, and tables.

- **Container:** Files in blob storage are stored in containers, subdivisions of a storage account's blob storage. Blob storage is divided into containers at the root level only – they cannot be nested.

- **Storage browser:** A web-based app used to manage Azure Storage accounts, hosted in the Azure portal.

- **Azure Storage Explorer:** A free desktop app used to manage Azure Storage accounts.

- **Bandwidth:** A term used by Microsoft to describe the movement of data into and out of Azure data centers. Outbound data movements incur a fee, sometimes referred to as an *egress charge*.

For SSIS Developers

Most core Azure Data Factory concepts have familiar parallels in SSIS. Table 2-1 lists some equivalent ADF and SSIS concepts.

Table 2-1. *Equivalent concepts in ADF and SSIS*

ADF concept	Equivalent in SSIS
Pipeline	Package
Activity	Task (on control flow surface)
Copy activity	Used in this chapter like a File System Task. In Chapter 3, you will explore more advanced behavior where it acts like a basic Data Flow Task
Linked service	Project-scoped connection manager (with no schema metadata)
Dataset	Schema metadata, stored in various different places (such as a flat file connection manager or OLE DB data flow source)
Integration runtime	SSIS Windows service
Set of pipelines in ADF Studio	SSIS project open in Visual Studio
Set of pipelines published to an ADF instance	SSIS project deployed to SSIS catalog

CHAPTER 3

The Copy Activity

Data integration tasks can be divided into two groups: those of *data movement* and those of *data transformation*. In Chapter 2, you created an Azure Data Factory pipeline that copied data from one blob storage container to another – a simple data movement using the *Copy activity*. The Copy activity is the core tool in Azure Data Factory for moving data from one place to another, and this chapter explores its application in greater detail.

The data movement performed in Chapter 2 was *unstructured*. By choosing the *Binary copy* option when you used the Copy data tool, you told the Copy activity explicitly to disregard files' internal structure. You didn't define or try to infer any information about data structures within individual files, simply copying them from one place to another as blobs.

One of the Copy activity's powerful features is its ability to infer and persist data structures – *schemas* – for files. In combination with multi-file handling capabilities, this provides simple but powerful support for loading file-based data into structured data stores like relational databases. In the next section, you will add an Azure SQL Database instance to your Azure resource group to enable you to explore this functionality.

Prepare an Azure SQL Database

Azure SQL Database (or *Azure SQL DB*) is one of a number of Azure-based SQL Server services. It provides a platform-as-a-service (PaaS) database engine, fully managed so that you don't have to worry about administration requirements like backups, patching, and upgrades. It is based on Microsoft's SQL Server database management system, so you can continue to interact with it using familiar client tools like SQL Server Management Studio or Azure Data Studio.

© Richard Swinbank 2024
R. Swinbank, *Azure Data Factory by Example*, https://doi.org/10.1007/979-8-8688-0218-8_3

Create the Database

To create your Azure SQL DB:

1. In the Azure portal, create a new resource of type *Azure SQL*.

2. When prompted *How do you plan to use the service?*, choose "Single database" from the *Resource type* dropdown on the *SQL databases* tile, as shown in Figure 3-1. Click the *Create* button below the dropdown on the same tile.

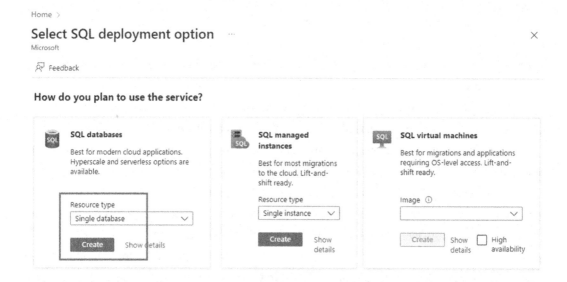

Figure 3-1. *SQL deployment options in the Azure portal*

3. Select the subscription and resource group that contains your ADF instance, then choose a name for your database. Below the *Server* dropdown box, click *Create new*.

4. The *Create SQL Database Server* blade appears (Figure 3-2). Provide a globally unique server name and specify the same location as your ADF instance. Choose the *Authentication method* of "Use SQL authentication", then enter a server admin login and password. Click *OK*.

The result of this process is not a traditional SQL Server instance, but a *logical* SQL Server. The logical server is a container for a group of one or more Azure SQL databases and provides services for all the databases in the group, including network settings and AAD-based administration.

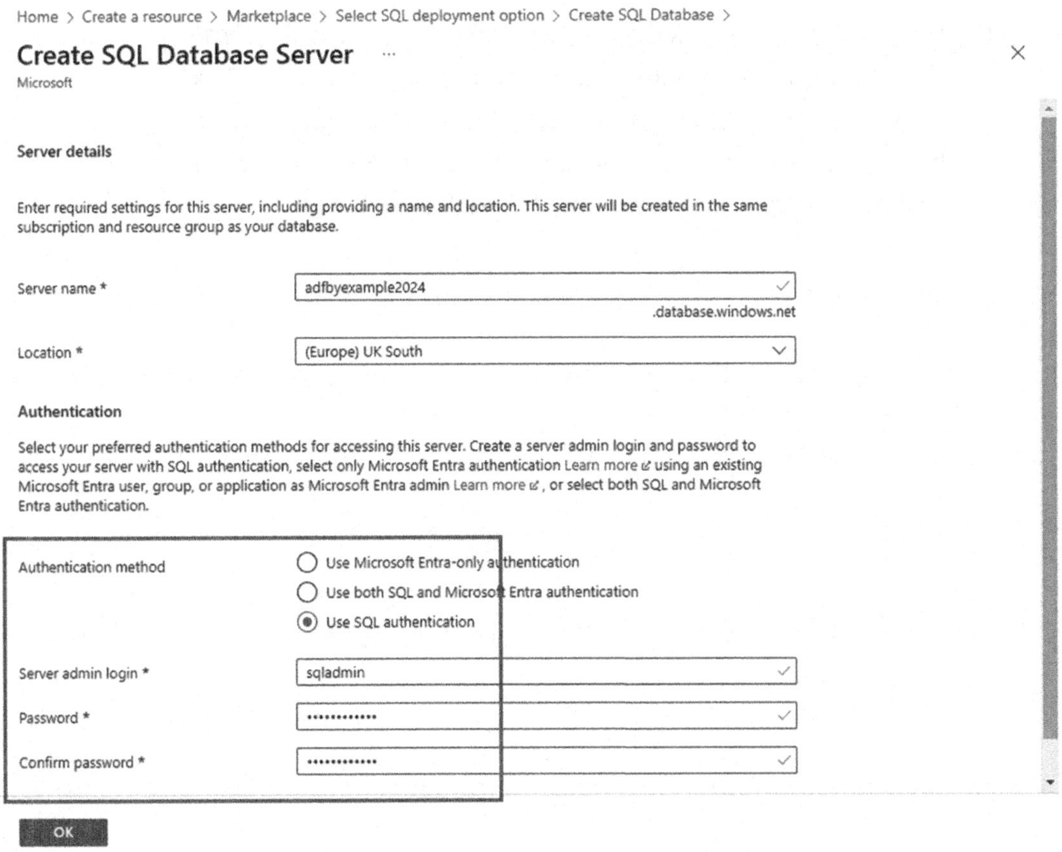

Home > Create a resource > Marketplace > Select SQL deployment option > Create SQL Database >

Create SQL Database Server   ...

Microsoft

Server details

Enter required settings for this server, including providing a name and location. This server will be created in the same subscription and resource group as your database.

Server name *	adfbyexample2024
	.database.windows.net
Location *	(Europe) UK South

Authentication

Select your preferred authentication methods for accessing this server. Create a server admin login and password to access your server with SQL authentication, select only Microsoft Entra authentication Learn more ✎ using an existing Microsoft Entra user, group, or application as Microsoft Entra admin Learn more ✎ , or select both SQL and Microsoft Entra authentication.

Authentication method	○ Use Microsoft Entra-only authentication
	○ Use both SQL and Microsoft Entra authentication
	◉ Use SQL authentication
Server admin login *	sqladmin
Password *	••••••••••••
Confirm password *	••••••••••••

OK

Figure 3-2. *Create SQL Database Server blade*

5.   Back in the *Create SQL Database* blade, ensure that *Want to use SQL elastic pool?* is set to "No", then set the *Workload environment* to "Development".

The development environment option configures a database with a minimal level of serverless compute. The serverless tier does not reserve compute resource in advance and is billed on usage only – this is a low-cost choice suitable for learning and development.

Note   By default, databases on the serverless compute tier are paused after one hour of inactivity. This keeps running costs down but means that when you return to the database after an inactive period, you may need to wait a few minutes before you can connect successfully.

6.   When you have specified server and database details, the *Create SQL Database* blade should look something like Figure 3-3. Click *Review + create*, then after validation click *Create*. (I am purposely bypassing the four remaining tabs – *Networking, Security, Additional settings*, and *Tags* – and accepting their default values.)

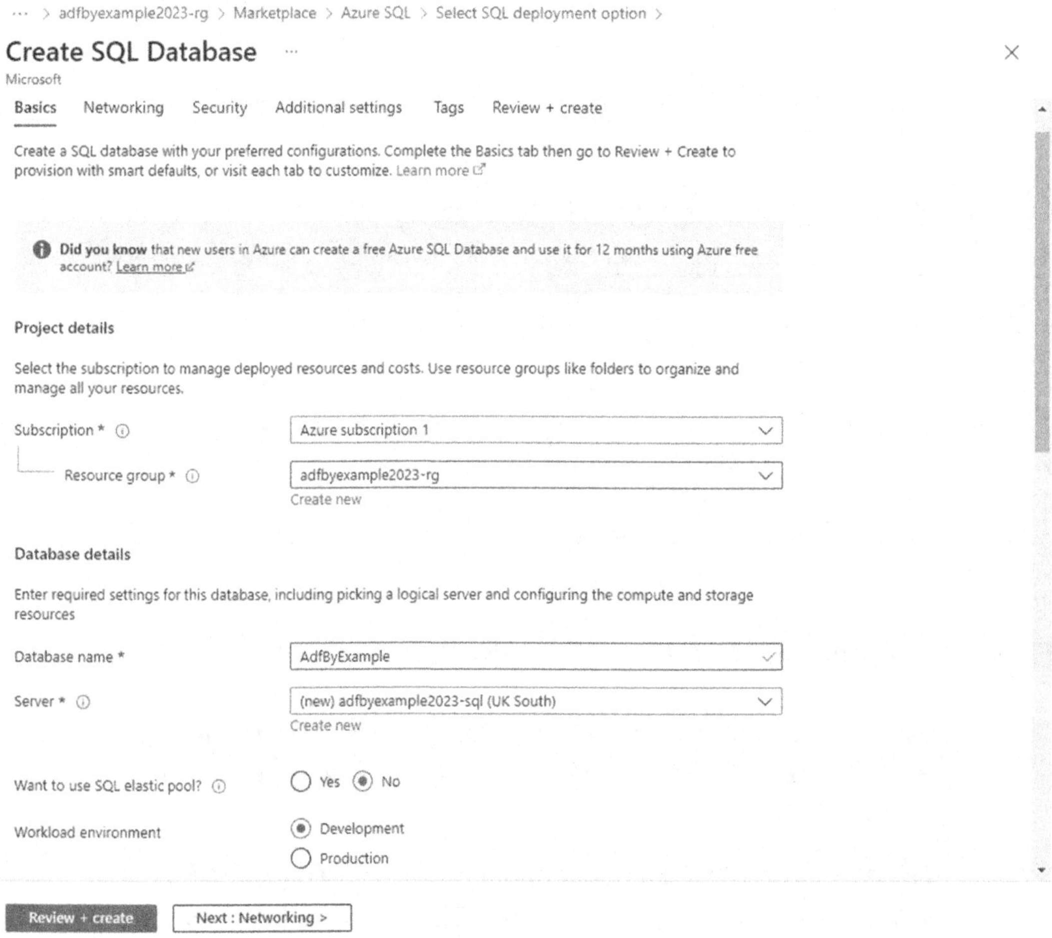

Figure 3-3. *Completed Create SQL Database blade*

7. The deployment process creates two new resources in your resource group: your new Azure SQL Server database and the logical SQL server that contains it. A notification message is displayed when deployment is complete, including a *Go to resource* button. Click the button to open the portal's SQL database blade (Figure 3-4).

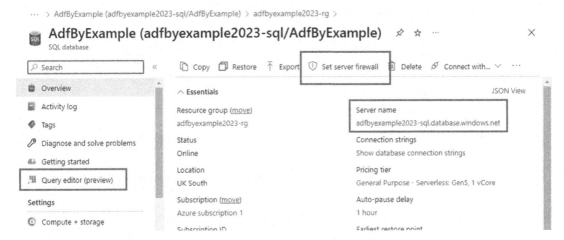

Figure 3-4. *Azure portal SQL Database blade, indicating important features*

8. Your database is now created, but you will be unable to access it until you have configured a server firewall rule to allow you in. At the top of the SQL database blade, click the *Set server firewall* button (indicated in Figure 3-4) to open the logical SQL server's *Networking* page.

9. On the *Networking* page's *Public access* tab (Figure 3-5), set *Public network access* to "Selected networks". This provides additional options: Use the + *Add your client IPv4 address* button to add your public IP address. Further down the blade, tick the *Allow Azure services and resources to access this server* check box – this will allow your ADF instance to access the server. Click *Save*.

Note   A more robust security posture is recommended for most Azure SQL Database deployments, but this configuration is acceptable for our immediate learning purposes.

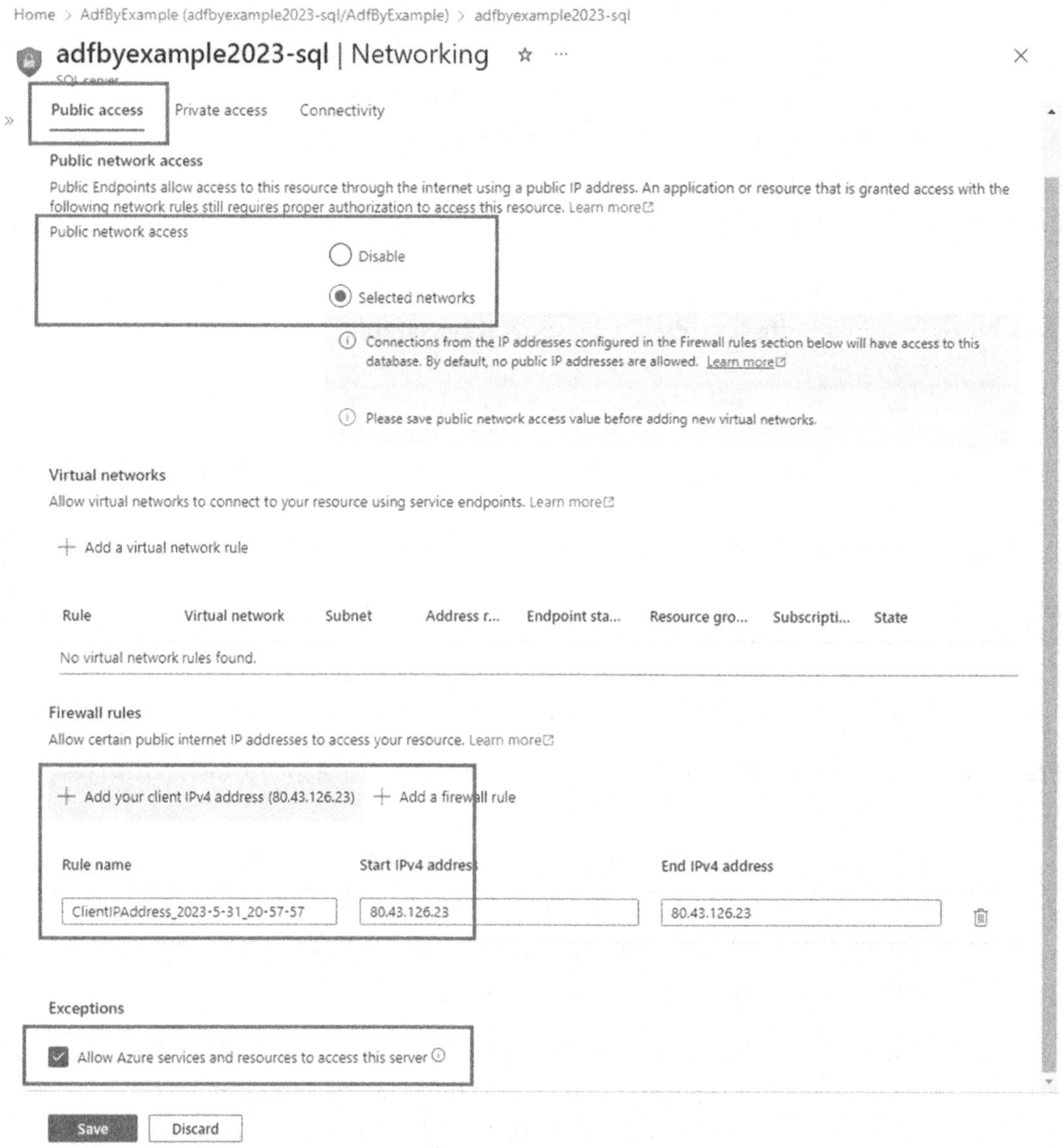

Home > AdfByExample (adfbyexample2023-sql/AdfByExample) > adfbyexample2023-sql

adfbyexample2023-sql | Networking ☆ ⋯   ×
SQL server

| Public access | Private access | Connectivity |

Public network access

Public Endpoints allow access to this resource through the internet using a public IP address. An application or resource that is granted access with the following network rules still requires proper authorization to access this resource. Learn more⧉

Public network access

      ○ Disable

      ◉ Selected networks

      ⓘ Connections from the IP addresses configured in the Firewall rules section below will have access to this database. By default, no public IP addresses are allowed. Learn more⧉

      ⓘ Please save public network access value before adding new virtual networks.

Virtual networks

Allow virtual networks to connect to your resource using service endpoints. Learn more⧉

 ＋ Add a virtual network rule

| Rule | Virtual network | Subnet | Address r... | Endpoint sta... | Resource gro... | Subscripti... | State |

No virtual network rules found.

Firewall rules

Allow certain public internet IP addresses to access your resource. Learn more⧉

 ＋ Add your client IPv4 address (80.43.126.23)   ＋ Add a firewall rule

Rule name	Start IPv4 address	End IPv4 address
ClientIPAddress_2023-5-31_20-57-57	80.43.126.23	80.43.126.23 🗑

Exceptions

☑ Allow Azure services and resources to access this server ⓘ

[Save] [Discard]

Figure 3-5. *Configure logical SQL Server networking*

Create Database Objects

Connection to your Azure SQL DB instance is possible using a number of client tools, for example:

- SQL Server Management Studio (SSMS) installed on your computer

- Azure Data Studio (ADS) installed on your computer

- The online SQL DB Query editor

To use SSMS or ADS, you will need to connect to the server, using its fully qualified domain name, with the username and password you configured in the previous section. The location of the server's name on the SQL database blade is indicated in Figure 3-4 – in this example, it is `adfbyexample2023-sql.database.windows.net`. To use the online query editor, click *Query editor (preview)* (also indicated in Figure 3-4) and log in with the same credentials.

Once you have connected successfully, you will be able to create database objects. Listing 3-1 provides SQL code to create a new table in your database – source code samples used in this book are available from the book's GitHub repository, located at `https://github.com/Apress/Azure-Data-Factory-by-Example-Second-Edition`. Copy and paste the SQL statement into the client tool of your choice and run the query.

Listing 3-1. Table creation script for dbo.Sales_LOAD

```
CREATE TABLE dbo.Sales_LOAD (
  RowId INT NOT NULL IDENTITY(1,1)
, Retailer NVARCHAR(255) NULL
, SalesMonth DATE NULL
, Product NVARCHAR(255) NULL
, ManufacturerProductCode NVARCHAR(50) NULL
, SalesValueUSD DECIMAL(18,2) NULL
, UnitsSold INT NULL
, CONSTRAINT PK__dbo_Sales_LOAD PRIMARY KEY (RowId)
);
```

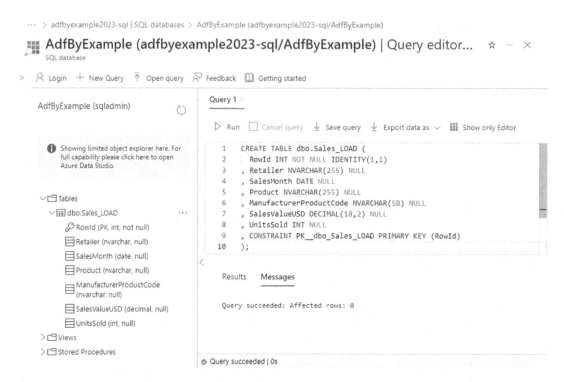

Figure 3-6. *Azure SQL DB's online query editor*

Figure 3-6 shows the online query editor after running the query, with the object explorer sidebar's *Tables* node refreshed and expanded to show the result.

Import Structured Data into Azure SQL DB

You have now created all the resources you need in order to start using ADF pipelines to move data between files in blob storage and SQL database tables. In this section, you will learn how to create pipelines that copy data from *structured* data files. Structured data formats are essentially *tabular* – file data is stored in rows, each of which contains the same number of fields. Comma-separated values (CSV) files are a common structured data format.

Create the Basic Pipeline

You will now create a pipeline to copy CSV file data into your Azure SQL Database. Recall from Chapter 2 that this requires a dataset and linked service at either end of the data movement and a Copy activity to connect the two.

Create the Database Linked Service and Dataset

Start by creating a linked service for your new Azure SQL DB, as follows:

1. Open ADF Studio and navigate to the management hub. Under *Connections* in the hub sidebar, select *Linked services*.

2. Click the + *New* button at the top of the *Linked services* page, then search for and select *Azure SQL Database*. Click *Continue*.

3. Complete the *New linked service (Azure SQL Database)* flyout (Figure 3-7). Use the account selection method "From Azure subscription," then select your subscription, server name, and database name. Choose the authentication type "SQL authentication" and supply your database server username and password.

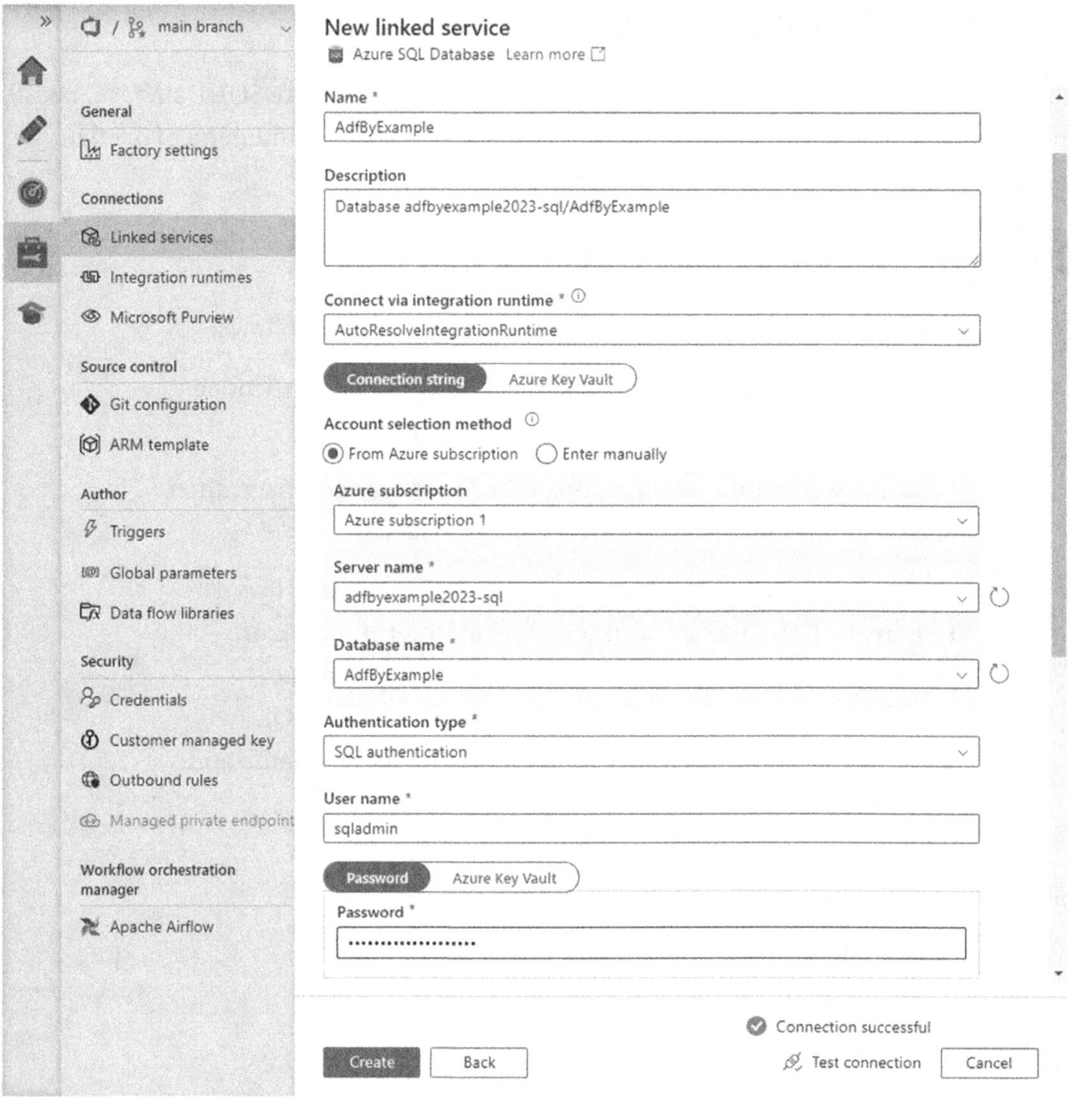

Figure 3-7. *New linked service (Azure SQL Database) flyout*

4. Use the *Test connection* button to verify your input values, then click *Create*. As when you created your storage account, the SQL DB linked service will be published immediately, to allow ADF to store the server password securely.

Now create a dataset to represent the table dbo.Sales_LOAD you created in the previous section:

1. Navigate to the authoring canvas. The *Factory Resources* explorer lists resources defined in your ADF Studio session – these are the resource definitions loaded from your working branch in Git. Each resource type section header includes a count of the number of resources (e.g., 1 pipeline, 2 datasets). Hover over the datasets count to reveal an ellipsis *Dataset Actions* button (indicated in Figure 3-8).

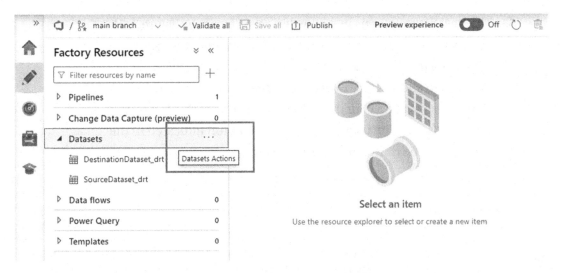

Figure 3-8. *Datasets Actions button in the Factory Resources explorer*

2. Click the *Datasets Actions* button to access the Dataset Actions menu. It contains two items: *New dataset* and *New folder*. Folders help organize resources inside your factory and can be nested. Create a new folder and name it "Chapter3" (you may also like to create a "Chapter2" folder to contain the datasets created by the Copy data tool – if you do this, you can simply drag the existing datasets and drop them into that folder).

3. The "Chapter3" folder shows a resource count (currently zero) and an Actions menu button. Choose *New dataset* from the Actions menu, then search for and select *Azure SQL Database*. Click *Continue.*

4.   Name the dataset "ASQL_dboSalesLoad" and select the new SQL
     DB linked service from the dropdown. A *Table name* dropdown
     appears – select the dbo.Sales_LOAD table, then click *OK*.

Tip   You may wish to adopt a naming convention for factory resources. My
preference is to avoid prefixes that indicate a resource's type, because resource
types are usually clear from their contexts. I do, however, find prefixes indicating a
dataset's storage type to be useful (e.g., "ASQL" for Azure SQL DB datasets).

---

5.   The new dataset opens in a new design surface tab (Figure 3-9).
     On the right-hand side, you see the tabbed *Properties* flyout,
     displaying the dataset's name and description. The flyout's
     Related tab allows you to see which pipelines refer to a dataset, a
     feature also available for other factory resources. You can toggle
     the flyout's visibility using the *Properties* button indicated in the
     figure – use the button to close the flyout.

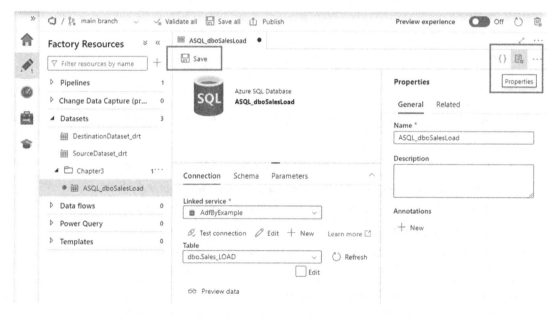

Figure 3-9. *Editing a dataset in the authoring canvas*

6. To the left of the Properties button, the *Code* button (braces or {} icon) allows you to inspect – and if you wish edit – a factory resource's definition as JSON. Click the button to view the code flyout, then click *Cancel* to close it.

7. The tabbed configuration pane below the design surface contains configuration information for the selected resource – in this case, the new dataset. The tabs present in the configuration pane vary between resource types. Select the *Schema* tab to inspect the schema of the `dbo.Sales_LOAD` table.

8. ADF Studio indicates unsaved changes in a number of ways. A gray dot appears to the left of your dataset's name in the Factory Resources explorer and to the right of its name on the design surface tab. In the navigation sidebar, the number "1" in a yellow circle below the pencil icon indicates that your session contains a total of one unsaved change. Click *Save* (indicated in Figure 3-9) to commit your dataset change and push it to your Git repository. Alternatively, you can click *Save all* in the factory header bar to commit and push all changes. Make sure that you save your changes regularly.

Note   ADF Studio is more tightly coupled to Git than is the case in other development environments. An ADF Studio session has no permanent storage of its own, so changes are saved directly to your linked Git repository. Every *Save* you make in ADF Studio is a Git commit that is immediately pushed to your Azure DevOps or GitHub repository.

Create a DelimitedText File Dataset

The pipeline you create will load sample CSV data from your blob storage account into an Azure SQL Database table. You created a linked service to connect to the storage account in Chapter 2 – you can reuse it to create a dataset representing a source CSV file.

1. Create a new dataset in the "Chapter3" folder by selecting *New dataset* from the folder's Actions menu, then select *Azure Blob Storage*. Click *Continue*.

2. On the *Select format* flyout, choose *DelimitedText* and click *Continue*.

3. Name the dataset "ABS_CSV_SweetTreats" – the file you are about to import is a CSV file in Azure Blob Storage (ABS) and contains sales data for a retailer called Sweet Treats. Select your existing blob storage linked service, then click the *Browse* button (folder icon) to the right of the *File path* fields.

4. Browse into the "sampledata" container until you find the "SampleData" folder. Navigate to the "SweetTreats/Apr-20" subfolder path and select the file "Sales.csv". Click *OK* to select the file and dismiss the file chooser.

5. Ensure that the *First row as header* check box is ticked, then click *OK* to create the dataset.

6. The new dataset opens in another design surface tab – click *Save* to commit and push the dataset definition to Git.

Create and Run the Pipeline

You are now ready to create the pipeline. Before you start, you may wish to move the pipeline from Chapter 2 into a "Chapter2" pipelines folder.

1. In the Factory Resources explorer, create a "Chapter3" folder under *Pipelines*, then select *New pipeline* from the folder's Actions menu.

2. A new pipeline tab opens with the *Properties* flyout displayed. The new pipeline has a default name like "pipeline1" – change its name to "ImportSweetTreatsSales" and add a description, then close the flyout.

3. If you need more space on the design surface, collapse the Factory Resources explorer by clicking the left chevrons («) button to the right of the *Factory Resources* heading.

4. To the left of the design surface is the Activities toolbox, headed *Activities*. Expand the *Move and transform* group, then drag a *Copy data* activity from the toolbox and drop it onto the canvas. The configuration pane below the canvas automatically expands to allow you to configure the activity.

5. The Copy data activity is generally referred to simply as the *Copy activity*. On the *General* tab of the configuration pane, change the name of your Copy activity to "Import sales data."

Caution   Activity names may contain alphanumeric characters, hyphens, underscores, and spaces, but names cannot start or end with a space. Although ADF Studio may appear to accept terminal spaces in activity names, they are automatically removed when the pipeline is saved.

---

6. On the *Source* tab, select the "ABS_CSV_SweetTreats" dataset, and on the *Sink* tab, choose the dataset "ASQL_dboSalesLoad". Azure Data Factory refers to pipeline data destinations as *sinks*.

7. In the design surface toolbar (immediately above the surface), click *Save* to commit and push your changes, then *Debug* to run the pipeline.

Pipeline run information is displayed on the *Output* tab of the pipeline's configuration pane (shown in Figure 3-10). Hovering over the name of the Copy activity on the *Output* tab reveals three icons for accessing information on the activity's *Input*, *Output*, and *Details*.

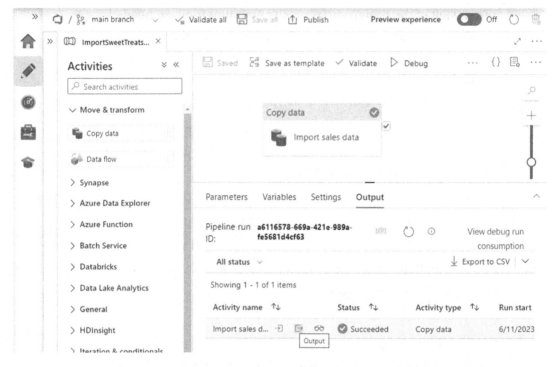

Figure 3-10. *Design surface with pipeline configuration pane's Output tab*

The Copy activity's output is a JSON object containing data about the activity run – the first part of an example output is shown in Figure 3-11. Notice particularly the following attributes:

- **filesRead:** The number of files read by the Copy activity run (in this example, one file)

- **rowsRead:** The total number of source rows read by the activity run

- **rowsCopied:** The number of sink rows written by the activity run

Figure 3-11. First part of a Copy activity run's output JSON object

Verify the Results

Return to the SQL client of your choice and verify that the dbo.Sales_LOAD table now contains the number of rows reported by the Copy activity run.

You may wish also to inspect the contents of the April 2020 "Sales.csv" file to verify that its contents have been correctly uploaded. The first few rows of the file are shown in Listing 3-2. In particular, notice the field names in the first row of the file – they match column names in the database table exactly. During pipeline creation, you did not map CSV fields to table columns yourself, but the Copy activity inferred the mapping automatically using matching column names.

Listing 3-2. The first few rows of the Sales.csv file

```
SalesMonth,Retailer,Product,SalesValueUSD,UnitsSold
"01-Apr-2020","Sweet Treats","Schnoogles 8.81oz",3922.31,409
"01-Apr-2020","Sweet Treats","Creamies 10.57oz",3057.18,502
"01-Apr-2020","Sweet Treats","Caramax 6.59oz",1147.37,443
```

For SSIS developers   In Chapter 2, I compared the Copy activity to an SSIS File System Task, but here it provides functionality like a simple Data Flow Task containing two components: a flat file data source and a SQL Server destination.

Process Multiple Files

The sample dataset includes six months of sales data for Sweet Treats. Each month's file has the same name – "Sales.csv" – and like April 2020's file is found in a folder named for the month to which it relates. The dataset you created in the previous section identifies April's data file specifically, but the Copy activity supports wildcard behavior that enables you to specify multiple files for processing.

1. In the ADF Studio design surface for your sales data import pipeline, click the Copy activity to select it. The configuration pane for the activity automatically expands below the canvas.

Tip   When selected, an activity on the design surface displays additional activity-specific functions including *Delete*, *View source code*, and *Clone*. The *Add activity* function is introduced in Chapter 6.

---

2. Select the *Source* tab, then change the *File path type* to "Wildcard file path." This means that the original file path specified in the dataset will no longer be used. Fields for wildcard paths are displayed (Figure 3-12).

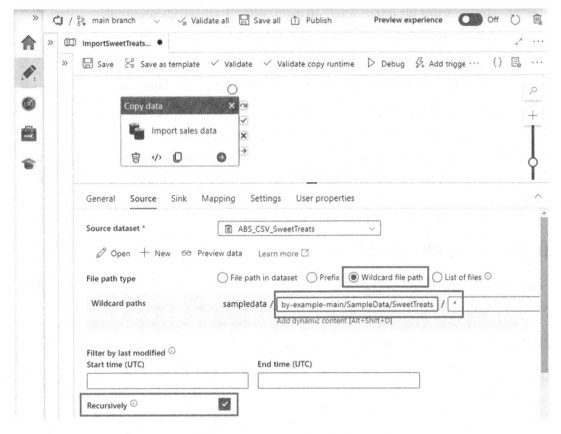

Figure 3-12. *Wildcard file path in the Copy activity source*

3. The container portion of the blob storage path is populated
    automatically from the "ABS_CSV_SweetTreats" dataset. In the
    Wildcard folder path field, enter "azure-data-factory-by-example-
    main/SampleData/SweetTreats" (the path to the "SweetTreats"
    folder). The path ends with "SweetTreats" and has no leading or
    trailing slash character.

Note   Unlike Windows environments, Azure Blob Storage file paths are case-
sensitive, and paths are delimited using the *forward*-slash character ("/").

---

4. In *Wildcard file name*, enter an asterisk (*"*"*) – this indicates that all files found in the "SweetTreats" folder are to be imported.

5. Scroll down and ensure that the *Recursively* check box is ticked. This indicates that files matching the wildcard path in any nested subfolder of "SweetTreats" are to be included.

Save your changes, then click *Debug* to run the pipeline. When complete, look at the Copy activity's Output JSON. This time, you will notice that the activity read a total of 6 files and 684 rows – all of the "Sales.csv" files for the six months between April and September 2020.

Truncate Before Load

Return to your SQL client of choice and run the query in Listing 3-3 to count the number of records loaded for each month.

Listing 3-3. Count records loaded per month

```
SELECT
  Retailer
, SalesMonth
, COUNT(*) AS [Rows]
FROM [dbo].[Sales_LOAD]
GROUP BY
  Retailer
, SalesMonth;
```

As expected, there are now rows present for each of the six months, but notice that the row count for April is roughly twice that of the other months. This is because you have loaded April's data twice – once when you ran your pipeline for the first time, then a second time while loading all six months' data. To use the dbo.Sales_LOAD table correctly, it must be truncated before each load activity.

This requirement can be supported using built-in Copy activity functionality provided for SQL database sinks. On the activity's *Sink* tab in ADF Studio, add this SQL command to the *Pre-copy script* field (Figure 3-13):

```
TRUNCATE TABLE dbo.Sales_LOAD
```

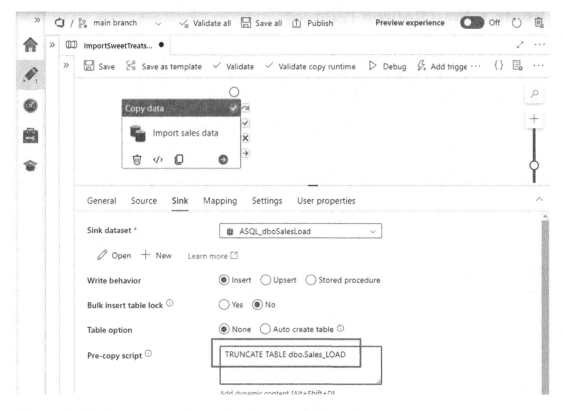

Figure 3-13. *Pre-copy script in the Copy activity sink*

This SQL command will be executed at the database containing the sink dataset every time the Copy activity runs, before any data is copied.

Run the pipeline again by clicking *Debug* – notice that debug mode allows you to run your revised pipeline without having saved your changes – then check the table's row counts again, using the script in Listing 3-3. This time, you will find that a similar number of rows is reported for each of the six months.

Map Source and Sink Schemas

The pipeline you created in the previous section relies on the Copy activity's ability to infer column mappings by matching names in the source files and sink table. In this section, you will discover what happens when source and sink column names do not match and how to handle that situation.

Create a New Source Dataset

The pipeline you're about to create will load data for a different retailer called Candy Shack. Its source data is also supplied in CSV files, so you can base its source dataset on "ABS_CSV_SweetTreats" by *cloning* it and editing the clone.

1. Figure 3-14 shows ADF Studio with the *Factory Resources* explorer expanded. Hovering over the right-hand end of the "ABS_CSV_SweetTreats" dataset (below the "Chapter3" folder pipeline count) reveals the ellipsis *Actions* button – click it to access the dataset's Actions menu, then select *Clone*.

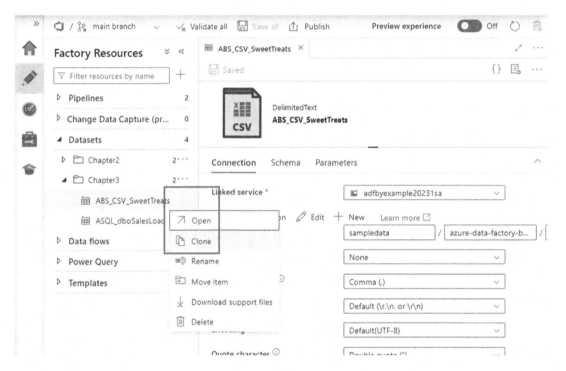

Figure 3-14. *Actions menu for ADF dataset*

2. *Clone* creates a copy of the original dataset and opens it in ADF Studio. The new dataset is automatically given a new name, based on the original – when it opens, the *Properties* flyout appears so that you can rename it. Change its name to "ABS_CSV_CandyShack" and close the flyout.

3. Edit the dataset's *File path* by browsing to the "CandyShack" folder nested below the "sampledata" container and choosing file "2020-04.csv".

4. Click *Save all* to save the new dataset and any unsaved changes.

Create a New Pipeline

The pipeline itself is very similar to the one you created to load Sweet Treats data. Clone the "ImportSweetTreatsSales" pipeline in the same way that you cloned the dataset, and amend it as follows:

1. Name the new pipeline "ImportCandyShackSales."

2. Change the Copy activity's *Source dataset* – using the dropdown list, select "ABS_CSV_CandyShack".

3. Still on the *Source* tab, edit *Wildcard paths*, replacing the reference to the folder "SweetTreats" with "CandyShack" (making sure that you leave the rest of the path intact).

4. Click *Debug* to run the pipeline. When pipeline execution stops, you will discover that the Copy activity run has a status of "Failed".

5. To the right of the activity's reported "Failed", an *Error* button (speech bubble icon) is displayed. Click *Error* to view information about why the activity failed.

The error pop-up window describing the activity failure is shown in Figure 3-15. Notice particularly the text "The column SkuCode is not found in target side." This indicates that a field called "SkuCode" was found in the source data, but that the sink table contains no corresponding field of the same name.

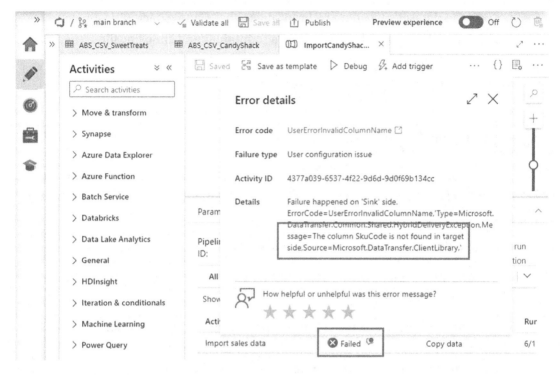

Figure 3-15. Copy activity error details

Configure Schema Mapping

For this Copy activity to succeed, you must first map source columns to sink columns explicitly, as follows:

1. Select the *Mapping* tab on the Copy activity's configuration pane and click the *Import schemas* button. Wait a few moments while ADF Studio retrieves schema information from a Candy Shack source file and the database sink table.

2. ADF Studio attempts to map imported source and sink columns automatically, displaying error or warning messages where necessary. Figure 3-16 shows the initial results of importing the two schemas.

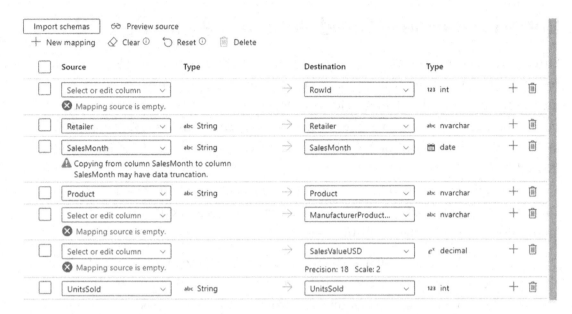

Figure 3-16. *Imported Candy Shack source and database sink schemas*

3. Additional controls to the right of each column mapping enable you to delete the mapping or to insert a new one. In this example, the destination [RowId] database column is an integer identity generated automatically by the database, so the mapping can be deleted – use the trash can icon to the right of the [RowId] mapping to do so. The source file contains no field corresponding to [ManufacturerProductCode], so remove this mapping too.

4. The dropdown lists for each field mapping allow you to select participating source and destination field name mappings. The source field corresponding to the destination [SalesValueUSD] column is called simply "SalesValue" – select it from the list.

5. Click *Debug* to run the pipeline again, this time successfully. Use Listing 3-3 in your SQL client to verify that six months' sales data for Candy Shack has been loaded into dbo.Sales_LOAD. Notice that the previously loaded Sweet Treats data has been removed by the activity's Pre-copy script.

Import Semi-structured Data into Azure SQL DB

Structured, tabular data files – such as the CSV files described in the previous section – resemble database tables in structure. In contrast, nontabular or *semi-structured* data formats use embedded metadata to identify data elements and frequently contain nested components. Common semi-structured data formats include JSON and XML; in this section, you will author a pipeline using the Copy activity's features for handling JSON data.

The sample data for loading is a collection of monthly sales data reports for a confectionery retailer called Sugar Cube. The Sugar Cube sales report format has the following features, as shown in Listing 3-4:

- The JSON document has a Month field identifying the month to which the report relates, a Company field identifying Sugar Cube, and a Sales field containing a list of individual product sales summaries.

- Each product sales summary identifies a product by name and manufacturer code, reporting the quantity sold (Units) and the total sales revenue (Value) for that product during the reporting month.

Listing 3-4. Start of a Sugar Cube sales report file

```
{
  "Month": "01-apr-2020",
  "Company": "Sugar Cube",
  "Sales": [
    {
      "Product": "Schnoogles 8.81oz",
      "ManufacturerProductCode": "CS-20147-0250",
      "Units": 745,
      "Value": 6995.55
    },
```

Create a JSON File Dataset

The new pipeline will load sample JSON data from your blob storage account into Azure SQL DB. In the previous section, you created the "ABS_CSV_CandyShack" dataset by cloning "ABS_CSV_SweetTreats", but in this case, you must create a new dataset from scratch. A dataset's file type can only be specified when the dataset is created – to load JSON data, you must first create a JSON blob storage dataset.

1. On the "Chapter3" folder's *Actions* menu in the *Factory Resources* explorer, click *New dataset*.

2. Select the *Azure Blob Storage* data store and click *Continue*.

3. On the *Select format* flyout, choose *JSON*. Click *Continue*.

4. Name the dataset "ABS_JSON_SugarCube" and select your existing storage account linked service. When the *File path* option appears, browse to the "SugarCube" subfolder in the "sampledata" container and find the file "April.json". Click *OK* to select the file.

5. Click *OK* to create the new dataset, then save it.

Create the Pipeline

Create a new pipeline named "ImportSugarCubeSales," either by cloning one of your existing "Chapter3" pipelines or from scratch. Add a Copy activity to the pipeline (unless you have cloned an existing pipeline) and configure the activity's source and sink as follows:

- **Source:** Choose the "ABS_JSON_SugarCube" dataset and select *File path type* "Wildcard file path." Under *Wildcard paths*, set the *Wildcard folder path* to "azure-data-factory-by-example-main/SampleData/SugarCube" (omitting the year and quarter subfolders) and specify "*.json" as *Wildcard file name*. Ensure that the *Recursively* check box is ticked.

- **Sink:** Choose your Azure SQL DB dataset and ensure that *Pre-copy script* is configured to truncate the destination database table.

Configure Schema Mapping

Select the Copy activity's *Mapping* configuration tab and click *Import schemas*.
Figure 3-17 shows the initial mapping, generated automatically by ADF Studio.

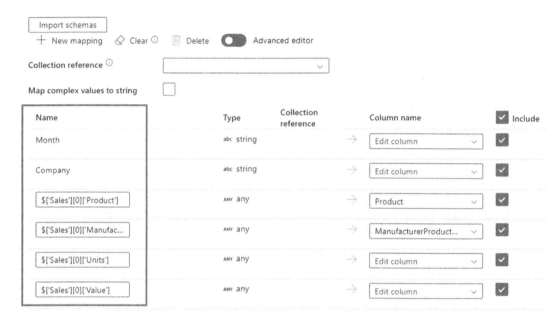

Figure 3-17. *Imported Sugar Cube source and database sink schemas*

The *Name* column (indicated in the figure) identifies source attributes detected in
the JSON file. The top-level "Month" and "Company" attributes appear as labels, while
every other attribute's name appears as an editable text box containing a JSON path
expression. In fact, even the labels have an underlying JSON path – to see this, enable
the *Advanced editor* on the *Mapping* tab. As you can see in Figure 3-18, this shows the
underlying JSON path expressions used to extract all source attribute values.

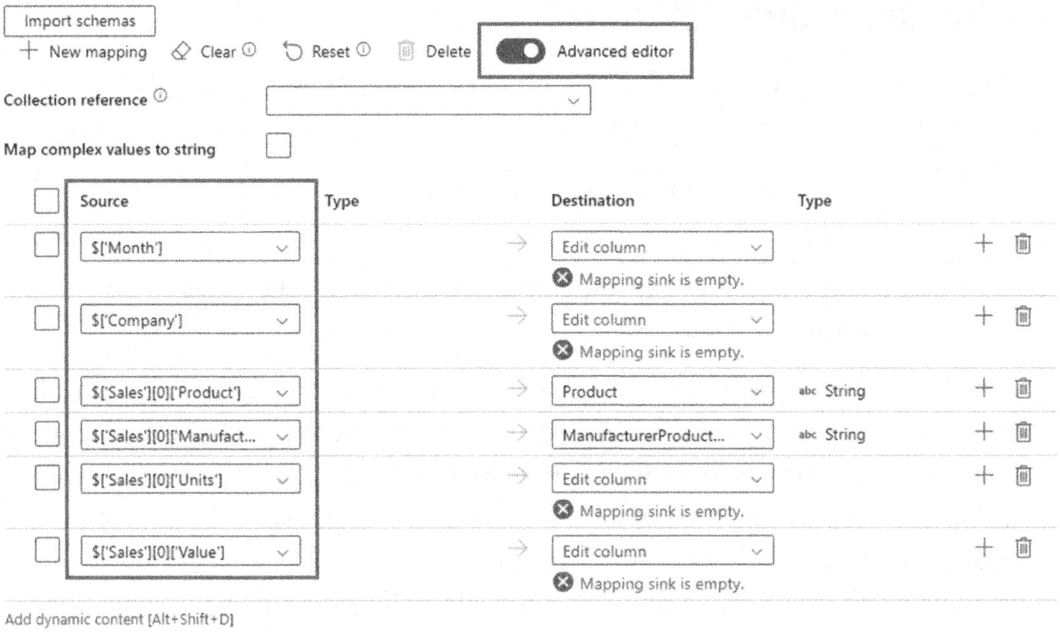

Figure 3-18. *Advanced mapping editor showing JSON path expressions*

We'll look at the JSON paths in more detail in a moment, but for the time being, notice that the final part of each path contains the name of a sales summary field. The "Product" and "ManufacturerProductCode" source fields have already been mapped to matching destination column names. Map the remaining JSON path expressions to their corresponding database table columns:

- $['Month'] → SalesMonth

- $['Company'] → Retailer

- $['Sales'][0]['Units'] → UnitsSold

- $['Sales'][0]['Value'] → SalesValueUSD

Now run the pipeline. When you inspect the results using your SQL client, you will discover that you have loaded exactly six rows.

Set the Collection Reference

The nested structure of JSON objects allows them to represent normalized data structures. The Sugar Cube sales report format contains the following relationships:

- Each report file contains exactly one monthly sales report JSON document.

- Each sales report JSON document contains many product sales summaries.

The *Collection reference* property on the Copy activity's *Mapping* configuration tab controls what an output row of data represents: in this case, either an individual product sales summary or the entire monthly report document. By default, *Collection reference* is set to the JSON document root, so the six rows loaded when you ran the pipeline correspond to the six Sugar Cube report files.

To understand the values selected for loading by ADF, review the path expressions shown in Figure 3-18. The leading "$" character refers to the root of the JSON document, so the expression $['Month'] means "the *Month* attribute in the root of the JSON document." In contrast, the sales summary paths all begin with $['Sales'][0], referring specifically to the first sales summary object in the file (counting from zero). $['Sales'] [0]['Units'] means "the *Units* attribute in the *first* element of the array named *Sales*."

To load each sales summary object as a separate row, use the *Collection reference* dropdown (above the list of column mappings) to change the collection reference to "$['Sales']." Figure 3-19 illustrates how doing this also updates the sales summary source expressions, making them relative to the new collection reference.

Figure 3-19. *JSON path expressions relative to the mapping's collection reference*

Run the pipeline again, then use your SQL client to verify that 100–120 rows have been loaded for each month.

The Effect of Schema Drift

Use your SQL client to look at the Sugar Cube data loaded for September 2020 (using a query such as the one shown in Listing 3-5).

Listing 3-5. Select September's Sugar Cube data

```
SELECT *
FROM [dbo].[Sales_LOAD]
WHERE Retailer = 'Sugar Cube'
AND SalesMonth = '2020-09-01';
```

A close inspection of the query results reveals that every row of data for September has no value in the database table's [Product] column. This has been caused by a small change to the sales report's JSON structure, introduced in that month. Listing 3-6 shows the start of the September file, in which you can see that the product name field, formerly called "Product," is now called "Item."

Listing 3-6.   Start of the September 2020 Sugar Cube sales report file

```
{
  "Month": "01-sep-2020",
  "Company": "Sugar Cube",
  "Sales": [
    {
      "Item": "Schnoogles 8.81oz",
      "ManufacturerProductCode": "CS-20147-0250",
      "Units": 643,
      "Value": 6745.07
    },
```

The result of renaming the "Product" field is that it appears simply to have been omitted, which ADF has accepted without error. JSON handling by the Copy activity is necessarily tolerant of missing fields, because optional elements may not always be present in a JSON object.

There is no simple fix here, but it illustrates the point that you cannot rely on JSON schema mappings to detect schema drift. Unlike when loading a structured data file, schema drift may not cause failure. In Chapter 6, you will add a basic data quality check on loaded data to improve pipeline robustness.

Understanding Type Conversion

When moving or transforming data, integration processes must mediate differences in type systems used by source and sink data stores. The `string` type shown for the "Month" and "Company" source fields in Figure 3-17 is a JSON data type, while the types of the corresponding sink fields shown in Figure 3-19 (`date`, `nvarchar`) are native to SQL Server. Data conversion between these two type systems takes place via a third: Azure Data Factory *interim data types* (IDTs).

The Copy activity performs a three-step type conversion to translate data from a source type system to the sink type system:

1. Convert the native source type into an ADF interim type.

2. Convert the interim type to a possibly different interim type compatible with the sink type.

3. Convert the sink-compatible interim type into a native sink type.

This knowledge isn't essential for successful use of the Copy activity, but it may help you to understand the behavior of schema mappings between different formats. For example, CSV files have no consistent type system, so ADF treats all incoming fields as strings and automatically converts them to the String interim data type (as can be seen in the source types shown in Figure 3-16).

IDTs allow Azure Data Factory to support an ever-growing range of supported data stores in a scalable way. Without IDTs, adding support for a new kind of data store would require Microsoft to specify type conversions between the new store and every other existing kind of data store. This task would grow in size with every addition to the list of supported data stores. Using IDTs means that to extend support to new kinds of data store, ADF needs only to be able to convert the new store's data types to and from its own interim data type system.

For SSIS developers   ADF's approach to mediating type conversions via an intermediate type system will be familiar from SSIS Data Flow Tasks. Integration Services data types (e.g., DT_STR, DT_WSTR, and DT_I4) perform the same role in SSIS, providing extensible support for arbitrary pairings of source and destination type systems.

Transform JSON Files into Parquet

So far, in this chapter, you have used ADF's ability to read data from CSV and JSON files and its ability to write data to Azure SQL DB tables. The fact that the Copy activity's source and sink are both described using ADF *datasets* means that you can just as easily extract data from a SQL database and write it out to CSV or JSON files. Similarly, you could use the Copy activity to read data from CSV files and write it out as JSON – or in fact to read data from *any* supported dataset type and write it to any other.

Apache *Parquet* is a compressed, column-oriented structured data storage format. Analytics applications that process large numbers of rows benefit from a column-oriented format, because data in columns outside the scope of a given analysis need not be read. Individual columns often contain only a few distinct values, allowing column data to be heavily compressed for efficient storage and retrieval. For these reasons, Parquet format is frequently chosen for data lake storage of tabular data.

The confectionery retailer Handy Candy reports sales data in the form of individual sales transaction JSON messages. Listing 3-7 contains one such message object. In this section, you will create a pipeline to ingest these messages and output them in Parquet format. This ingestion pattern is frequently used to integrate new data into a data lake, but in this case, you will simply emit the Parquet file to Azure blob storage.

Listing 3-7. Handy Candy sales transaction message

```
{
  "TransactionId": "0C90CC54-392B-4322-BB23-B4B34CE403D9",
  "TransactionDate": "2020-06-08",
  "StoreId": "114",
  "Items": [
    {
      "Product": "Boho 2.82oz",
      "Price": 2.89
    }
  ]
}
```

Create a New JSON Dataset

In order to be able to import the schema of the Handy Candy message file, you need a JSON dataset that refers to a message file in the "HandyCandy" subfolder of the SampleData folder.

1. Either create a new JSON dataset using your blob storage account or clone "ABS_JSON_SugarCube". Name the new dataset "ABS_JSON_HandyCandy".

2. Set the dataset's *File path* by selecting one of the message files in the "sampledata" container's "HandyCandy" subfolder.

Create a Parquet Dataset

Create a new dataset in the "Chapter3" datasets folder with the following properties:

- **Data store:** Azure Blob Storage.

- **File format:** Parquet.

- **Name:** Enter "ABS_PAR_HandyCandy".

- **Linked service:** Choose your existing blob storage linked service.

- **File path:** Specify *Container* "output," *Directory* "datalake," and *File* "HandyCandy.parquet".

Before you click *OK* on the *Set properties* flyout, ensure that *Import schema* is set to "None."

Tip   If no "output" container exists when the pipeline is executed, the pipeline will create one automatically.

Create and Run the Transformation Pipeline

Create a new pipeline named "IngestHandyCandyMessages" in the "Chapter3" pipelines folder, then drag a Copy activity onto the design surface. Configure the activity as follows:

- **Source:** Choose the "ABS_JSON_HandyCandy" dataset and select *File path type* "Wildcard file path." Under *Wildcard paths*, set *Wildcard folder path* to "azure-data-factory-by-example-main/SampleData/ HandyCandy" and *Wildcard file name* to "*.json".

- **Sink:** Choose the "ABS_PAR_HandyCandy" dataset and set *Copy behavior* to "Merge files." This instructs ADF to merge incoming JSON message files into a single Parquet output file.

- **Mapping:** On the Mapping tab, click *Import schemas*. Verify that the imported schema matches the message structure shown in Listing 3-7. Enable the Mapping tab's *Advanced editor*, then select "$['Items']" from the *Collection reference dropdown*. Ensure that the source JSON path expressions are updated relative to the new collection reference. A Parquet file schema includes the data types of its columns – specify output column types as shown in Figure 3-20.

The destination field names shown in Figure 3-20 were generated automatically by the mapping tool but you can change them if you wish.

Figure 3-20. *Prepared mapping for the JSON to Parquet transformation*

Run the pipeline. When execution is complete, inspect your storage account's "output" container to verify that the Parquet file is present. Compression of columnar data means that the output file is about one-quarter of the total size of the input JSON files.

If you wish to verify the contents of the Parquet file, inspect it using the *Preview data* option on the "ABS_PAR_HandyCandy" dataset's *Connection* configuration tab.

Performance Settings

In addition to the tabs you have already explored, the Copy activity's configuration pane features a *Settings* tab. Two of these settings relate to activity performance – others are covered later in the book.

Data Integration Units

The main focus of this chapter has been how to copy data using the Copy activity, without paying a great deal of attention to performance. This has not been a problem because the sample datasets are small, but when working with larger, real-world datasets, you may be able to improve copy performance by adjusting default performance characteristics.

The Copy activity's resources are measured in *data integration units* (DIUs), a single measure that combines CPU, memory, and network usage. You can increase the power allocated to a Copy activity by increasing the maximum number of DIUs available to it, specified using the *Maximum data integration unit* option on the *Settings* tab.

The default setting for the Data integration unit is "Auto," which means that the number of DIUs allocated is determined automatically, based on information about your source and sink data stores. If you wish, you can increase the maximum DIU allocation above the default, but bear in mind that doing so may increase the financial cost of executing the activity. Conversely, the default DIU value for many scenarios is four, so you may wish to reduce your execution cost – particularly in learning and development scenarios – by limiting the number of DIUs to its minimum value of two.

You can see the number of DIUs used by a Copy activity execution in the `usedDataIntegrationUnits` field of the execution's JSON output (as shown in Figure 3-11). More information about DIUs and Copy activity performance is available at `https://learn.microsoft.com/en-us/azure/data-factory/copy-activity-performance-features`.

Degree of Copy Parallelism

The *Degree of copy parallelism* option allows you to override the Copy activity's default degree of parallelism. The degree of parallelism actually used at runtime appears in the `usedParallelCopies` field of the execution's JSON output. You can see how this varies even within your sample data pipelines – the Handy Candy ingestion pipeline processes many more files and exhibits a higher degree of parallelism. Automatic scale-out behavior of this kind is a key advantage of serverless services such as Azure Data Factory.

The default degree of parallelism is also determined automatically and varies based on information about your source and sink data stores. While it might seem tempting to override the default, Microsoft's advice is that the best data throughput is usually achieved with the default behavior. As in the case of DIUs, a more common use case might be to throttle parallelism, to avoid overloading a source data store.

Chapter Review

At the beginning of this chapter, I described the Copy activity as being the core tool for data *movement* in Azure Data Factory. While this is true, you will now have gained an appreciation of some of the data *transformation* capabilities also provided by the activity, enabling you to convert datasets between storage formats.

Conversion between data formats has three requirements:

- The ability to read data from a source format

- The ability to write data to a sink format

- Support for mapping elements from source data into the sink format

Azure Data Factory provides read/write functionality for a large number of storage formats and services by means of its rich library of linked services and dataset types. The abstract concept of a dataset allows the Copy activity to transform data between any source/sink dataset pairing, using ADF's interim data type system to manage type conversions between the two.

Key Concepts

The key concept for this chapter is the *Copy activity*. This powerful activity supports data movement and transformation between a wide variety of storage formats and services. Related concepts include the following:

- **Unstructured file:** A file treated as having no internal data structure – a blob. The Copy activity treats files as unstructured when a binary copy is specified.

- **Structured file:** A file with a tabular data structure such as CSV or Parquet.

- **Parquet file:** A column-oriented, compressed structured file format supporting efficient storage and querying of large volumes of data.

- **Semi-structured file:** A file with a nontabular, frequently nested data structure, such as XML or JSON.

- **Collection reference:** Nested data structures can represent multiple collections of data simultaneously. In a Copy activity schema mapping, the collection reference indicates which collection is to be transformed into data rows.

- **Sink:** Azure Data Factory refers to data pipeline destinations as sinks.

- **Interim data type:** The Copy activity converts incoming data values from their source types to ADF interim data types and then converts the resulting values to corresponding sink system types. This approach decouples source and sink type systems, reducing the complexity of supporting different kinds of storage system.

- **Data integration unit (DIU):** A DIU is a measure of computing power incorporating CPU, memory, and network usage. Power is allocated to Copy activity executions as a number of DIUs; the cost of an execution is determined by the duration for which it was allocated those DIUs.

- **Degree of parallelism (DoP):** A Copy activity can be performed in parallel using multiple threads to read different files simultaneously. The maximum number of threads used during an activity's execution is its degree of parallelism; the number can be set manually for the activity, but this is not advised.

- **Azure SQL DB:** Azure-based, PaaS SQL Server service.

- **Logical SQL Server:** Logical grouping of Azure SQL Databases for collective management.

- **Online query editor:** Web-based query editor available for use with Azure SQL DB (and other Azure database platforms).

Azure Data Factory Studio

As a result of working through this chapter, many of ADF Studio's features will now be familiar to you. Figure 3-21 shows ADF Studio's authoring canvas subdivided into its various regions:

- Region 1 is the *Factory Resources* explorer. From here, you used the various Actions menus to create and clone pipelines and datasets and to organize them into folders.

- Region 2 is the *Activities toolbox*. This contains the Copy activity, used extensively throughout this chapter, among others.

- Region 3 contains tabs for open resources such as pipeline or dataset definitions.

- Region 4 is the *design surface toolbar*. Its controls include the *Debug* button to run pipelines and the *Properties* flyout toggle. The code editor (braces icon) allows you to edit factory resources' JSON definitions directly.

- Region 5 is the *design surface*, a visual editor used to interact with pipeline activities. Display tools for search, zoom, and auto-alignment are on its right-hand edge.

- Region 6 is the design surface's *configuration pane*.

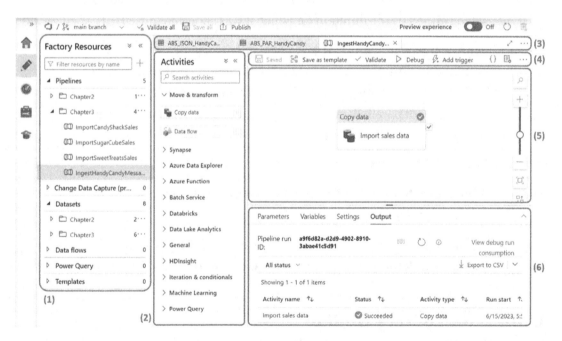

Figure 3-21. *Regions in the ADF Studio authoring canvas*

The configuration pane contains settings tabs specific to the currently selected object, for example, a pipeline, dataset, or activity. These vary widely depending on the selected object. In this chapter, you saw configuration options for

- Azure SQL DB and CSV file datasets (Figures 3-9 and 3-14)

- CSV datasets as sources (Figure 3-12)

- SQL DB datasets as sinks (Figure 3-13)

- Structured and semi-structured schema mapping (Figures 3-16 to 3-20)

- Pipeline debug execution output (Figure 3-10)

The wide range of available connectors means that the list of dataset configuration options is very large. My intention here is not to provide an exhaustive introduction to all connector types, but to introduce a few common datasets and to provide you with the tools to find your own way around.

For SSIS Developers

The Copy activity was introduced in Chapter 2, in a role similar to that of an SSIS File System Task. This chapter has extended its use to something like a rudimentary Data Flow Task. Abstracting sources and sinks as datasets enables the activity to behave like a combined SSIS source and destination component – for arbitrary pairings of supported data store – but it cannot perform intermediate per-row transformations familiar from the SSIS data flow surface. True Data Flow Task functionality will be introduced in Chapters 7 and 9.

Like SSIS, ADF achieves flexible transformation between source and destination type systems by using an intermediate type system of its own. As with Integration Services data types, this means that each kind of connector need only be concerned with type conversions into and out of ADF interim data types.

CHAPTER 4

Pipeline Expressions

The pipelines you authored in Chapter 3 have at least one thing in common: the values of all their properties are *static* – that is to say that they were determined at development time. In very many places, Azure Data Factory supports the use of *dynamic* property values – determined at runtime – through the use of *pipeline expressions*.

The main focus of this chapter is to introduce you to pipeline expressions, but you will also start to encounter more pipeline activities. The Copy activity is sufficiently broad and important to have deserved a chapter to itself, but from now on, you will start to make use of a wider variety of activities found in the Activities toolbox.

Explore the Pipeline Expression Builder

Pipeline expressions can be used in ADF Studio wherever you see the text *Add dynamic content [Alt+Shift+D]* – you may already have noticed this message appearing below text or other input fields as you edit them. Figure 4-1 shows the *Wildcard folder path* field (on the Copy activity's *Source* tab) with focus so that the message is visible.

© Richard Swinbank 2024
R. Swinbank, *Azure Data Factory by Example*, https://doi.org/10.1007/979-8-8688-0218-8_4

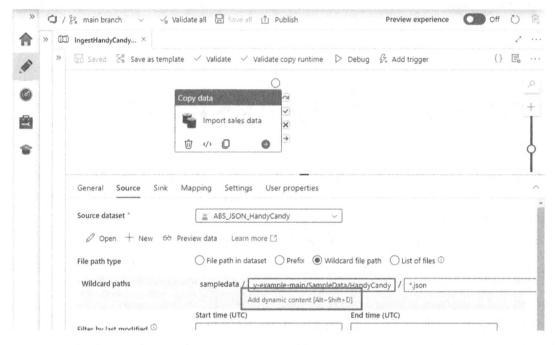

Figure 4-1. *Add dynamic content [Alt+Shift+D] appears when editing a field*

The message itself is a link to launch ADF Studio's *Pipeline expression builder*. As the message suggests, you can also launch the expression builder for a field by pressing *Alt+Shift+D* when the field has focus. Figure 4-2 shows the opened expression builder.

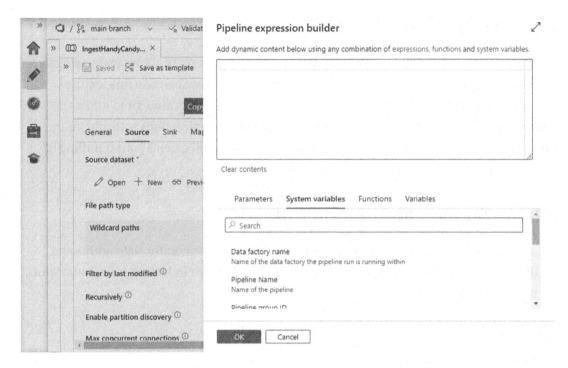

Figure 4-2. *Pipeline expression builder in ADF Studio*

Pipeline expressions make use of literal values, properties of factory resources, and a variety of expression functions. The lower half of the pipeline expression builder is a tabbed library of available parameters, variables, functions, and resource properties. The *Search* box at the top of each tab enables you to locate required elements quickly.

A later part of this chapter is concerned with user variables. Before that, you will start to use system variables and functions to add to pipeline functionality. We will return to pipeline parameters in Chapter 5.

Caution   ADF pipeline expressions are *case-sensitive* – when entering expressions by hand, make sure that you use the correct case when referring to a function, variable, or property.

Use System Variables

Among its source dataset configuration options, the Copy activity allows you to specify additional columns that can be copied to the activity sink. You can use this feature to duplicate an existing column, to include an additional static value, or to add a value determined at runtime. A common use case for dynamic values is to add audit information to incoming source data. In this section, you will extend your handling of Sweet Treats data by adding audit values in this way.

Enable Storage of Audit Information

Before proceeding, extend the [dbo].[Sales_LOAD] table to accommodate additional audit information. Use your SQL client to run the script given in Listing 4-1 against your Azure SQL Database.

Listing 4-1. Add columns to [dbo].[Sales_LOAD]

```
ALTER TABLE [dbo].[Sales_LOAD]
ADD PipelineRunId UNIQUEIDENTIFIER NULL
  , SourceFileName NVARCHAR(1024) NULL;
```

Create a New Pipeline

Create a new pipeline by cloning your "ImportSweetTreatsSales" pipeline from Chapter 3. Name the cloned pipeline "ImportSweetTreatsSales_Audit", then create a "Chapter4" folder for pipelines and move the new pipeline into it.

Add New Source Columns

Select the new pipeline's Copy activity. Add new source columns like this:

1. Navigate to the *Source* tab and scroll down until you find the *Additional columns* section.

2. Add a new column by clicking the + *New* button. Give it the name "SourceFileName" and leave its value set to the default $$FILEPATH. This special reserved variable indicates to ADF that the runtime source file path is to be provided as the field's value – it is not a true pipeline expression and can only be used here.

Caution   Make sure that the new column names are exactly as specified here. The Sweet Treats pipeline relies on ADF's inferred, case-sensitive schema mapping – the source and sink dataset column names must match for the mapping to succeed.

3. Add a second new column called "PipelineRunId." Expand the new field's *VALUE* field dropdown, then select "Add dynamic content" (indicated in Figure 4-3). The Pipeline expression builder opens automatically.

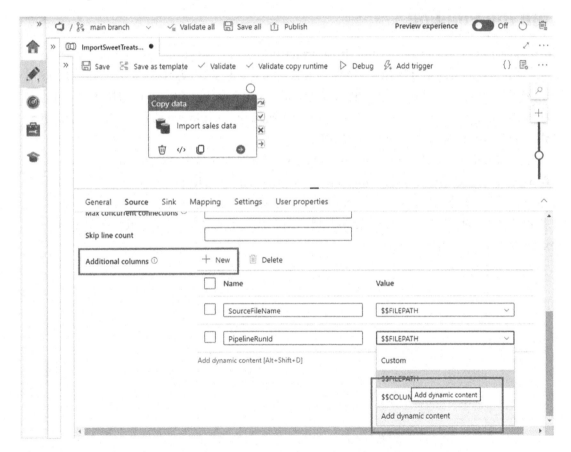

Figure 4-3. *Adding additional columns with dynamic content*

Caution   Be sure to use the "Add dynamic content" option in the *VALUE* field dropdown, not the similar link below the list of additional column names. The link's purpose is to permit the entire additional columns list to be defined using a single pipeline expression.

---

4. In the pipeline expression builder, select *Pipeline run ID* from the *System variables* tab. The text `@pipeline().RunId` appears in the expression pane at the top of the builder. Click *OK*.

Run the Pipeline

Run the pipeline and wait for it to finish execution, then use your SQL client to inspect the contents of the [dbo].[Sales_LOAD] table – Figure 4-4 shows the two new database columns populated with a pipeline run ID value and a source file path. (The file path is not the full, absolute path to the file in blob storage but is relative to the source dataset's folder path – this is the behavior of `$$FILEPATH`.)

The pipeline run ID inserted into the new column is a *globally unique identifier (GUID)*. GUIDs are used to identify pipeline runs in the same way they are used to identify almost everything in Azure. The value of the run ID – "3242688c-9d58-43e7-8e0b-8664209dbfd7" in Figure 4-4 – is the value returned by the expression `@pipeline().RunId`.

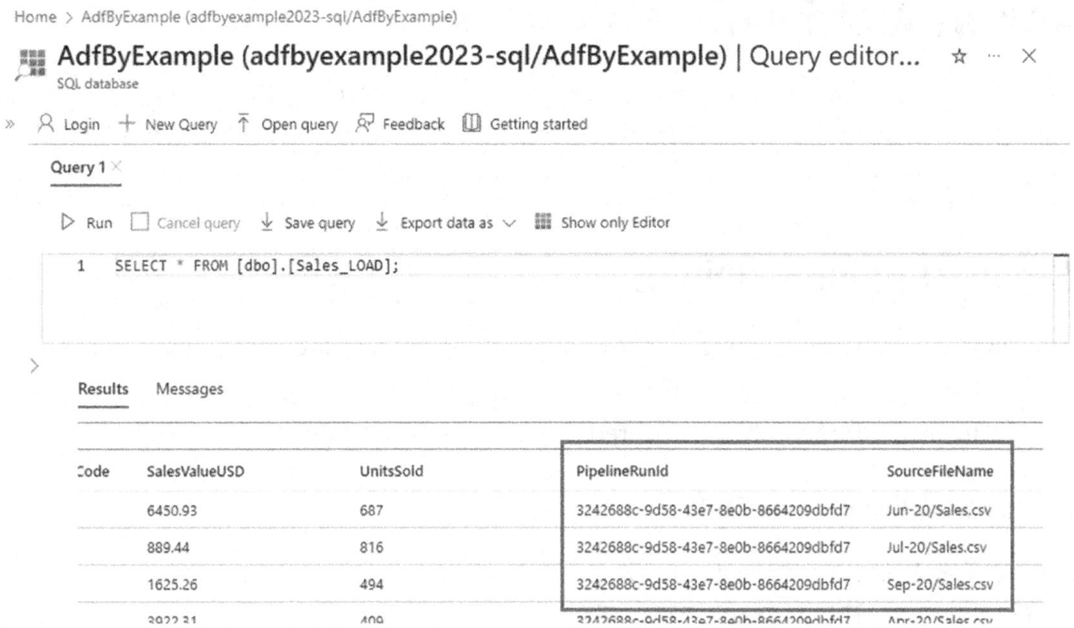

Figure 4-4. *Query results showing populated audit columns*

The purpose of a pipeline expression's initial @ symbol is to indicate to ADF that what follows is to be evaluated as an expression. If you omit the @ symbol, the expression becomes a fixed value: in this case, the string "pipeline().RunId". Such an omission would cause this pipeline to fail, because the string is not a valid value for the sink column's UNIQUEIDENTIFIER SQL type.

Tip   You must use the pipeline expression builder to create pipeline expressions – if you enter them directly into a field, ADF Studio stores them as string values. Fields that contain literal values are displayed with a white background; those containing expressions are light blue. This effect can be seen in Figure 4-7, later in this chapter.

Access Activity Run Properties

In this section, you will extend your pipeline to write some audit information about the pipeline's execution into your Azure SQL Database. You will do this using ADF's *Stored procedure activity*.

Create Database Objects

After the Copy activity is complete, your pipeline will call a stored procedure to record some information about the pipeline's execution in a database log table. Use Listings 4-2 and 4-3 to create the log table and stored procedure in your database.

Listing 4-2. Create a log table

```
CREATE TABLE dbo.PipelineExecution (
  RunSeqNo INT IDENTITY PRIMARY KEY
, PipelineRunId UNIQUEIDENTIFIER UNIQUE NOT NULL
, RunStartDateTime DATETIME NULL
, RunEndDateTime DATETIME NULL
, RunStatus NVARCHAR(20) NULL
, FilesRead INT NULL
, RowsRead INT NULL
, RowsCopied INT NULL
, Comments NVARCHAR(1024) NULL
);
```

Listing 4-3. Create a logging stored procedure

```
CREATE PROCEDURE dbo.LogPipelineExecution (
  @PipelineRunId UNIQUEIDENTIFIER
, @RunEndDateTime DATETIME
, @FilesRead INT
, @RowsRead INT
, @RowsCopied INT
) AS
```

```
INSERT INTO dbo.PipelineExecution (
  PipelineRunId
, RunEndDateTime
, FilesRead
, RowsRead
, RowsCopied
) VALUES (
  @PipelineRunId
, @RunEndDateTime
, @FilesRead
, @RowsRead
, @RowsCopied
);
```

Add Stored Procedure Activity

The Stored procedure activity is found in the *General* group of ADF Studio's Activities toolbox.

1. Open the "ImportSweetTreatsSales_Audit" pipeline in ADF Studio and drag a Stored procedure activity from the toolbox onto the design surface. The configuration pane below the design surface expands automatically – on the activity's *General* tab, name it "Log pipeline outcome."

2. The new activity is to be executed *after* the Copy activity has completed successfully. To enforce this, hold the left mouse button down over the green tick mark "handle" on the Copy activity's right-hand edge, then drag the mouse pointer over the Stored procedure activity.

   Releasing the left mouse button here creates an *activity dependency*. Figure 4-5 shows the pipeline configured with the correct dependency – the effect of this dependency is to prevent the Stored procedure activity from executing until the Copy activity has completed successfully.

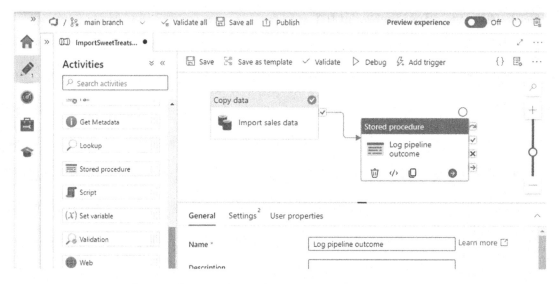

Figure 4-5. *Stored procedure activity dependent on the Copy activity*

Tip   To delete an activity dependency, right-click the dependency arrow and select *Delete* from the pop-up menu, or left-click to select it and hit your *Delete* key. These options are also available for pipeline activities, in addition to the *Delete* button (trash can icon) visible when an activity is selected.

---

3. Select the Stored procedure activity's *Settings* tab. It contains two mandatory input fields – choose your Azure SQL Database *Linked service*. After doing so, you will be able to select the newly created stored procedure from the *Stored procedure name* dropdown.

4. Below the *Stored procedure parameters* section heading is an *Import* button – click it to import the stored procedure's parameters from its definition in the database.

5. Use the pipeline expression builder to set the value of the parameter "PipelineRunId" as before, using the *Pipeline run ID* system variable.

6. Set the "RunEndDateTime" parameter to use the current UTC
   date and time. This is available using the *utcnow* function,
   found in the *Date Functions* section of the expression builder's
   Functions tab.

Note   Pipeline expression date functions return *strings*, because the expression language has no date or time types. The language has six types: string, integer, float, boolean, arrays, and *dictionaries*. A dictionary is a collection of named elements.

---

7. The values of "FilesRead," "RowsRead," and "RowsCopied" will
   be taken from the Copy activity's output JSON object – recall
   the activity output you encountered in Chapter 3. Open the
   pipeline expression builder for the "FilesRead" stored procedure
   parameter. Notice that the expression builder now includes an
   Activity outputs tab – this is because the pipeline contains an
   activity prior to the Stored procedure activity.

8. The *Activity outputs* tab includes a list of output properties
   available from predecessor activities, in this case, the pipeline's
   Copy activity. Click the output subtitled "Import sales data activity
   output" and observe that the text `@activity('Import sales
   data').output` appears in the expression pane.

9. `activity('Import sales data')` refers to the activity named
   "Import sales data," and the `.output` suffix specifies the activity's
   output object. To identify a field within the object, you must add
   another dot, followed by its JSON path expression. The `filesRead`
   field is in the root of the output object, so its path is simply the
   field's name. Add `.filesRead` to the expression pane so that the
   expression reads `@activity('Import sales data').output.
   filesRead` (as shown in Figure 4-6). Click *OK*.

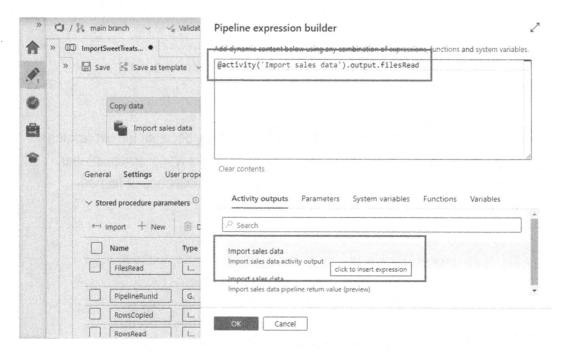

Figure 4-6. *Pipeline expression to obtain filesRead value from predecessor "Import sales data" activity output*

10. Set the "RowsRead" and "RowsCopied" parameter values in the
     same way. Table 4-1 provides the full list of stored procedure
     parameters and corresponding pipeline expressions for [dbo].
     [LogPipelineExecution].

Table 4-1. *Pipeline expressions for [dbo].[LogPipelineExecution] stored procedure parameters*

Parameter name	Pipeline expression
FilesRead	@activity('Import sales data').output.filesRead
PipelineRunId	@pipeline().RunId
RowsCopied	@activity('Import sales data').output.rowsCopied
RowsRead	@activity('Import sales data').output.rowsRead
RunEndDateTime	@utcnow()

For SSIS developers   The Stored procedure activity is conceptually similar to the SSIS Execute SQL Task, but it does not support the execution of arbitrary SQL statements, nor can it return a result set – these capabilities are provided by other ADF activities. Activity dependencies have behavior comparable to that of SSIS precedence constraints and are discussed in greater detail in Chapter 6.

Run the Pipeline

Run the pipeline, then use your SQL client to inspect the contents of the two tables: [dbo].[PipelineExecution] and [dbo].[Sales_LOAD].

- [dbo].[PipelineExecution] contains a single row containing pipeline execution information. You can verify the values in columns [FilesRead], [RowsRead], and [RowsCopied] by comparing them to the Copy activity output (on the *Output* tab of the pipeline's configuration pane). Notice that the *Output* configuration tab now lists two activity executions: the Copy activity and the Stored procedure activity.

- Rows in [dbo].[Sales_LOAD] have a [PipelineRunId] value matching that recorded in [dbo].[PipelineExecution]. This value can be found displayed in ADF Studio at the top of the pipeline's *Output* configuration tab.

Use the Lookup Activity

The audit information copied into [dbo].[PipelineExecution] is available in ADF's own pipeline run history, but storing it alongside sales data supports *lineage tracking* – recording when and how each record was brought into [dbo].[Sales_LOAD].

In this scenario, describing pipeline executions using GUIDs can be unwieldy or inconvenient. For example, using an integer identifier for lineage tracking – in place of the [PipelineRunId] in table [dbo].[Sales_LOAD] – has the desirable effect of reducing database row size.

ADF's *Lookup activity* is used to obtain small amounts of information from an ADF dataset for use in a pipeline's execution. In this section, you will use the Lookup activity to retrieve a log row's integer identity value (already allocated in [dbo]. [PipelineExecution]) and use it in place of the pipeline's execution GUID.

Create Database Objects

In the previous section, you inserted a log table row *after* the Copy activity had completed. Now you will need to insert a row *before* copying starts, in order to generate and return its identity value. You will update the same row afterward to add pipeline execution information. Using your SQL client, run the code given in Listings 4-4 and 4-5 to create two new stored procedures.

Listing 4-4. Create [dbo].[LogPipelineStart]

```
CREATE PROCEDURE dbo.LogPipelineStart (
  @PipelineRunId UNIQUEIDENTIFIER
, @RunStartDateTime DATETIME
, @Comments NVARCHAR(1024) = NULL
) AS
INSERT INTO dbo.PipelineExecution (
  PipelineRunId
, RunStartDateTime
, Comments
) VALUES (
  @PipelineRunId
, @RunStartDateTime
, @Comments
);
SELECT SCOPE_IDENTITY() AS RunSeqNo;
```

Listing 4-5. Create [dbo].[LogPipelineEnd]

```
CREATE PROCEDURE dbo.LogPipelineEnd (
  @RunSeqNo INT
, @RunEndDateTime DATETIME
, @RunStatus VARCHAR(20)
```

```
, @FilesRead INT
, @RowsRead INT
, @RowsCopied INT
) AS
UPDATE dbo.PipelineExecution
SET RunEndDateTime = @RunEndDateTime
   , RunStatus = @RunStatus
   , FilesRead = @FilesRead
   , RowsRead = @RowsRead
   , RowsCopied = @RowsCopied
WHERE RunSeqNo = @RunSeqNo;
```

The stored procedure shown in Listing 4-4 returns a result set consisting of one row and one column, containing the unique INT value inserted into the log table. To use this value in place of ADF's pipeline run ID, some additional modification to table [dbo]. [Sales_LOAD] is necessary. Run the code given in Listing 4-6 to replace the table's 16-byte UNIQUEIDENTIFIER [PipelineRunId] column with a smaller 4-byte INT field.

Listing 4-6. Alter logging table

```
ALTER TABLE dbo.Sales_LOAD
DROP COLUMN PipelineRunId;
ALTER TABLE dbo.Sales_LOAD
ADD RunSeqNo INT;
```

Configure the Lookup Activity

You're now ready to revise your "ImportSweetTreatsSales_Audit" pipeline in ADF Studio.

1. Drag a Lookup activity from the *General* section of the Activities toolbox onto the design surface and name it "Lookup RunSeqNo." Create a dependency to ensure that the Copy activity executes after the Lookup activity has succeeded. Figure 4-7 shows the correctly configured dependency.

2. Select the Lookup activity so that its configuration pane is displayed, then open its *Settings* tab. Recall that the Lookup activity obtains data from a dataset, so the tab offers you a dataset dropdown – choose the Azure SQL DB dataset you have been using to copy data into [dbo].[Sales_LOAD]. Ensure that the *First row only* check box is ticked.

3. Previously, you were able to override the file path configured in a blob storage dataset by specifying a wildcard path in the Copy activity – here you will override the Azure SQL DB dataset's configuration in the same way. The dataset was created to represent the [dbo].[Sales_LOAD] table, but you can override this setting to represent other result sets, such as other tables (or views), SQL queries, or stored procedures that return a result set. Set *Use query* to "Stored procedure" to indicate that you will be executing a stored procedure.

4. When you set *Use query* to "Stored procedure," ADF Studio offers you a dropdown *Stored procedure name* list. Choose your new [dbo].[LogPipelineStart] procedure, then click the *Import parameter* button to acquire its list of parameters.

5. Set the values of "PipelineRunId" and "RunStartDateTime" as before, using pipeline expressions `@pipeline().RunId` and `@utcnow()`. The new stored procedure also has a "Comments" parameter – leave it NULL for now, by ticking the *Treat as null* check box.

Figure 4-7 shows the correctly completed *Settings* pane for the Lookup activity.

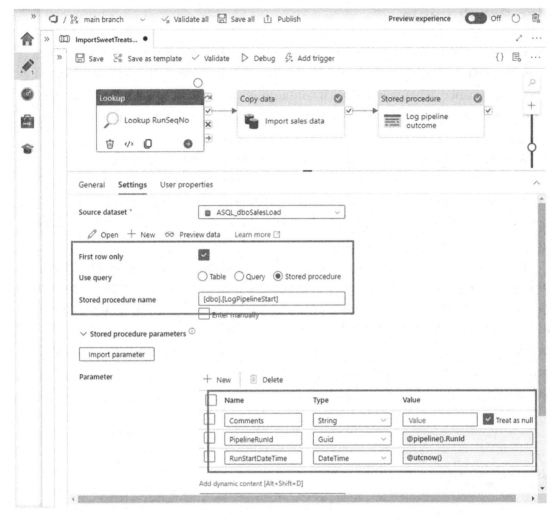

Figure 4-7. *Lookup activity configured with settings and dependencies*

For SSIS developers   Do not confuse ADF's Lookup activity with the Lookup transformation in SSIS – ADF Studio's design surface is equivalent to the SSIS control flow surface, so there is no stream of rows being processed here. A closer comparison is the use of an SSIS task to populate a package variable – for example, using an Execute SQL Task to retrieve a result set of one or more rows. The result set functionality absent from ADF's Stored procedure activity is present instead in the Lookup activity.

Use Breakpoints

To make use of the Lookup activity's output, you must read the value(s) you need from its execution output object. The exact JSON path required depends on the structure of the value returned: what field names it contains and whether it contains only one row or more. A simple way to find the JSON path in the activity execution's output object is to run the activity.

ADF Studio enables you to stop a pipeline's execution at a certain point using an activity *breakpoint*. When an activity is selected on the design surface – such as the Lookup activity in Figure 4-7 – a red circle is displayed above its top-right corner. To set a breakpoint on the activity, click inside the circle. When the breakpoint is set, the circle is filled red – to remove the breakpoint, click the filled circle.

Figure 4-8 shows the pipeline with a breakpoint set on the Lookup activity. The pipeline's other activities are grayed out because setting the breakpoint disables them – the activity where the breakpoint is set will still be executed. Unlike other IDEs you may be familiar with, ADF Studio does not permit you to resume execution after the breakpoint has been hit – a pipeline executes up to and including the first activity with a breakpoint set, but no further. The breakpoint tooltip visible in the figure describes this behavior as *Debug until*.

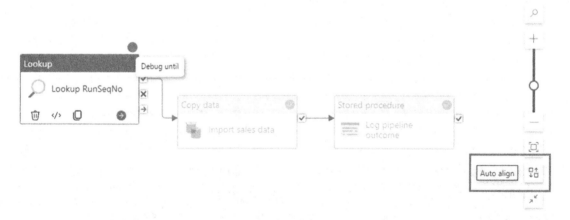

Figure 4-8. *Pipeline design surface showing breakpoint set on Lookup RunSeqNo*

Tip   To arrange activities neatly on the design surface, use the *Auto align* button, found at the bottom of the column of display tools on the right-hand side of the canvas (indicated in Figure 4-8).

Set a breakpoint on the Lookup activity as shown in Figure 4-8, then run the pipeline. When execution is complete, inspect the activity's output JSON in the pipeline's *Output* configuration tab. Figure 4-9 shows the output pane, highlighting the area of interest – the JSON path to the value returned by the stored procedure is `firstRow.RunSeqNo`.

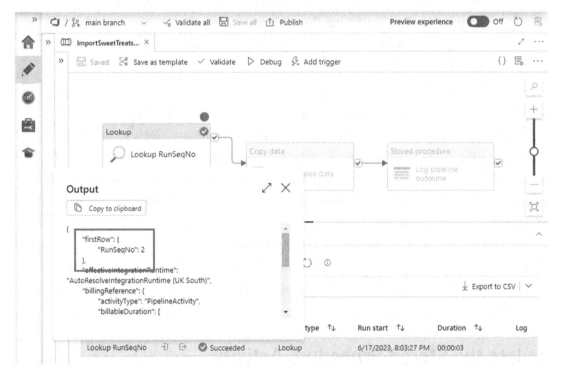

Figure 4-9. *The Lookup activity's Output object*

Use the Lookup Value

With the lookup value's JSON path, you can now use the value in the Copy activity.

1. Select the pipeline's Copy activity and open its *Source* configuration tab. Scroll down until you find the *Additional columns* section.

2. Change the name of the "PipelineRunId" column to "RunSeqNo." Recall that the activity is using a case-sensitive inferred mapping, so the column name must match that of the new database table column exactly.

3. Open the pipeline expression builder for the "RunSeqNo" column's *VALUE* field and remove the existing expression – there is a *Clear contents* link below the expression pane.

4. Select the output subtitled "Import RunSeqNo activity output" from the *Activity outputs* tab, then add a dot and the JSON path identified earlier. Verify that the expression reads `@activity('Lookup RunSeqNo').output.firstRow.RunSeqNo`, then click *OK*.

The *Activity outputs* tab offers various prepared snippets when building pipeline expressions – for example, you may have noticed the "Lookup RunSeqNo first row" option. This expression returns the entire `firstRow` object and is available at development time because you checked the Lookup activity's *First row only* check box. However, no snippets are provided for properties inside the `firstRow` object because they are not known until runtime (when they have been returned in the database result set).

Similarly, although the pipeline expression builder detects invalid syntax automatically, ADF Studio cannot detect invalid JSON paths during development. Ensure that you test thoroughly any activity that uses a JSON path to access runtime properties.

Update the Stored Procedure Activity

You must now update your pipeline's Stored procedure activity to use the new stored procedure specified in Listing 4-5.

1. Select the Stored procedure activity and open its *Settings* configuration tab. Select "[dbo].[LogPipelineEnd]" from the *Stored procedure name* dropdown list.

Tip   If you cannot see the stored procedure in the dropdown list, click the *Refresh* button to the right of the dropdown – this will reload the list from the database. If the field itself appears to be a text box instead of a dropdown list, verify that the *Enter manually* check box is not ticked.

2. Under *Stored procedure parameters*, click the *Import* button to import the new procedure's parameters. Set expressions for the values of parameters "FilesRead," "RowsCopied," "RowsRead," and "RunEndDateTime" as before.

3. Set the value of "RunSeqNo" to use the same expression as in the previous section (based on the output of the Lookup activity). Set "RunStatus" to "Done" – this is a string literal, so you can enter it directly into the field without launching the pipeline expression builder.

Notice that output values from both the Lookup activity and the Copy activity are available for use by the Stored procedure activity in pipeline expressions. An activity's output properties are available for use by any activity that is dependent on it, either directly or indirectly.

Run the Pipeline

Ensure that you have unset the breakpoint from the previous section, then run the pipeline. When execution has successfully completed, use your SQL client to inspect table contents. You should find that

- The latest row in [dbo].[PipelineExecution] – the row with the greatest [RunSeqNo] value – contains values for both [RunStartEndTime] and [RunEndDateTime].

- The value of [RunSeqNo] in [dbo].[Sales_LOAD] matches the value in the latest [dbo].[PipelineExecution] row.

The value of [RunSeqNo] in [dbo].[PipelineExecution] is the value that was created and returned by the Lookup activity and then subsequently used in the pipeline's Copy and Stored procedure activities.

> **Note**   You will also notice an incomplete row in [dbo].[PipelineExecution] where
> an execution started but did not finish – this is the record created when you ran
> the pipeline up to the Lookup activity's breakpoint.

User Variables

In the previous section, you used the pipeline expression

```
@activity('Lookup RunSeqNo').output.firstRow.RunSeqNo
```

in two places – once in the Copy activity, then again in the Stored procedure activity. Having to use the same expression twice is not ideal, because if something changes (e.g., the name of the activity or of the returned field), you will need to update the expression in every place in which it appears. You can eliminate this redundant code by using a *user variable*.

Create a Variable

User variables are created at the level of the pipeline.

1. Click somewhere in blank space on the design surface to open the configuration pane containing pipeline-level settings.

2. Select the *Variables* tab and click the + *New* button to create a new variable.

3. A variable requires a name, a type, and optionally a default value. Name the variable "RunSeqNo" and set its type to "Integer."

> **Tip**   ADF supports four types of user variable: String, Boolean, Integer, or Array.

4. Specify a default value of "-1". Providing a default value for "RunSeqNo" doesn't make much sense from the perspective of this pipeline's purpose, but setting one makes it easier to detect bugs in cases where the variable has not been assigned properly.

Set a Variable

Variable assignment is implemented by two ADF activities, both found in the *General* section of the Activities toolbox:

- The *Set variable* activity sets the value of a variable, overwriting its default or any previous value.

- The *Append variable* activity appends an element to the end of an Array-type variable.

Set the "RunSeqNo" variable for use in your pipeline as follows:

1. Drag a Set variable activity onto the design surface and name it "Set RunSeqNo." The variable must be set to the value obtained by the Lookup activity, so create a dependency between the two activities.

2. On the Set variable activity's configuration pane, select the *Settings* tab and accept the default *Variable type* of "Pipeline variable". Choose the "RunSeqNo" variable from the *Name* dropdown. A *Value* field appears below the dropdown.

3. Click the *Value* field to reveal the *Add dynamic content* link. Open the pipeline expression builder.

4. On the expression builder's *Activity outputs* tab, click *Lookup RunSeqNo first row* – if this option is missing, verify that the Set variable activity is dependent on the Lookup activity.

5. The prepared expression snippet refers to the Lookup activity's `firstRow` object. Complete the path to the RunSeqNo property by adding `.RunSeqNo`.

6. Although limited in number, variable types are *strict*. Without further modification, this variable assignment will fail, because the value obtained by the Lookup activity is of type Float, not Integer. To convert the value to an integer, wrap it in the *int* function (found in the *Conversion Functions* section of the expression builder's *Functions* tab).

7. Click *OK* to close the pipeline expression builder.

Figure 4-10 shows the pipeline expression builder for the Set variable activity, containing the completed pipeline expression:

```
@int(activity('Lookup RunSeqNo').output.firstRow.RunSeqNo)
```

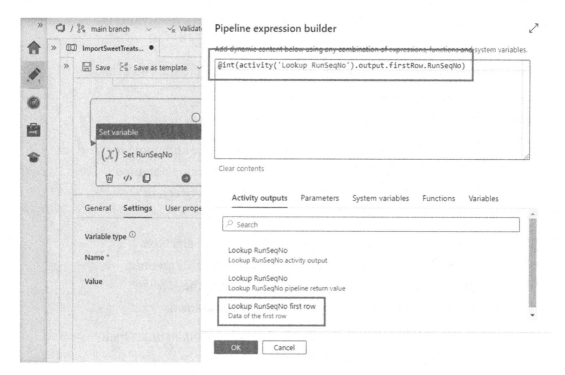

Figure 4-10. *Pipeline expression to set the RunSeqNo variable*

Use the Variable

Variables are scoped at the pipeline level, so they can be used by any of the pipeline's activities. You must create activity dependencies as necessary to ensure that a variable is not used until it has been set.

1. Create a dependency between the Set variable activity and the Copy activity. The new chain of dependencies means that the direct dependency between the Lookup and Copy activities is redundant – you can delete it. Figure 4-11 shows the correctly configured dependency chain.

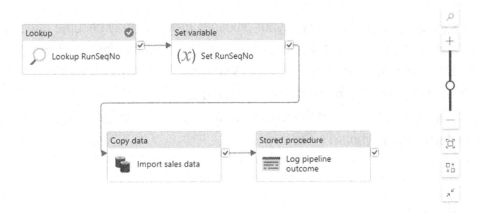

Figure 4-11. *Dependencies used to ensure that variables are set correctly and not accessed until ready*

2. Open the Copy activity's *Source* configuration tab and open the pipeline expression builder for the "RunSeqNo" column (in the *Additional columns* section).

3. Remove the existing expression using the *Clear contents* link, then select the *Variables* tab that now contains the "RunSeqNo" variable. Click it to add it to the expression pane, then click *OK*.

4. Unlike system variables that use the property-like syntax `pipeline().property`, a user variable is referred to using the collection-like syntax `variables('variableName')`. The expression pane should now contain the expression `@variables('RunSeqNo')`.

5. Open the Stored procedure activity's *Settings* configuration tab and update the expression for the "RunSeqNo" parameter so that it too uses the new variable.

6. Finally, run the pipeline and verify that it continues to function correctly.

Tip   As the number of activities in your pipelines grows, it may become difficult to see them all on screen at the same time. You can move the canvas viewport around by clicking and dragging in canvas whitespace, or by using your cursor keys or mouse wheel. Alternatively, change the display zoom level using the display tools on the right-hand side of the canvas, or by using your mouse wheel while holding down your keyboard's *Ctrl* key.

Array Variables

The decision to use a variable of type "Integer" in the previous section was appropriate because the Lookup activity returned a single row. Ticking the *First row only* check box enforces this behavior (no matter how many rows are returned by the source dataset).

With the check box left unticked, the Lookup activity returns a JSON array called value. The array contains one element for each row returned by the dataset, up to a maximum of 5000 rows or 4MB of data. To store this value for reuse in the pipeline, assign it to a variable of type "Array."

A frequent requirement for array values is the ability to iterate over them, processing each element individually but in the same way. ADF activities for doing this are introduced in Chapter 6.

Concatenate Strings

While using the pipeline expression builder, you will have noticed that there are six groups of expression functions:

- *String* functions, which operate on strings (e.g., *concat*, *substring*)

- *Math* functions, which perform mathematical operations (*add*, *max*)

- *Logical* functions, which return either true or false (*equals*, *if*)

- *Date* functions, which return strings representing dates (*utcnow*, *addhours*) – recall that the pipeline expression language has no date or time types

- *Collection* functions, which act on arrays and dictionaries (*length, contains*)

- *Conversion* functions, which convert values into different data types (e.g., *string*) or representations (e.g., *base64*)

In this section, you will use the *concat* function to build a message by concatenating several strings together. The message will be logged using the [dbo].[LogPipelineStart] stored procedure's "Comments" parameter.

1. On the design surface, open the Lookup activity's *Settings* configuration tab.

2. Untick the *Treat as null* check box on the "Comments" parameter and open the pipeline expression builder to set its value.

3. Click the *concat* function – found in the *String Functions* section of the pipeline expression builder's *Functions* tab – to add it to the expression pane.

4. The function takes a list of string arguments separated by commas. Literal string values are surrounded by single quotes. Between the function's parentheses, enter the first argument `'Pipeline '` (including a final space after the word "Pipeline"). The expression should now read @concat(`'Pipeline '`).

5. Add a second argument by inserting a comma after the first, then selecting *Pipeline Name* from the *System variables* tab.

6. Add a third string literal argument `' executed in '` and a fourth by selecting the system variable *Data factory name*. The entire expression should now read `@concat('Pipeline ',pipeline(). Pipeline,' executed in ',pipeline().DataFactory)`. Click *OK* and run the pipeline.

When pipeline execution is complete, inspect the latest record in table [dbo]. [PipelineExecution] – its [Comments] field should contain something like "Pipeline ImportSweetTreatsSales_Audit executed in MyDataFactory" (depending on the name of your ADF instance).

Infix Operators

ADF's pipeline expression language contains no *infix* operators – all operations are implemented as functions. In the same way that you use `concat('a','b')` (instead of something like `'a' + 'b'`), all mathematical operations are invoked using functions found in the *Math Functions* section of the pipeline expression builder's *Functions* tab, for example:

- To calculate 1 + 2, you must use the *add* function: `add(1,2)`.

- Subtraction, multiplication, and division are implemented by the functions *sub*, *mul*, and *div*, respectively.

String Interpolation

Another approach to building string expressions is to use *string interpolation*. An interpolated string is a string value that contains *placeholder expressions* that are evaluated at runtime. A placeholder expression is contained in braces and preceded by the @ symbol like this: `@{placeholderExpression}`.

Interpolated strings are more readable than those built using the *concat* function – the equivalent of the function call you built in the previous section is

`Pipeline @{pipeline().Pipeline} executed in @{pipeline().DataFactory}`

Interpolated strings cannot be nested inside other pipeline expressions. If an interpolated string appears as a function argument, its placeholder expressions are not evaluated but are treated as string literals.

Escaping @

The initial @ symbol indicates to ADF that what follows it should be evaluated as a pipeline expression. If you need to specify a string literal that begins with the @ character, you must *escape* it by using it twice:

- `@add(1,2)` is a pipeline expression that evaluates to 3.

- `@@add(1,2)` is the string literal "@add(1,2)".

Chapter Review

Pipeline expressions allow you to specify many factory resource properties dynamically – values for such properties are evaluated at runtime using the configured expression. You can use an expression wherever the link *Add dynamic content [Alt+Shift+D]* appears, allowing you to launch the pipeline expression builder.

A pipeline expression can be a string literal (possibly containing placeholder expressions), a variable, or a function. Nesting of functions allows you to build complex, powerful expressions.

User variables are created at the pipeline level and accessible to all activities for the duration of a pipeline run. Use the Set variable activity to set or overwrite a variable's default or previously set value. The Append variable activity allows you to add elements to the end of an Array variable's value.

Key Concepts

- **Pipeline expression:** A pipeline expression is evaluated at pipeline execution time to determine a property value. Data types supported by the pipeline expression language are string, integer, float, boolean, array, or dictionary.

- **Array:** A collection of multiple values referred to as *elements*. Elements are addressed by an integer index between zero and one less than the array's length.

- **Dictionary:** A collection whose elements are referred to by name.

- **Pipeline expression builder:** An editor for pipeline expressions built into ADF Studio.

- **System variable:** System variables provide access to the runtime values of various system properties.

- **User variable:** Created to store String, Boolean, Integer, or Array values during a pipeline's execution.

- **Pipeline expression function:** One of a library of functions available for use in pipeline expressions. Function types include String, Math, Logical, Date, Collection, and Type conversions.

- **Interpolated string:** A string literal containing placeholder expressions.

- **Placeholder expression:** An expression embedded in an interpolated string, evaluated at runtime to return a string.

- **Escape:** String literals beginning with the @ character must be escaped to prevent their interpretation as pipeline expressions. @ is escaped by following it with a second @ character.

- **Stored procedure activity:** ADF activity that enables the execution of a database stored procedure, specifying values for the stored procedure's parameters as required.

- **Lookup activity:** ADF activity that returns one or more rows from a dataset for use during a pipeline's execution. In the case of SQL Server datasets, rows can be returned from tables, views, inline queries, or stored procedures.

- **Set variable activity:** ADF activity used to update the value of a user variable.

- **Append variable activity:** ADF activity used to add a new element to the end of an existing Array variable's value.

- **Activity dependency:** Constraint used to control the order in which a pipeline's activities are executed.

- **Activity output object:** JSON object produced by the execution of an ADF activity. An output object and its properties are available to any activity dependent on the source activity, either directly or indirectly.

- **Breakpoint:** An ADF Studio breakpoint allows you to run a pipeline, in debug mode, up to and including the activity on which the breakpoint is set (breakpoints do not exist in published pipelines). It is not possible to resume execution after hitting a breakpoint.

- **$$FILEPATH:** A reserved system variable that enables the Copy activity to label incoming file data with its source file. $$FILEPATH is available solely to populate additional columns in the Copy activity and cannot be used in pipeline expressions.

- **$$COLUMN:** A reserved system variable that enables the Copy activity to duplicate a specified column in incoming data. $$COLUMN is available solely to populate additional columns in the Copy activity and cannot be used in pipeline expressions.

- **Additional columns:** A Copy activity source can be augmented with additional columns, the values of which are specified by a pipeline expression, $$FILEPATH, $$COLUMN, or a hard-coded static value.

- **Lineage tracking:** The practice of labeling data as it is processed, to enable later identification of information related to its source and/or processing.

For SSIS Developers

This chapter introduced two new activities that have similar functions to SSIS activities. The correspondence is not exact:

- The Stored procedure activity allows you to execute a stored procedure. Unlike SSIS's Execute SQL Task, you cannot use it to execute arbitrary SQL code or to return a result set.

- The Lookup activity enables you to load small datasets. With a SQL connection, this is similar to the use of an Execute SQL Task to execute SQL code to return a result set, but the activity can also be used to load datasets of different kinds.

The order of activities' execution is controlled using activity dependencies. These are conceptually similar to SSIS precedence constraints but have some important differences that are discussed in Chapter 6.

Compared to SSIS in Visual Studio, ADF Studio's support for breakpoints is limited. All pipeline expression functions use the syntax `functionName(arguments)` – infix operators like "+" used in SSIS expressions are not supported.

CHAPTER 5

Parameters

Chapter 4 introduced pipeline expressions as a way of setting property values in factory resources at runtime. The examples presented used expressions to determine values for a variety of properties, all of which were under the internal control of the pipeline. But sometimes it is convenient to be able to inject external values into factory resources at runtime, either to share data or to create generic resources that can be reused in multiple scenarios. Injection of runtime values is achieved by using *parameters*.

Runtime parameters are supported not only by pipelines but also by datasets, linked services, and data flows. Data flows are introduced in Chapter 7 – this chapter looks at the use of parameters with the other factory resource types. Parameters can also be defined at the level of a data factory instance. Unlike other parameter types, these *global parameters* do not enable runtime value substitution but rather represent *constants*, shared by all pipelines.

You will be using an instance of Azure Key Vault to enable you to parameterize linked services securely, so in the first part of the chapter, you will create and configure your key vault.

Set Up an Azure Key Vault

Azure Key Vault provides a secure, cloud-based repository for cryptographic keys and other secrets such as database or storage account connection strings. In this section, you will add a key vault to your resource group, store a connection string inside it, and configure an Azure Data Factory linked service using the securely stored connection string.

© Richard Swinbank 2024
R. Swinbank, *Azure Data Factory by Example*, https://doi.org/10.1007/979-8-8688-0218-8_5

Create a Key Vault

Azure Key Vault instances are created and managed in the Azure portal.

1.   Open the portal and create a new resource of type *Key Vault*.

2.   Select the subscription and resource group that contains your ADF instance, then choose a globally unique *Key vault name*.

3.   Choose the *Region* closest to you geographically and ensure that the *Pricing tier* is set to "Standard". Accept the rest of the default values by clicking *Next*. Figure 5-1 shows the completed *Basics* tab of the *Create a key vault* blade.

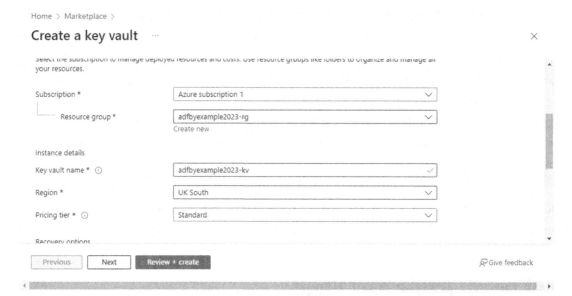

Figure 5-1.   *Create a key vault Basics tab*

4.   On the *Access configuration* tab, under *Permission model*, ensure that the *Azure role-based access control (recommended)* option is selected.

Note   Access to key vault contents can be authorized using *Azure role-based access control* (*Azure RBAC*) or a *key vault access policy*. Azure RBAC is the recommended authorization system and is the approach we will take here.

---

5. Click *Review + create* (I am purposely bypassing the *Networking* and *Tags* tabs).

6. After validation, click *Create*. Go to the new resource when deployment is complete.

Grant Access to Key Vault Secrets

Actions you take in Azure can be divided into two groups: *control plane* operations and *data plane* operations. Control plane operations enable the management of resources, for example, the creation of a key vault. Conversely, data plane operations affect resource configuration and content, such as the creation and use of key vault secrets.

Control plane operations and data plane operations are often secured separately. In the case of the key vault you created in the previous section, this means that – although you are the key vault's owner and have access to manage and even to delete it – you do not yet have access to create or use key vault secrets. No user or service may create or use secrets stored in your key vault until given the permissions necessary to do so.

Your data factory instance has an associated *managed identity* – a managed application registered in Microsoft Entra ID – which was created automatically when you created the data factory. The factory's managed identity can be used to authenticate requests made to other Azure services, such as a key vault. In this section, you will grant appropriate access to key vault secrets, first to the data factory's managed identity and then to yourself.

1. Open the portal blade for your key vault and select *Access control (IAM)* near the top of the sidebar menu. On the tabbed pane that appears, select the *Role assignments* tab, then from the + *Add* dropdown (indicated in Figure 5-2), select *Add role assignment*.

Figure 5-2. *Key vault role assignments on the Access control (IAM) page*

2. On the *Role* tab of the *Add role assignment* page, select the "Key Vault Secrets User" role in the *Job function roles* list. Click *Next*.

3. Under *Assign access to* on the *Members* tab, select the "Managed identity" option, then use the *+ Select members* link on the *Members* tab to open the *Select managed identities* flyout, shown in Figure 5-3.

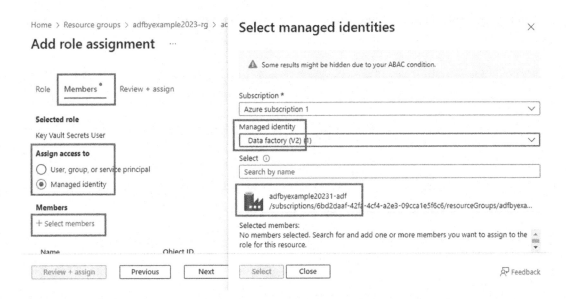

Figure 5-3. *Assigning an ADF managed identity to the Key Vault Secrets User role*

4. Ensure that your data factory's subscription is selected, then use the *Managed identity* dropdown (indicated in the figure) to select either *All system-assigned managed identities* or *Data factory (V2)*.

5. Managed identities matching your search criteria appear below the search fields – click on the entry for your data factory (indicated in the figure) to move it to the list of selected members. Click *Select* at the bottom of the flyout to close it.

6. Click the *Review + Assign* button, check your proposed role assignment, then click the button again.

7. Repeat steps 1 to 6, but this time

   a. In step 2, select the "Key Vault Secrets Officer" role

   b. In step 3, opt to assign access to a "User, group, or service principal"

   c. In step 4, search for and select your own user identity in the *Select members* flyout

Figure 5-4 shows the updated *Access control (IAM)* page containing the two new role assignments.

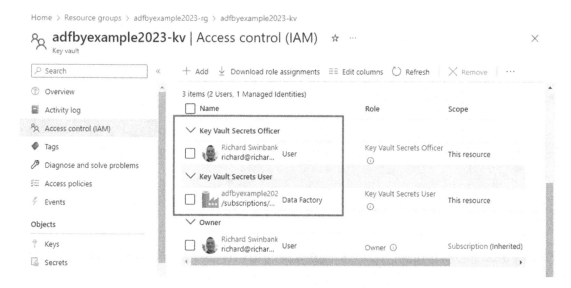

Figure 5-4. *Key vault access controls including new role assignments*

Create a Key Vault Secret

As a member of the "Key Vault Secrets Officer" role, you now have access to read and write key vault secrets. Your storage account's connection string can be found in the Azure portal – in this section, you will store its value securely in the new key vault.

1. Open the portal blade for your storage account (you can find it in the list of resources contained in your resource group or using the *Search resources, services and docs (G + /)* box in the portal toolbar).

2. Select *Access keys* from the sidebar's *Security + networking* group. In order to copy a key value, you must first click its *Show* button. Figure 5-5 shows the blade after showing the *key1 Connection String* value – the corresponding *Show* button has been replaced by *Hide*. The secret value is truncated in the screenshot.

Figure 5-5. *Storage account access keys*

3. Copy the *Connection string* value for *key1* to the clipboard using the copy button on the right-hand side of the field (indicated in the figure).

4. Return to the portal blade for your key vault and select *Secrets* from the sidebar's *Objects* group. At the top of the *Secrets* page, click the + *Generate/Import* button to add a new secret.

5. The *Create a secret* form is displayed. Paste the contents of the clipboard into the *Secret value* field, then enter a *Name* for the secret. Figure 5-6 shows the completed form for my "StorageAccountConnectionString" secret. Click *Create*.

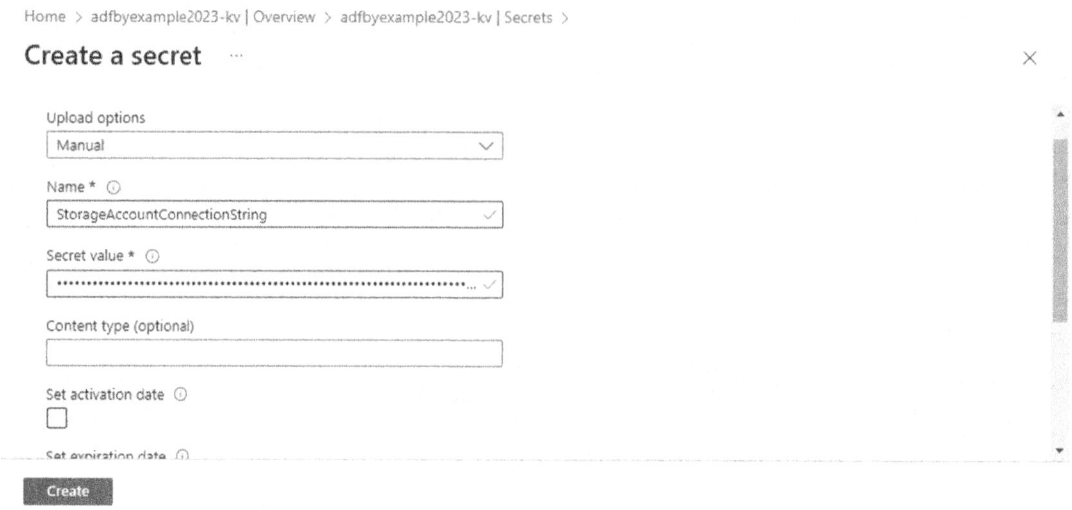

Home > adfbyexample2023-kv | Overview > adfbyexample2023-kv | Secrets >

Create a secret   ...   ✕

Upload options

| Manual | ⌄ |

Name * ⓘ

| StorageAccountConnectionString | ✓ |

Secret value * ⓘ

| •••... ✓ |

Content type (optional)

| |

Set activation date ⓘ

☐

Set expiration date ⓘ

Create

Figure 5-6. Creating a secret in the key vault

Create a Key Vault ADF Linked Service

Azure Data Factory accesses a key vault in exactly the same way it does other types of external resource: using a linked service. To refer to a key vault from within your data factory, you must create a linked service to represent it.

1. Open the ADF Studio management hub and select *Linked services* in the *Connections* section of its sidebar.

2. Click the + *New* button to add a new linked service, then search for and select the *Azure Key Vault* data store. Click *Continue*.

3. On the *New linked service* flyout, provide a *Name* for the key vault linked service, then select your key vault from the *Azure key vault name* dropdown.

4. Make sure that *Authentication method* is set to "System Assigned Managed Identity" – this ensures that ADF will connect to the key vault using the identity to which you have already granted access.

5. Figure 5-7 shows the completed flyout. Use the *Test connection* button to check the linked service configuration, and when successful, click *Create*.

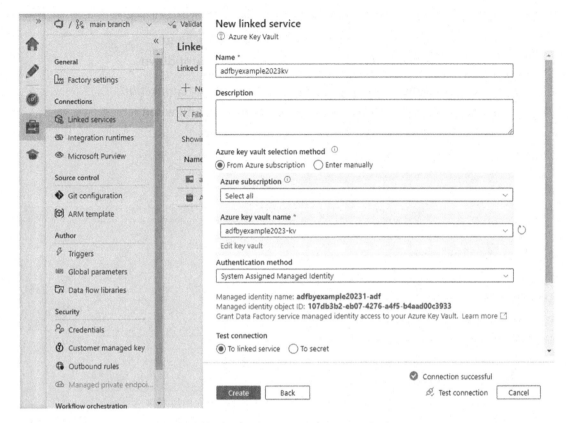

Figure 5-7. *Create linked service for Azure Key Vault*

Create a New Storage Account Linked Service

The data factory linked services that you created in Chapters 2 and 3 were published to
ADF immediately, to allow the associated connection credentials to be stored securely.
Using key vault secrets is a much better practice – in this section, you will create a new
storage account linked service that obtains the value of its connection string at runtime,
by referencing your key vault secret.

1. On the same *Linked services* page in the management hub, create
   another new linked service, this time using the *Azure Blob Storage*
   data store.

2. Ensure that *Authentication method* is set to "Account key," then
   use the toggle below that field to change the connection type from
   "Connection string" to "Azure Key Vault."

3. Select your key vault linked service from the *AKV linked service*
    dropdown, then select the name of your storage account
    connection string secret from the "Secret name" dropdown.

4. Figure 5-8 shows the completed flyout. Use the *Test connection*
    button to check the linked service configuration, and when
    successful, click *Create*.

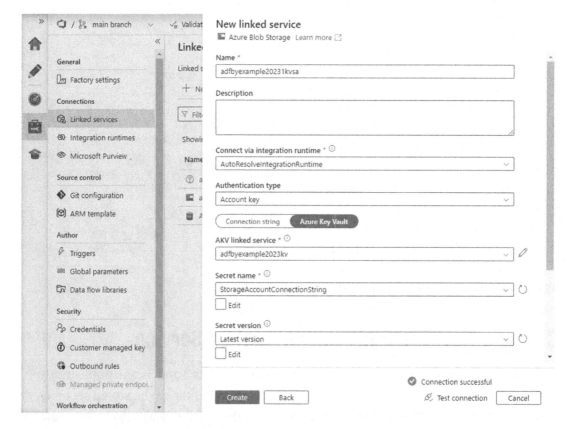

Figure 5-8. *Blob storage linked service using a key vault secret*

The new blob storage linked service obtains credentials from the key vault at
runtime, by obtaining the value of your named secret, authorized using the ADF
instance's managed identity. Unlike your previous storage account linked service, the
new linked service has not yet been published to ADF, because there is no longer any
part of its definition that requires secure storage.

Use Dataset Parameters

In Chapter 3, you created a number of ADF datasets, as and when you needed them, to represent different source files. The dataset "ABS_CSV_CandyShack" (shown in Figure 5-9) has the following features:

- It is of type *DelimitedText*, indicated in the canvas space at the top of the figure. Some properties shown on the *Connection* tab are specific to this file type – for example, *Column delimiter* and *Row delimiter*.

- It has a specified *Linked service*, a blob storage account.

- It has a *File path* consisting of a *container*, a *directory*, and a *file*. Each time you used a dataset with a file path, you overrode its directory and file settings using wildcard settings on the Copy activity's *Source* configuration tab.

- It has an associated file schema, visible on the *Schema* tab. When you used the "ABS_CSV_CandyShack" dataset, you overrode its schema with settings in the Copy activity's *Mapping* configuration tab. If that isn't clear, look at the Candy Shack dataset's *Schema* tab – it contains the schema for Sweet Treats data (from when you cloned the dataset). It does not match the schema stored in the Copy activity mapping.

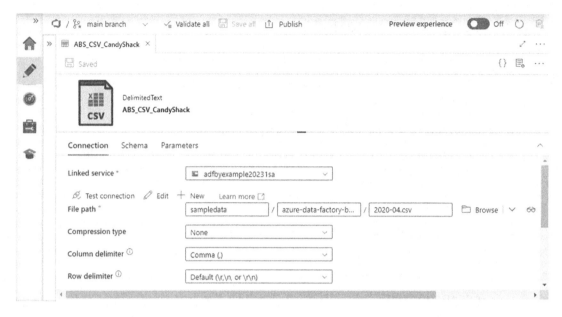

Figure 5-9. *"ABS_CSV_CandyShack" dataset configuration*

In fact, the "ABV_CSV_CandyShack" and "ABS_CSV_SweetTreats" datasets are equivalent and interchangeable – they are of the same type, use the same linked service, and specify the same container. The values where they differ – file path and schema – are provided at runtime by the Copy activity. The same is true of the two JSON file datasets used to represent Sugar Cube and Handy Candy data.

Interchangeable datasets are *redundant* – they can be replaced by a single, generic, reusable dataset. There are several advantages to generic datasets:

- You avoid having to create and maintain multiple equivalent datasets that differ only in file location and schema.

- A single generic dataset (replacing interchangeable datasets) can be clearly labeled as such. A source-specific dataset suggests a tighter coupling to its source location than is really the case.

- Your collection of datasets is smaller and easier to manage.

You could create a dataset like this with the knowledge you already have, but it would still require a hard-coded container name. In the following section, you will create a file-independent dataset by using *dataset parameters* to specify file path components at runtime.

Create a Parameterized Dataset

In ADF Studio, create a new "Chapter5" datasets folder, then create a new dataset inside it as follows:

1. On the *New dataset* flyout, choose *Azure Blob Storage*, then *Continue*.

2. Select *JSON* format, then *Continue*.

3. Name your dataset "ABS_JSON_<newlinkedservice>", where <newlinkedservice> is the name of the linked service you created in the previous section. Select that linked service from the *Linked service* dropdown.

4. Leave every other option with its default values and click *OK* to create the dataset. The dataset and its *Properties* flyout open automatically – close the *Properties* flyout.

The new dataset is not yet usable because it contains no file path information. To inject file path information at runtime, create and use dataset parameters as follows:

1. Select the new dataset's *Parameters* configuration tab and click the + *New* button.

2. Name the new parameter "Container" and ensure its type is "String." Leave its default value blank.

3. Create two more parameters called "Directory" and "File" in the same way, giving each one a default value of "." (period). The set of configured parameters is shown in Figure 5-10.

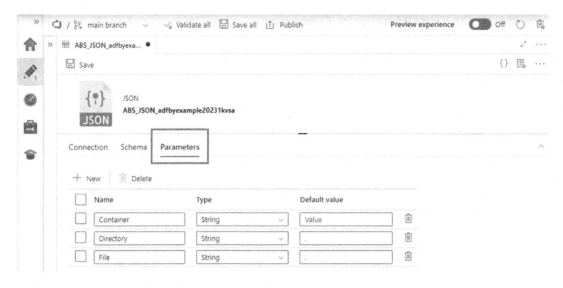

Figure 5-10. *Dataset parameter definitions*

4. Return to the *Connection* tab and click into *File path*'s *Container* field. The *Add dynamic content [Alt+Shift+D]* message appears – launch the pipeline expression builder.

5. You will notice that the options available for selection in the expression builder are different to those you encountered in Chapter 4. (For example, pipeline-related system variables are not available.) Locate the "Container" parameter on the *Parameters* tab and click on it.

6. The expression `@dataset().Container` appears in the expression pane. Click *OK*.

7. Repeat steps 4–6 for the *File path*'s *Directory* and *File* fields, using the corresponding dataset parameters. Save the dataset.

Figure 5-11 shows the dataset's *Connection* configuration tab using its three parameters.

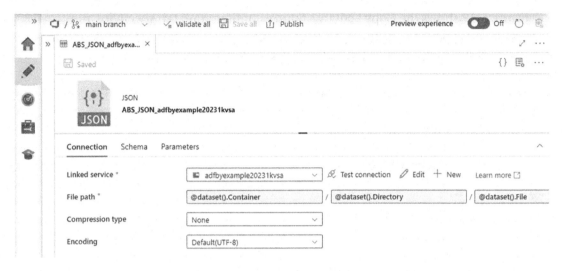

Figure 5-11. *JSON dataset with parameterized file path components*

Note   The syntax `dataset().ParameterName` identifies a parameter called "ParameterName" within the context of the dataset where the parameter is defined. The `dataset()` prefix can only be used inside a dataset definition and only to refer to that dataset's own parameters.

Use the Parameterized Dataset

Create a new "Chapter5" pipelines folder, then create a new pipeline by cloning Chapter 3's "ImportSugarCubeSales" pipeline. Drag the cloned pipeline into the "Chapter5" pipelines folder.

The cloned Sugar Cube pipeline contains a single activity – the Copy activity used to copy data from JSON files into your Azure SQL DB.

1. Select the Copy activity, then open its *Source* configuration tab.

2. Change its *Source dataset* from "ABS_JSON_SugarCube" to your new, parameterized dataset. When you select a parameterized dataset, a *Dataset properties* region appears below the *Source dataset* dropdown – this is where you specify values or pipeline expressions for the dataset's parameter(s).

3. Enter the value "sampledata" for the "Container" parameter.

145

Figure 5-12 shows the Copy activity's *Source* configuration tab specifying the container name. Run the pipeline and use your SQL client to verify that Sugar Cube data has been read using the parameterized dataset and loaded correctly.

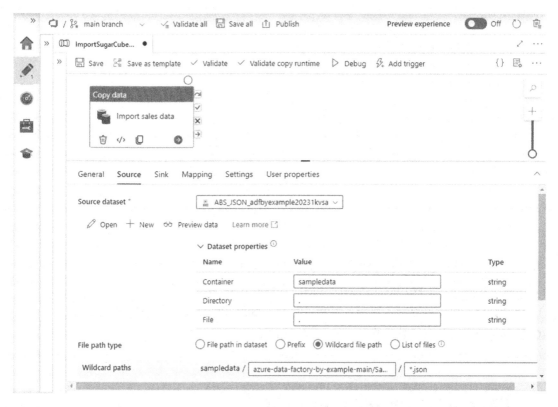

Figure 5-12. *Copy activity configured to pass dataset parameters*

Tip   You can make a dataset parameter *optional* by giving it a default value – if no value is provided at runtime, the default value is used instead. In this example, the default values of the dataset's "Directory" and "File" parameters were overridden (because the Copy activity specified a *File type path* of "Wildcard file path"), but without them, you would still have to supply parameter values for the pipeline to be valid.

Reuse the Parameterized Dataset

Repeat the steps from the previous section, this time cloning Chapter 3's "IngestHandyCandyMessages" pipeline into the "Chapter5" folder. Run the resulting pipeline and check the results. (Recall that this pipeline transforms source JSON messages into a Parquet file in blob storage, so you must inspect the file to assess the effect of the pipeline.)

The major result here is that both pipelines are now using the same source dataset – in fact, any pipeline reading JSON data from your blob storage account could use this dataset. This is a significant improvement:

- You need fewer source datasets – you could choose to create a single parameterized dataset for each combination of blob storage linked service and file type.

- The parameterized source dataset is generic by design. Anyone looking at the dataset in future is in no danger of believing that the dataset is coupled to any specific file location.

Given that all the source data is in the "sampledata" container, it would be reasonable to ask why parameterize the dataset container at all. How your source data is organized is a consideration here:

- If your source data is in multiple containers, a parameterized dataset provides useful reusability.

- If your source data is guaranteed always to occupy a single container, then a dataset with a hard-coded container name relieves you of providing a parameter value every time you use it.

If your source data is in multiple storage accounts, you might want to go a step further and implement a generic dataset per file type. This would require linked service connection details to be injected at runtime, which is the subject of the next section.

Use Linked Service Parameters

By parameterizing the dataset in the previous section, you increased its reusability, because it can now be used to refer to any JSON file in the underlying storage account. A dataset that could refer to any JSON file in *any* storage account would be even more reusable but would require the storage account also to be specified at runtime.

The storage account used by a dataset is specified in the linked service it uses and can be provided at runtime using a *linked service parameter*. Passing a storage account connection string as a parameter value would be possible, but insecure. Configuring a linked service to use a key vault secret means that the same effect can be achieved securely, by allowing the secret's name to be passed in as a parameter.

Create a Parameterized Linked Service

In the first part of this chapter, you created a key vault and added a secret – your storage account's connection string. You created a new storage account linked service, using the corresponding key vault secret name to access the connection string value at runtime. In this section, you will create a parameterized linked service for blob storage accounts, enabling you to pass different secret names in at runtime – this will enable the linked service to be used to connect to different storage accounts.

1. Open ADF Studio's management hub and select *Linked services* in the *Connections* section of its sidebar.

2. Click the + *New* button to add a new linked service, then select the *Azure Blob Storage* data store and click *Continue*.

3. Call the new linked service "AnyBlobStorage" – it could be used to connect to any Azure storage account.

4. Scroll down to the bottom of the *New linked service* flyout and expand the *Parameters* section. Click + *New* to create a new linked service parameter.

5. Name the new parameter "ConnectionSecretName" and ensure its type is "String", then return to the top of the flyout.

6. Using the button below the *Authentication method* dropdown, change the connection type to *Azure Key Vault*. Select the key vault linked service you created earlier from the *AKV linked service* dropdown.

7. By default, a dropdown list of available secrets is automatically provided in the *Secret name* field. Tick the *Edit* check box to convert the field to a text box, then click into the field – the *Add dynamic content [Alt+Shift+D]* link appears.

8. Use the link to launch the pipeline expression builder, then
    select "ConnectionSecretName" from the list of linked
    service parameters. The expression @linkedService().
    ConnectionSecretName appears in the expression pane. Click
    OK. Figure 5-13 shows the parameter being defined and used in
    the *New linked service* flyout.

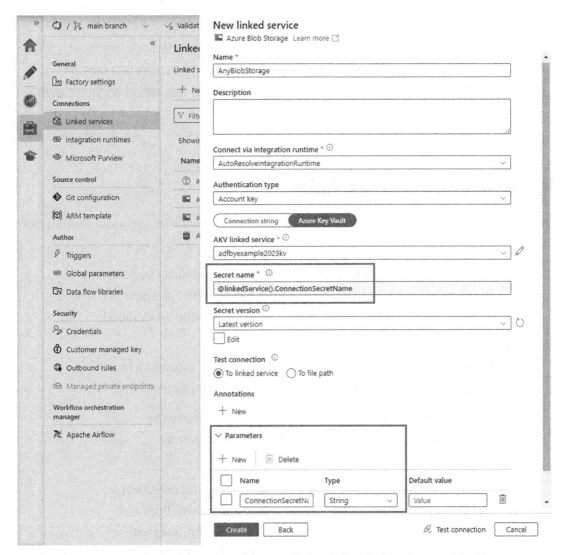

Figure 5-13. *Linked service parameter definition and use*

9. Click *Test connection* at the bottom of the flyout. ADF Studio
    now prompts you to supply a value for the parameter
    "ConnectionSecretName" – enter the name of the key vault
    secret that contains your storage account connection string, then
    click *OK*.

10. When the test has successfully completed, click *Create* to save the
    new linked service.

Note   As in the case of datasets, the `linkedService()` syntax can only be
used inside a linked service definition and only to refer to the linked service's own
parameters.

Increase Dataset Reusability

Use your parameterized linked service to implement a dataset with greater reusability as
follows:

1. Return to the authoring canvas and create a new dataset by
    cloning the parameterized dataset from earlier in the chapter.
    Name it "ABS_JSON" – it will be able to represent any JSON file(s)
    in any Azure blob storage account.

2. On the cloned dataset's *Parameters* configuration tab, add a fourth
    String parameter called "LinkedServiceConnectionSecret."

3. On the dataset's *Connection* configuration tab, choose the
    "AnyBlobStorage" linked service from the *Linked service*
    dropdown.

4. Selecting a parameterized linked service displays a *Linked service
    properties* region below the *Linked service* dropdown. Populate
    the linked service's "ConnectionSecretName" parameter with
    a pipeline expression that returns the value of the dataset's
    "LinkedServiceConnectionSecret" parameter.

5.   Test your linked service parameter value by clicking
Test connection (on the right of the *Linked service*
dropdown). ADF Studio will prompt you for a value for
"LinkedServiceConnectionSecret" – provide the name of the key
vault secret containing your storage account connection string.
When the test has successfully completed, save your changes.

Figure 5-14 shows the configuration of the new parameterized dataset using the
parameterized linked service. This dataset can be used to refer to any JSON file in any
Azure blob storage account for which a connection string is stored in your key vault.

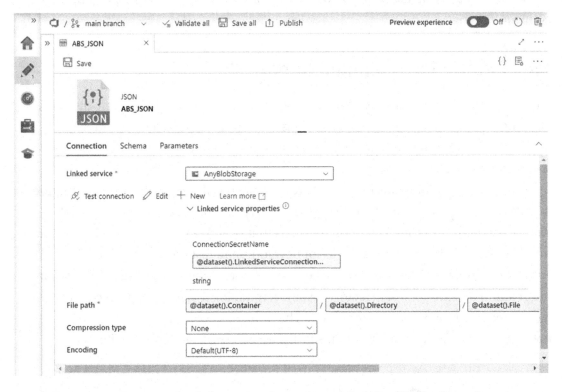

Figure 5-14. *Parameterized dataset using a parameterized linked service*

Use the New Dataset

To test the new dataset, clone the Sugar Cube pipeline you created earlier in the chapter. Change the Copy activity's source dataset to "ABS_JSON" and supply the two mandatory parameter values:

- Set "ContainerName" to the value "sampledata."

- Set "LinkedServiceConnectionSecret" to the name of the key vault secret containing your storage account connection string.

Verify the results using your SQL client and/or the *Output* tab in the pipeline's configuration pane.

Why Parameterize Linked Services?

Parameterizing ADF datasets is a powerful way to avoid creating file-specific datasets, allowing a single dataset to be reused for files of the same type in different folder locations. Similarly, a parameterized linked service can be reused for different data stores of the same storage type.

One reason for doing this might be to reduce the number of linked services required in order to connect to multiple stores of the same type – for example, multiple blob storage accounts. Another important reason is that your Azure tenant is likely to contain multiple Azure Data Factory instances for development, testing, and production. Parameterizing linked services using a key vault allows you to centralize configuration information outside your data factory instance, reducing the complexity of copying factory resources between environments. The publication of ADF resources and management of multiple environments is discussed in greater depth in Chapter 10.

Use Pipeline Parameters

The sample data files you uploaded to your blob storage account in Chapter 2 include sales data for another customer of fictional confectionery manufacturer ABC – an online retailer named "Desserts4All." Desserts4All reports sales of ABC's products in CSV files, using exactly the same format as Sweet Treats.

You could reuse your Sweet Treats pipeline to load data for Desserts4All, but file location information for the pipeline – the *Wildcard folder path* and *Wildcard file name* – is hard-coded in the Copy activity. In this section, you will use *pipeline parameters* to specify their values at runtime, creating a single pipeline that can process sales data from either vendor.

Create a Parameterized Pipeline

Start by cloning your Chapter 4 pipeline – "ImportSweetTreatsSales_Audit" – into the "Chapter5" folder. Name the new pipeline "ImportSTFormatFolder."

1. Below the design surface, in the pipeline's configuration pane, you will find a *Parameters* tab – select it.

2. Use the + *New* button to create a new parameter of type "String." Name it "WildcardFolderPath." Repeat the process to create a "String" parameter called "WildcardFileName," giving it a default value of "*.csv". Figure 5-15 shows the completed *Parameters* tab.

Figure 5-15. *Pipeline parameter definitions*

3. Select the pipeline's Copy activity and open its *Source* configuration tab. Click the *Wildcard folder path* component of *Wildcard paths* and launch the pipeline expression builder.

4. Select the *Parameters* tab – here you will find listed the pipeline parameters you created in step 2. Select the "WildcardFolderPath" parameter.

5. The expression `@pipeline().parameters.WildcardFolderPath` appears in the expression pane – pipeline parameters are referred to using the syntax `pipeline().parameters.ParameterName`. Click *OK*.

6. Repeat steps 3–5 for the *Wildcard file name* component of *Wildcard paths*, this time choosing the "WildcardFileName" parameter.

Note   The `pipeline()` syntax can be used in any of a pipeline's activities and is used to refer to system variables (e.g., `pipeline().RunId`) as well as to parameters. The syntax `pipeline().parameters.ParameterName` eliminates the risk of name conflicts between pipeline parameters and system variables.

Run the Parameterized Pipeline

When you run the parameterized pipeline, ADF Studio prompts you to supply values for the pipeline's parameters.

1. Provide parameter values required for Sweet Treats data (Figure 5-16 shows the relevant inputs) and click *OK* to run the pipeline. Notice that "WildcardFileName" is prepopulated with the default value you specified for the parameter.

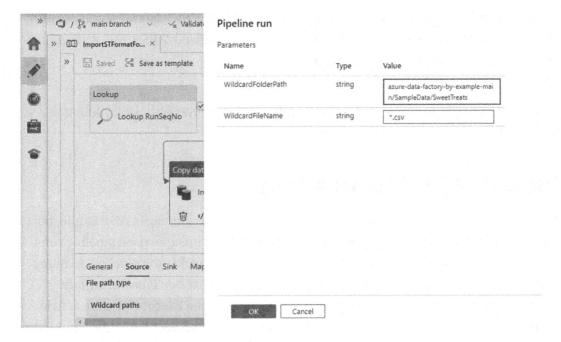

Figure 5-16. *Parameter inputs required for the pipeline run*

2. Inspect the contents of database tables [dbo].[PipelineExecution] and [dbo].[Sales_LOAD] to verify that Sweet Treats data has been loaded successfully.

3. Run the pipeline again, this time providing parameter values for Desserts4All data. For "WildcardFolderPath," edit the value you used for Sweet Treats data, replacing the final "SweetTreats" folder name with "Desserts4All." Use the same "WildcardFileName" value ("*.csv").

4. Inspect the contents of database tables [dbo].[PipelineExecution] and [dbo].[Sales_LOAD] again, verifying that this time the data loaded relates to Desserts4All.

As you have just demonstrated, the new pipeline can now load data stored in the Sweet Treats file format from whichever folder you choose. Note that the Copy activity in the new pipeline is still using the "ABS_CSV_SweetTreats" dataset. The pipeline runs successfully because the activity overrides the dataset's directory and path at runtime (and all your source data is in the same blob storage container), but this gives the pipeline's definition an inconsistent appearance.

A cleaner approach would be to create a reusable "ABS_CSV" dataset, similar to the "ABS_JSON" dataset you created earlier. Create a parameterized "ABS_CSV" dataset now and test it – you will need it again in Chapter 6.

Tip   Don't forget to specify *First row as header* in the new "ABS_CSV" dataset.

Use the Execute Pipeline Activity

Inputting parameter values manually is acceptable while developing in ADF Studio, but most pipeline executions do not take place interactively. In unsupervised pipeline runs, parameter values must be supplied by whichever process invokes the pipeline. In many cases, this process will be another ADF pipeline, using the *Execute Pipeline activity*.

In this section, you will create a new pipeline that uses the Execute Pipeline activity to run the "ImportSTFormatFolder" pipeline twice – once for Sweet Treats data and once for Desserts4All.

1. Create a new pipeline in the "Chapter5" folder and name it "ImportSweetTreatsAndDesserts4All".

2. Drag an Execute Pipeline activity onto the design surface. This activity is found in the *General* section of the Activities toolbox.

3. Name it appropriately, then on the activity's *Settings* configuration tab, select "ImportSTFormatFolder" from the *Invoked pipeline* dropdown. When you do so, input fields for the pipeline's parameters appear immediately below.

4. Ensure that the *Wait on completion* check box is ticked, then supply parameter values for Sweet Treats data, as before.

5. Repeat steps 2–4, this time supplying parameter values for Desserts4All data.

6. Create an activity dependency between the two activities (to prevent them from running simultaneously). Figure 5-17 shows the configured pipeline and the Execute Pipeline activity's *Settings* configuration tab.

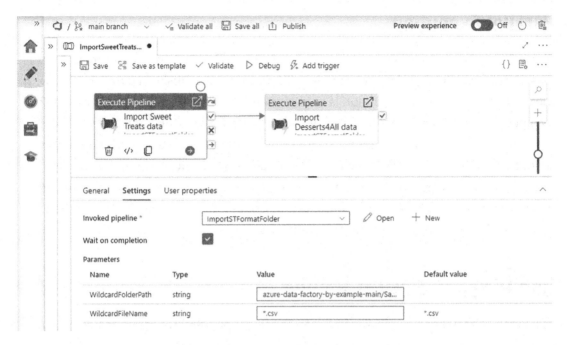

Figure 5-17. *Sequential Execute Pipeline activities*

Run the pipeline and verify that two new log records have been created in database table [dbo].[PipelineExecution]. Table [dbo].[Sales_LOAD] will only contain data loaded by the second Execute Pipeline activity, because the loading pipeline's Copy activity truncates the sink table before copying in new data. The pipelines you have developed so far do not persist loaded data, but in Chapter 6, you will extend the loading pipeline to transfer data into a table for permanent storage.

The *Output* tab on the pipeline's configuration pane contains two rows, one for each Execute Pipeline activity. The output from each activity includes the pipeline run ID of the pipeline execution it invoked, displayed as a link – follow the link to view activity run information for the invoked pipeline.

For SSIS developers   When choosing a pipeline for the Execute Pipeline activity, you are offered a fixed dropdown list – there is no option to launch the pipeline expression builder. Unlike SSIS's Execute Package Task, you cannot specify a pipeline name using a parameter or variable. (Even in SSIS, this requires the value of the task's DelayValidation property to be "true" – the concept of delayed validation is not supported in ADF.)

157

Parallel Execution

The activity dependency between the two Execute Pipeline activities forces them to run sequentially – without it, the two activities will run simultaneously, in parallel. Even with the dependency in place, execution is only sequential because the first activity waits for its pipeline run to complete – this is the effect of the *Wait for completion* check box.

In this case, the two activities must run sequentially because the invoked pipeline is poorly designed for parallel execution. Both executions truncate the sink table independently, so running them in parallel might allow one execution to truncate data while the other is in the process of loading it. In Chapter 6, you will revise the loading pipeline's design to make it safe for parallelization.

Use Pipeline Return Values

Pipeline parameters allow values to be injected into a pipeline run by the process that triggers it (e.g., by an Execute Pipeline activity in another pipeline). A feature added recently to ADF is the ability to return values from a completed pipeline run, back to the calling Execute Pipeline activity.

Return a Value from a Pipeline

Values to be returned by a pipeline are defined using the Set variable activity – you may have noticed when using the activity in Chapter 4 that it offers a *Variable type* of "Pipeline return value". Unlike pipeline variables, pipeline return values are created directly in the Set variable activity and do not need to be defined separately.

Modify the "ImportSTFormatFolder" pipeline you created in the previous section as follows:

1. Add a Set variable activity to the pipeline and make it dependent on the existing Set variable activity (used to set the value of the "RunSeqNo" variable).

2. Use the new activity's *General* configuration tab to change its name to "Set return value".

3. On the activity's *Settings* configuration tab, change its type to "Pipeline return value", then use the + *New* button (indicated in Figure 5-18) to create a new return value.

4. Set the return value's *Name* to "PipelineRunSeqNo" and its *Type* to "Expression". Use the *Value* field to launch the pipeline expression builder and select the "RunSeqNo" variable from the *Variables* tab.

The completed *Settings* configuration tab is shown in Figure 5-18.

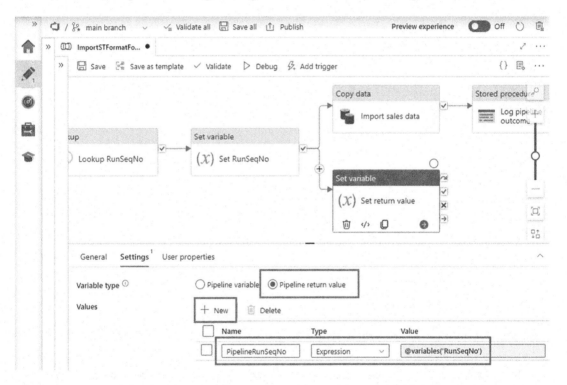

Figure 5-18. *Pipeline return value defined using the Set variable activity*

Note   Use the "Expression" type to return values determined at runtime, such as an output from an earlier activity. Other types are used to return literal values of the corresponding type, defined at development time.

Reference Pipeline Return Values

You can run your modified pipeline directly without error, but you have no way yet of inspecting its return values. A pipeline run's return values, if defined, are exposed in the output JSON object of the Execute Pipeline activity that triggers it.

Unlike the outputs of other activities, the Execute Pipeline activity's output object cannot be inspected directly in ADF Studio – as Figure 5-19 illustrates, the IDE presents it as a clickable link to the corresponding pipeline run.

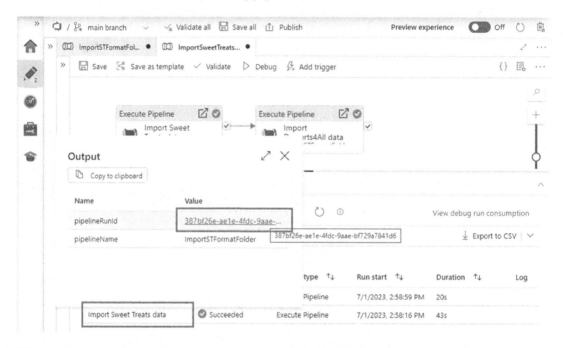

Figure 5-19. *Execute Pipeline activity output auto-formatted by ADF Studio*

Although not visible in ADF Studio, pipeline return values are nonetheless present in the Execute Pipeline activity's output object, as an attribute named "pipelineReturnValue". Modify your "ImportSweetTreatsAndDesserts4All" to collect RunSeqId values returned by each of its Execute Pipeline activities.

1. In the "ImportSweetTreatsAndDesserts4All", define a new pipeline variable of type "Integer". Name it "ReturnedValue".

2. Add a Set variable activity to the design surface, making it dependent on the second of the two Execute Pipeline activities, as shown in Figure 5-20.

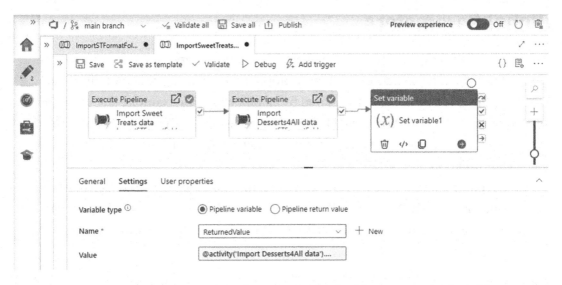

Figure 5-20. *Assigning a variable the value returned by an invoked pipeline*

3. Configure the Set variable activity to assign a value to the "ReturnedValue" array variable. Use the pipeline expression builder to create an expression referencing the "PipelineRunSeqId" value returned by the invoked pipeline. For example, the full expression truncated in Figure 5-20 is `@activity('Import Desserts4All data').output.` `pipelineReturnValue.PipelineRunSeqNo`.

4. Run the pipeline. When complete, use the output of the Set variable activity to determine the value returned to the Execute Pipeline activity. Verify that it matches the value recorded in the database for the pipeline.

Warning   For pipeline return values to be available in the Execute Pipeline activity's output, the activity's *Wait on completion* check box must be ticked.

The example given here demonstrates how pipeline return values can be handled, but for simplicity does not make further use of them. Real-world use cases might include returning a copied row count from each invoked pipeline run (maintaining a total row count in the calling pipeline) or allowing a parent pipeline to take responsibility for log entries by returning information for logging from each child run.

Global Parameters

Unlike the other parameter types covered earlier in the chapter, *global parameters* are not a means of injecting different values at runtime. The role of global parameters is instead to provide *constant* values, shared by all pipelines. For example, if your Azure tenant contains separate Azure Data Factory instances for development, testing, and production, a global parameter is a convenient way to store nonsensitive instance-specific information.

Global parameters are created and edited on the *Global parameters* page of ADF Studio's management hub. Figure 5-21 shows parameters being used to identify the factory's resource group and to indicate that this is the development environment.

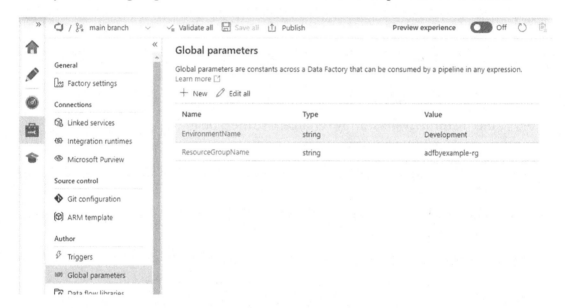

Figure 5-21. *Global parameter editor in ADF Studio*

Global parameters can be referenced in pipeline expressions, within the scope of pipeline activities, and are available for selection in the pipeline expression builder. The syntax used to refer to a global parameter is

`pipeline().globalParameters.ParameterName`

For example, the "EnvironmentName" global parameter shown in Figure 5-21 would be referred to in a pipeline expression using `pipeline().globalParameters.EnvironmentName`.

Chapter Review

In this chapter, you defined parameters for pipelines, datasets, and linked services. Parameters allow a factory resource to require that certain data values be provided at runtime, exploiting those values by using them in pipeline expressions.

A common use case for parameters is to allow factory resources to be defined generically. This allows reuse, reducing clutter in your data factory and preventing unnecessary reimplementation of frequently used components. Reusable linked services may require sensitive connection information to be passed in at runtime – Azure Key Vault secrets provide a secure way to do this.

The degree to which you choose to parameterize factory resources depends heavily on your own use cases and usage patterns. As you continue to use ADF, you will find other places in which design decisions can only be made in the context of your own specific technical requirements.

A real-world data platform is likely to contain many pipelines responsible for individual data processing tasks. The ability to define which pipelines are to run, under what conditions, and in what order is an important requirement, typically referred to as *orchestration*. The Execute Pipeline activity plays a key role in coordinating the execution of multiple pipelines, and in Chapter 6, you will explore additional controls to orchestrate more sophisticated workflows.

Key Concepts

- **Runtime parameter:** A placeholder in a factory resource definition for a value substituted at runtime. Pipeline, dataset, and linked service parameters are runtime parameters; global parameters are not.

- **Optional parameter:** A runtime parameter can be made optional by defining a default value for it. If a value is not supplied at runtime, the default value is substituted for the parameter instead.

- **Reusability:** Runtime parameters enable factory resources to be defined in a reusable way. The behavior of reusable resources is modified by supplying different parameter values at runtime.

- **Global parameter:** A constant value defined at development time and shared by all pipelines. Global parameters are referred to in expressions, within the scope of pipeline activities, using the syntax `pipeline().globalParameters.ParameterName`.

- **Pipeline parameter:** Runtime parameter for an ADF pipeline, supplied when pipeline execution begins. Pipeline parameters are referred to in expressions, within the scope of pipeline activities, using the syntax `pipeline().parameters.ParameterName`.

- **Pipeline return value:** A value determined during a pipeline run, returned when pipeline execution is complete. Pipeline return values are defined using the Set variable activity and are made available to the calling pipeline in the output of the Execute Pipeline activity.

- **Dataset parameter:** Runtime parameter for an ADF dataset. Dataset parameters are referred to in expressions, within the scope of the same dataset, using the syntax `dataset().ParameterName`.

- **Linked service parameter:** Runtime parameter for an ADF linked service. Linked service parameters are referred to in expressions, within the scope of the same linked service, using the syntax `linkedService().ParameterName`.

- **Orchestration:** Orchestration refers to the coordination of multiple ETL pipelines and activities, determining which pipelines are to run, under what conditions, and in what order.

- **Execute Pipeline activity:** ADF pipeline activity used to execute another pipeline within the same data factory instance. The Execute Pipeline activity plays an important role in ETL orchestration.

- **Azure Key Vault:** A secure repository for secrets and cryptographic keys.

- **Secret:** A name/value pair stored in an Azure Key Vault. The value usually contains sensitive information such as service authentication credentials. A secure way to handle this information is to refer to the secret by name – a service that requires the secret's value may retrieve it from the vault by name, if permitted to do so.

- **Service principal:** An identity created for use with an application or service – such as Azure Data Factory – enabling the service to identify itself to external resources requiring authentication and authorization.

- **Managed identity:** A managed identity associates a service principal with an instance of Azure Data Factory (or other Azure resources). A *system-assigned managed identity* is created automatically for new ADF instances created in the Azure portal and is automatically removed if and when its factory is deleted.

- **Control plane operation:** Control plane operations enable the management of resources, for example, the creation of a key vault or a storage account.

- **Data plane operation:** Data plane operations affect resource configuration and content, such as the creation and use of key vault secrets, or the reading and writing of files in blob storage.

- **Azure role-based access control (Azure RBAC):** An authorization system used throughout Azure to control access to resources on both the control plane and the data plane.

- **Access policy:** A legacy authorization system used in Azure Key Vaults to control access to key vault contents on the data plane. Azure RBAC is recommended over access policies for key vault data plane security.

For SSIS Developers

ADF pipeline parameters are conceptually similar to SSIS package parameters. As in SSIS packages, pipeline parameters are specified as part of the pipeline definition and can be referred to anywhere within the pipeline's activities.

Data factory linked services most closely resemble SSIS's project-level connection managers but behave somewhat differently. SSIS connection managers do not support external injection of parameters – package-level connection managers are parameterized using SSIS expressions that reference package parameters or variables.

The concept of a variable or parameter scoped to the exact level of the connection manager is not found in SSIS. Project-level connection managers can make use of project parameters, but the scope of these is project-wide (much like the factory-wide scope of ADF's global parameters).

ADF's Execute Pipeline activity serves the same purpose as SSIS's Execute Package Task, but invoked pipelines can only be specified at design time. SSIS allows you to override this constraint by setting the Execute Package Task's DelayValidation property to true, but ADF activities have no comparable setting.

SSIS packages are frequently executed using SQL Server Agent jobs, requiring the agent's service account (or proxy) to be granted access to external resources. An ADF instance's managed identity serves the same purpose as a domain account used to run the SQL Server agent service – it enables processes executed by the factory to be authenticated and authorized against external data stores and services.

CHAPTER 6

Controlling Flow

In Chapter 4, you began building ADF pipelines containing more than one activity, controlling their order of execution using activity dependencies configured between them. Activity dependencies are among a range of tools available in ADF for controlling a pipeline's flow of execution.

Chapter 5 introduced the Execute Pipeline activity, enabling one pipeline to trigger the execution of another. The ability to do this is fundamental to the orchestration of large ETL workflows, allowing them to be composed of smaller, more manageable pipelines.

In this chapter, you will develop more sophisticated control flows using activity dependencies with different *dependency conditions*. You will also encounter other ADF activities with the specific purpose of controlling flow. To begin with, you will create a new pipeline to use with some of these activities.

Create a Per-File Pipeline

The pipelines you built in previous chapters exploited the Copy activity's ability to describe multi-file sources using directory and file name wildcards. This chapter's pipelines will introduce finer-grained file load controls, making use of a pipeline that loads a single specified file.

1. Create a clone of the "ImportSTFormatFolder" pipeline from Chapter 5 and move it into a new "Chapter6" pipelines folder. Name the new pipeline "ImportSTFormatFile."

2. Open the new pipeline's *Parameters* configuration tab. Rename the two existing parameters to "Directory" and "File" and remove any default value settings.

© Richard Swinbank 2024
R. Swinbank, *Azure Data Factory by Example*, https://doi.org/10.1007/979-8-8688-0218-8_6

3. Select the "Import sales data" Copy activity and open its *Source* tab. You will immediately see error messages relating to the original parameter names (which no longer exist) – remove the two invalid expressions. Change the source's *File path type* to "File path in dataset."

4. Change the activity's *Source dataset*, selecting your "ABS_CSV" parameterized dataset from Chapter 5. In the *Dataset properties* region, ensure that the value of the "Container" parameter is set to "sampledata", then update the "Directory" and "File" dataset parameter values to use the pipeline parameters of the same names. You will also need to provide the name of your blob storage connection string key vault secret – Figure 6-1 shows the configuration of the Copy activity's source.

5. On the *Settings* tab of the pipeline's first activity – the Lookup activity named "Lookup RunSeqNo" – extend the "Comments" parameter pipeline expression to include the file being loaded, for example, `Pipeline @{pipeline().Pipeline} executed in @{pipeline().DataFactory} - loading file "@{pipeline(). parameters.Directory}/@{pipeline().parameters.File}"`.

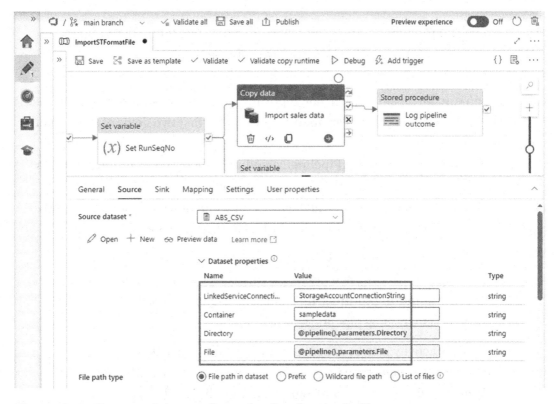

Figure 6-1. *Copy activity configured to load a single file*

Save and run the pipeline. You will be prompted to supply values for the pipeline's "Directory" and "File" parameters – specify the full path and file name of a Sweet Treats or Desserts4All sales data file (e.g., "azure-data-factory-by-example-main/SampleData/Desserts4All" and "04-20.csv"). When execution is complete, verify the results in the [dbo].[PipelineExecution] and [dbo].[Sales_LOAD] database tables.

Use Activity Dependency Conditions

A third retailer – "Naughty but Nice" – supplies sales data in the Sweet Treats format. The "NaughtyButNice" folder (in the same place as the "SweetTreats" and "Desserts4All" folders) contains corresponding data files. Run the "ImportSTFormatFile" pipeline again, this time with these parameters:

- For "Directory," enter "azure-data-factory-by-example-main/SampleData/NaughtyButNice".

- Set "File" to "NBN-202006.csv".

Tip   You will be rerunning the pipeline using these values a number of times –
you may wish to set them as the parameters' default values.

When you run the pipeline, it will fail, reporting a type conversion error. This is due
to a corrupted data file – a comma is missing between the first two fields of a few records
in the middle of the file.

The execution record in [dbo].[PipelineExecution] is incomplete for the pipeline's
execution, because its final Stored procedure activity was not reached. Using the log
table alone, it is not possible to determine whether the pipeline has failed or is simply
still running. You can improve this situation by logging the pipeline's failure.

1. Create a copy of the activity "Log pipeline outcome," the pipeline's
   final Stored procedure activity. To do this, select the activity to
   reveal its authoring controls, then click the *Clone* button. Rename
   the new activity "Log pipeline failure."

2. The new activity is to be executed only if the Copy activity fails. To
   configure this, select the Copy activity. Hold the left mouse button
   down over the red cross mark handle on its right-hand edge.

3. Drag the mouse pointer to the new Stored procedure activity, then
   release the mouse button to create a *Failure* activity dependency.
   Figure 6-2 shows the two dependencies now configured on the
   Copy activity.

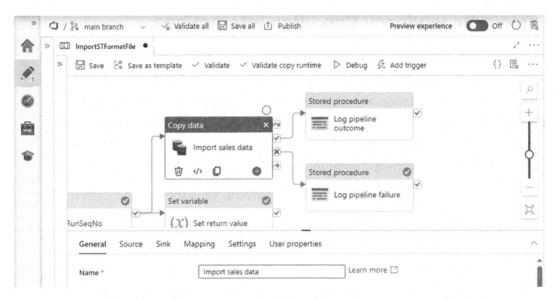

Figure 6-2. *Copy activity followed by activity dependencies with Success and Failure conditions*

4. The "Log pipeline failure" activity will now execute only if the
    Copy activity fails. Open the activity's *Settings* configuration tab
    and scroll down to the *Stored procedure parameters* section.
    Change the value of the "RunStatus" stored procedure parameter
    to "Failed."

Save and run the pipeline, using the same parameter values as before. In the pipeline configuration pane's *Output* tab, you will notice that the Copy activity data fails but that the new failure-logging task is then executed. The log record in the database table [dbo]. [PipelineExecution] shows the pipeline's execution with a [RunStatus] value of "Failed."

Tip   As you drag the design surface viewport around to see different activities in a large pipeline, it is surprisingly easy to lose your place and end up looking at an empty screen! To recover this, right-click somewhere design surface whitespace and select *Zoom to fit* from the pop-up menu. After the surface has recentered, choose *Reset zoom level* (on the same right-click pop-up menu) to restore activities to their usual sizes.

Explore Dependency Condition Interactions

The selected Copy activity shown in Figure 6-2 has a total of four activity dependency handles – one for each of the four possible values for an activity dependency condition: *Success*, *Failure*, *Completion*, and *Skipped*. By combining the four condition values in different ways, you can achieve sophisticated flow control in your pipelines. In this section, you will create a simple testing pipeline to allow you to explore how different combinations of dependency condition interact with one another.

1. Create a new pipeline and drag a *Fail activity* onto the design surface (found in the *General* section of the Activities toolbox).

2. Use the Fail activity's *Settings* configuration tab to set its *Fail message* and *Error code* to values of your choice.

3. Drag two Set variable activities onto the design surface. Configure each one with a *Variable type* of "Pipeline return value" and corresponding return value. Figure 6-3 shows a Set variable activity configured in this way.

4. Connect the pipeline's three activities together into a chain – starting with the Fail activity – using *Success* activity dependencies.

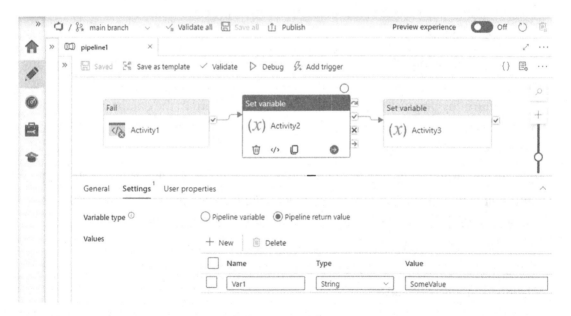

Figure 6-3. *Activity chain created to explore dependencies*

The resulting pipeline, shown in Figure 6-3, does not do useful data integration work – its purpose is simply to enable you to explore the effects of activity dependencies. The two Set variable activities will always succeed when executed, while the Fail activity always fails.

Run the pipeline. As you will expect, the first activity fails, and the next two do not run.

Understand the Skipped Condition

Right-click over the dependency between the second and third activities. The pop-up menu (shown in Figure 6-4) allows you to alter the dependency's condition – change it to *Skipped*.

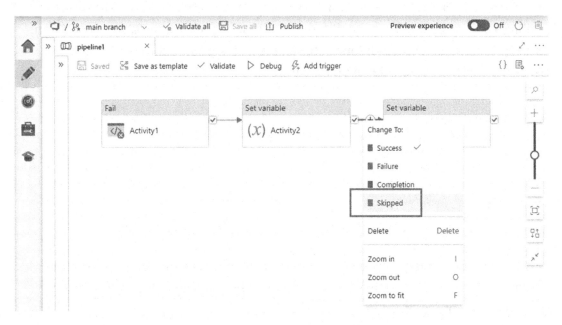

Figure 6-4. *Activity dependency right-click pop-up menu*

Run the pipeline again. This time

- Activity2 is not executed because its dependency condition requires Activity1 to succeed

- Activity3 is executed because its dependency condition requires Activity2 to have been skipped

Understand the Failed Condition

Right-click over the dependency between the first and second activities and change the dependency condition to *Failure*. Run the pipeline, noticing that

- Activity2 is executed because its dependency condition requires Activity1 to fail

- Activity3 is no longer executed because Activity2 has not been skipped

Combine Conditions

Drag the green tick mark handle from the second activity and drop it onto the third, creating a *Success* dependency condition, in addition to the existing *Skipped* condition. Figure 6-5 shows the two conditions between the activities. Run the pipeline again to discover that all three activities are now executed.

Figure 6-5. *Two dependency conditions between Activity2 and Activity3*

Change the condition between the first two activities back to *Success* and run the pipeline again. This time, Activity2 is not executed, but Activity3 still runs because the *Skipped* condition is met.

If multiple dependency conditions are set between a pair of activities, the second activity will be executed if *any* of the conditions are met. In this example, Activity3 will run if Activity2 succeeded OR if Activity2 was skipped.

Create Dependencies on Multiple Activities

Add a third Set variable task to your pipeline and configure it in the same way as the other two. Create a *Success* dependency condition by connecting the new activity's green tick mark handle to Activity2, as shown in Figure 6-6. Run the pipeline.

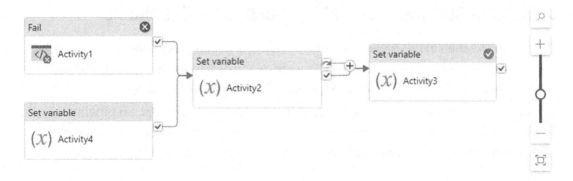

Figure 6-6. *Activity dependent on multiple predecessors*

On this run

- Activity2 is not executed because Activity1 fails

- Activity3 is executed because Activity2 is skipped

When an activity like Activity2 is dependent on the outcome of more than one prior activity, it is only executed if dependency conditions are met from *all* of its predecessors. In this example, Activity2 will run only if Activity1 succeeds AND if Activity4 succeeds.

Understand the Completion Condition

Change the dependency condition between the failing activity and the second activity to *Completion* and run the pipeline. This time, all four activities are executed.

Completion means "either *Success* or *Failure*" – creating the *Success* and *Failure* conditions separately has exactly the same effect. Activity2 is executed in this case because the following combined condition is true:

(Activity1 succeeded OR Activity1 failed) AND Activity4 succeeded

---

For SSIS developers   ADF activity dependency conditions are comparable to SSIS precedence constraints, with two main differences. First, for an activity to be executed, a dependency condition must be met for every activity on which it depends – ADF activity dependencies have no equivalent to SSIS precedence constraints' configurable LogicalAnd property. Second, SSIS supports the use of expressions in precedence constraints, while ADF does not.

Debugging Activities Subject to Dependency Conditions

The examples earlier in this section focus on the effect of dependency conditions themselves, rather than on the activities they connect. In a real-world development scenario, you will need to debug the behavior both of activities and of the dependencies that connect them.

A recently-introduced ADF feature enables you to deactivate selected pipeline activities and to specify the outcome of an deactivated activity. Figure 6-7 shows the "ImportSTFormatFile" pipeline from earlier in the chapter, with the Copy activity selected and deactivated.

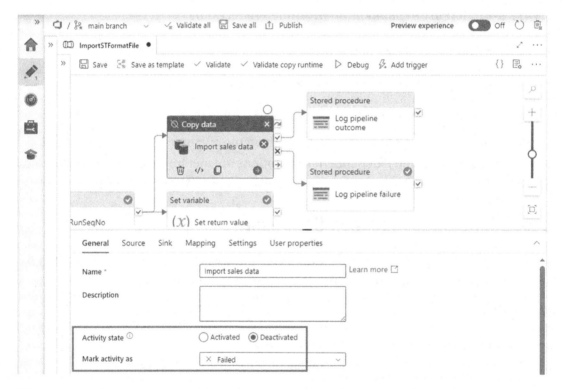

Figure 6-7. *Copy activity with activity state set to Deactivated and outcome set to Failed*

The *Activity state* property on the Copy activity's *General* configuration tab is set to "Deactivated", and the value of *Mark activity as* is "Failed". The effect of these settings is that the Copy activity does not run but is reported to have failed, which in this pipeline causes the "Log pipeline failure" Stored procedure activity (indicated in the figure) to run. Using this setting at development time enables you to test different outcome paths for activities, without having to manufacture those outcomes artificially.

Tip An activity's state can be modified on its *General* configuration tab as shown in Figure 6-7, or can be changed via the pop-up menu accessed by right-clicking the activity on the design surface.

The *Activity state* property is available on all activities. Unlike breakpoints, introduced in Chapter 4, the effect of the property is not limited to debugging runs in ADF Studio. If you wish to disable an activity in a published pipeline, you may do so by setting its activity state to "Deactivated". If you are using activity state for debugging purposes only – for example, to test multiple activity outcomes as described here – remember to reactivate the activity and save your pipeline when you have finished.

Understand Pipeline Outcome

You have been using the *Output* tab on the pipeline's configuration pane to inspect the outcomes of pipeline activities. In addition to individual activity outcomes, a pipeline execution has an overall outcome of its own, reported in ADF Studio's monitoring experience. To open the monitoring experience, click the *Monitor* button (gauge icon) in the navigation sidebar.

The monitoring experience is discussed in depth in Chapter 12. For the time being, select the *Pipeline runs* page, then ensure that the *Debug* tab is selected – the relevant controls are indicated in Figure 6-8.

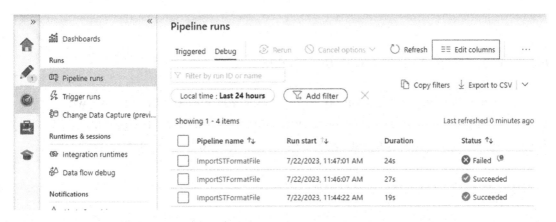

Figure 6-8. *Pipeline debug runs shown in the ADF Studio monitoring experience*

Figure 6-8 shows the result of running the "ImportSTFormatFile" pipeline three times, the third time loading the Naughty but Nice file "NBN-202006.csv", as you did earlier in the chapter. This pipeline run is reported to have failed, but not simply because the Copy activity failed. It is useful to be able to understand the combination of activity outcomes that produces this result.

A pipeline's execution outcome is determined as follows:

- The outcome of every "leaf" activity is inspected. A leaf activity is an activity that has no successor activities in the pipeline. Importantly, if a leaf activity is skipped, its predecessor is treated as a leaf activity for the purpose of evaluating the pipeline's outcome.

- If any leaf activity has *Failed*, the pipeline's outcome is also *Failed*.

Figures 6-9 and 6-10 illustrate the difference between these scenarios. In Figure 6-9, when Activity1 fails, then Activity2 is executed and Activity3 is skipped. Because Activity3 is a skipped leaf, Activity1 is considered to be a leaf instead – and because it has failed, the pipeline itself fails.

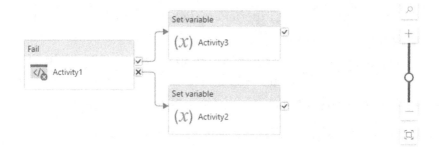

Figure 6-9. *When Activity1 fails, the pipeline fails*

Figure 6-10 shows the same pipeline with Activity3 removed. In this case, when Activity1 fails, then Activity2 is executed as before, but no activity is skipped. Activity3 is the only leaf activity, so when it succeeds, the pipeline also succeeds.

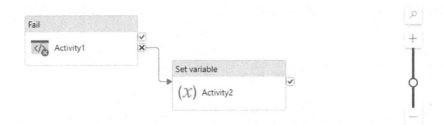

Figure 6-10. *When Activity1 fails, the pipeline succeeds*

In the case of the "ImportSTFormatFile" pipeline, one leaf activity is always skipped – if the Copy activity succeeds, the "Log pipeline failure" activity is skipped, but if the copy fails, "Log pipeline outcome" is skipped instead. This means that the pipeline's Copy activity is always treated as a leaf activity (as the predecessor of whichever Stored procedure activity has been skipped). This has the effect – in this example – that the pipeline's overall outcome is determined directly by the success or failure of the Copy activity.

Figure 6-11 shows an alternative version of "ImportSTFormatFile," modified to use a single Stored procedure activity with a *Completion* dependency condition.

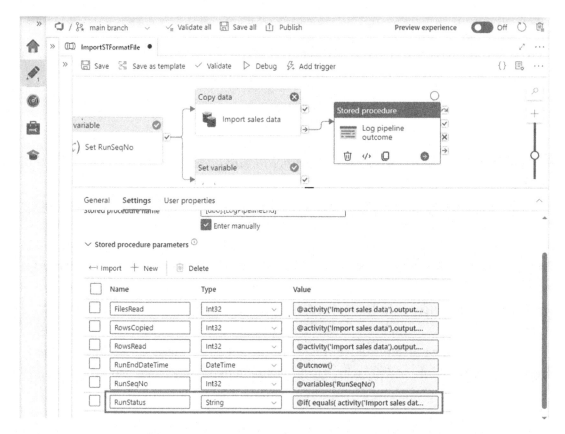

Figure 6-11. *A single Stored procedure activity used to report either success or failure*

An ADF pipeline expression is used to calculate the value of the stored procedure's "RunStatus" parameter (indicated in the figure). The full expression is given in Listing 6-1 – the code layout presented in the listing is used for readability and is also permitted in the ADF Studio pipeline expression builder.

Listing 6-1. Pipeline expression to calculate run status value

```
@if(
    equals(
        activity('Import sales data').output.executionDetails[0].status
        ,'Failed'
    )
```

```
    ,'Failed'
    ,'Done'
)
```

This version of the pipeline has only one leaf activity – "Log pipeline outcome" – which is executed whether the Copy activity succeeds or not. Assuming that the logging activity succeeds, the pipeline is reported to succeed even if the copy fails, because all its leaf activities have succeeded.

For SSIS developers   By default, any error that occurs during SSIS package execution causes the package to fail, but you can modify this behavior by preventing errors from propagating to the calling package or process. The way to meet this requirement in ADF is to understand the behavior of activity dependency conditions and to organize them to achieve the desired effect.

Raise Errors

Understanding why a pipeline is reported to fail allows you to control propagation of errors raised during a pipeline's execution. In contrast, sometimes you may wish to raise errors of your own, for example, if some invalid system state is detected.

The Fail activity introduced earlier in this chapter enables you to raise errors directly in this way, but this is not always necessary. For example, activities that execute T-SQL code will fail when an error is thrown from the underlying SQL database. Raising errors using T-SQL's RAISERROR or THROW statements is often more convenient than using an additional ADF Fail activity.

In Chapter 3, you encountered an issue with schema drift, where a renamed field in the Sugar Cube JSON schema caused product names to disappear from loaded data. The effect of this was to populate the [Product] field in [dbo].[Sales_LOAD] with NULLs in rows relating to September 2020 – this is an example of invalid state that you might choose to raise as an error.

Listing 6-2 provides a revised version of the [dbo].[LogPipelineEnd] stored procedure. The procedure inspects the database table's [Product] field, using RAISERROR to cause the loading pipeline to fail if NULLs are encountered. This provides a basic data quality check, converting undesirable data features into detectable pipeline failures. If you wish, modify your existing stored procedure using the script provided – to test it, you will need to create a new pipeline, combining the Sugar Cube data load from Chapter 3 with the logging functionality you developed after that.

Listing 6-2. [dbo].[LogPipelineEnd] raises an error if [Product] is NULL

```
ALTER PROCEDURE [dbo].[LogPipelineEnd] (
  @RunSeqNo INT
, @RunEndDateTime DATETIME
, @RunStatus VARCHAR(20)
, @FilesRead INT
, @RowsRead INT
, @RowsCopied INT
) AS
UPDATE dbo.PipelineExecution
SET RunEndDateTime = @RunEndDateTime
  , RunStatus = @RunStatus
  , FilesRead = @FilesRead
  , RowsRead = @RowsRead
  , RowsCopied = @RowsCopied
WHERE RunSeqNo = @RunSeqNo;
IF EXISTS (
  SELECT * FROM dbo.Sales_LOAD
  WHERE [Product] IS NULL
)
RAISERROR('Unexpected NULL in dbo.Sales_LOAD.[Product]', 11, 1);
```

Use Conditional Activities

There are a wide variety of different ways to handle data errors, depending on factors ranging from business data requirements to technical process control. So far, in this chapter, you have implemented pipelines that report loading failures, using activity dependencies to control whether pipeline execution succeeds or fails under those conditions.

Whether the loading pipeline fails or not, format errors in the Naughty but Nice sales file "NBN-202006.csv" cause loading to be abandoned – when an error is encountered, no rows are loaded. An alternative approach is to load whatever valid data you can, diverting other rows elsewhere to be inspected and handled later. In this section, you will use a Copy activity feature to divert errors and then use one of ADF's *conditional activities* to load records into a separate database table for inspection.

Divert Error Rows

The Copy activity includes a feature that allows you to redirect failed rows to a log file in blob storage. Configure that option as follows:

1. Clone the "ImportSTFormatFile" pipeline from earlier in the chapter. Name the clone "ImportSTFormatFile_Divert", then open the Copy activity's *Settings* configuration tab.

2. Scroll down to the *Fault tolerance* multiselect dropdown and select "Skip incompatible rows." Ensure that the *Enable logging* check box is ticked, causing additional *Logging settings* to be displayed.

3. In *Logging settings*, choose your Azure blob storage linked service from the *Storage connection name* dropdown.

4. You will be prompted for a *Folder path* and – if you have chosen a parameterized linked service – required *Linked service properties*. Accept the default values provided for *Logging level* and *Logging Mode*.

5. Click the *Browse* button to the right of the *Folder path* field, choose the blob storage "output" container, then click *OK*. Edit the *Folder path* value, appending "/errors".

Figure 6-12 shows the configured fault tolerance settings for the Copy activity.

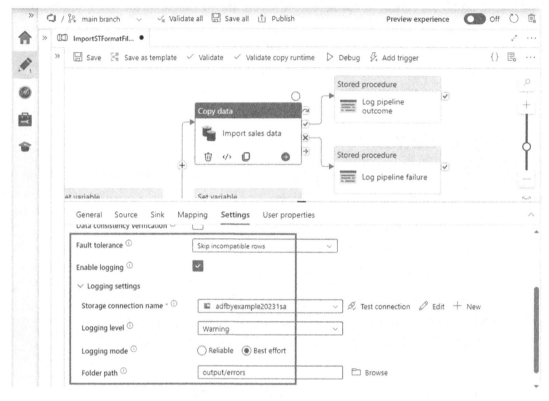

Figure 6-12. *Copy activity fault tolerance settings*

Tip   Copy activity logging can be enabled independent of fault tolerance settings. Setting *Logging level* to "Info" causes information about successfully copied files to be logged, in addition to skipped files and rows.

Run the modified pipeline, again loading the badly formatted Naughty but Nice sales file "NBN-202006.csv". This time, the Copy activity's new fault tolerance settings will enable it to succeed. When the pipeline has successfully completed, inspect the Copy activity's output JSON object (via the link in the *Output* tab on the pipeline's configuration pane). An example is shown in Figure 6-13, including the following information:

- **rowsRead:** The number of rows read from the source file.

- **rowsCopied:** The number of rows copied to your Azure SQL DB. This is fewer than the number of rows read but is greater than zero because correctly formatted rows have been loaded successfully into the database table.

- **rowsSkipped:** The number of rows not copied. These are the badly formatted rows in the source file.

- **logFilePath:** Skipped rows have been written into a log file specific to this activity run. The log file path ends in a GUID folder name – this is the activity run GUID that you can find on the right-hand side of the *Output* tab on the pipeline's configuration pane.

Figure 6-13. *Fault tolerance information in the Copy activity's output JSON*

Using the Azure portal's Storage browser for your storage account, browse to the log file's location. Download the ".txt" file you find there and open it in a text editor. Figure 6-14 shows a similar log file, also produced by loading "NBN-202006.csv". The log is a CSV file containing five columns, the fourth of which – "OperationItem" – contains the entire diverted row.

As this is a quote-enclosed CSV file, every double quote character in the original record has been escaped by preceding it with another. Even so, you can easily see that the problem records are missing a comma between the date and retailer fields (indicated in Figure 6-14).

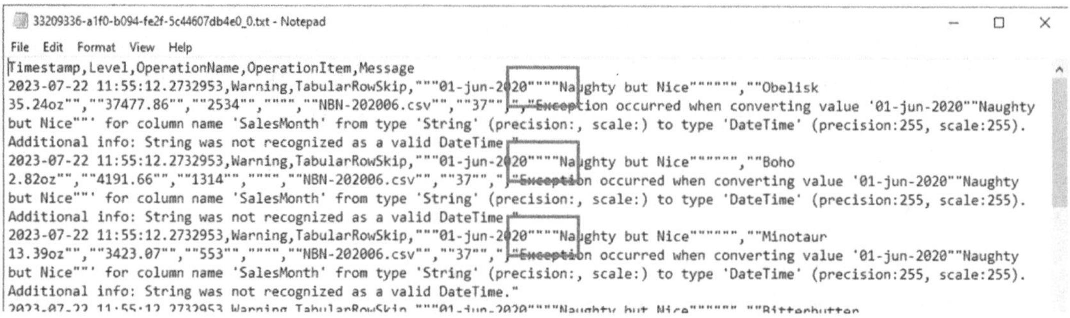

Figure 6-14. *Badly formatted source records in the Copy activity fault log*

Load Error Rows

A convenient way to inspect tabular log files is to collect their contents in a database table. In this section, you will add another Copy activity to load the log file into an error table. Create an error log table in your Azure SQL Database using the code in Listing 6-3.

Listing 6-3. Create a loading error table

```
CREATE TABLE dbo.LoadingError (
  [Timestamp] DATETIME2 NULL
, [Level] NVARCHAR(50) NULL
, [OperationName] NVARCHAR(50) NULL
, [OperationItem] NVARCHAR(4000) NULL
, [Message] NVARCHAR(4000) NULL
);
```

Create a New Sink Dataset

Your existing Azure SQL Database dataset contains a hard-coded table name in its definition – [dbo].[Sales_LOAD]. Create a new dataset (in a "Chapter6" datasets folder) to enable you to load log data into [dbo].[LoadingError], preferably by parameterizing the table's schema and name in the dataset definition.

Figure 6-15 shows an AQL SQL DB dataset using a table name specified by dataset parameters. You will get further use out of a parameterized table dataset in Chapter 7.

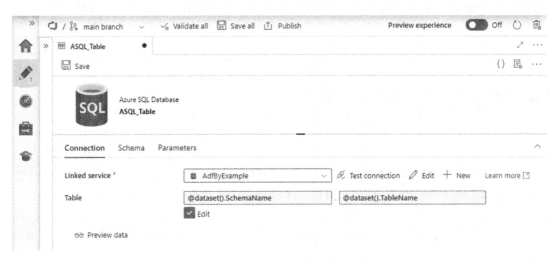

Figure 6-15. *Parameterized Azure SQL DB dataset*

Revise the Source Dataset

Open the "ABS_CSV" dataset you created in Chapter 5 and inspect the properties on its *Connection* configuration tab. So far, you have only been making changes to *File path* settings, but the dataset's properties can be configured to match many variations in file format. Notice in particular that the *Escape character* default is "Backslash (\)". As you saw in Figure 6-14, the log file's escape character is a double quote – change the selected value to "Double quote(")", then save the revised dataset.

When modifying shared resources such as datasets, take care not to introduce faults in pipelines or other resources that use them. The change is safe in this situation, because none of the source CSV files you have encountered so far contains escape characters. An alternative approach is to parameterize the escape character, giving the dataset parameter a default value of "\" to ensure backward compatibility.

Tip   The *Properties* flyout, available for datasets and other factory resources, includes a *Related* tab, identifying related factory resources. When modifying an existing resource, use the *Related* tab to find resources that may be affected by changes.

Use the If Condition Activity

The new Copy activity will use the log file path reported in the output of the original file copy. A log file is found in this location only when one or more records have been skipped – if no rows are skipped, then no file is created. Running the log file Copy activity when the log file does not exist would itself cause an error, so the activity can only be permitted to run if rows have been skipped.

You can control this behavior using an *If Condition* activity, found in the *Iteration & conditionals* section of the Activities toolbox.

1. Return to the "ImportSTFormatFile_Divert" pipeline, then drag an If Condition activity onto the design surface. Rearrange activity dependencies to place it between the "Import sales data" Copy activity and the "Log pipeline outcome" (log success) Stored procedure activity, as shown in Figure 6-16. Name the activity "If rows skipped."

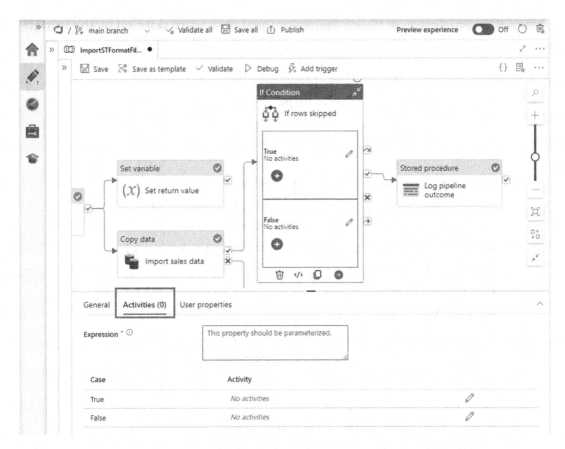

Figure 6-16. *If Condition activity added to the ImportSTFormatFile_Divert*
pipeline

2. Select the If Condition's *Activities* configuration tab (indicated
   in the figure). It contains an *Expression* field and two *cases*: *True*
   and *False*. The two cases are containers for other activities – the
   activities contained in the *True* case are executed when the
   pipeline expression in the *Expression* field evaluates to true; those
   in the *False* case when it does not.

3. Click the *Expression* field to launch the pipeline expression
   builder. Enter a pipeline expression that evaluates to true if any
   rows were skipped by the prior Copy activity. A possible choice is
   given in Listing 6-4.

Listing 6-4. Pipeline expression to determine if rows were skipped by the Import sales data Copy activity

```
@greater(
    activity('Import sales data').output.rowsSkipped
    , 0
)
```

4. Below the *Expression* field, click the pencil icon on the right of the *True* case – this opens a new design surface showing the case's activities, currently none. (Alternatively, use the pencil icon displayed in the activity graphic on the design surface.) The breadcrumb trail in the top left contains the pipeline name, the If Condition activity name, and *True activities*, indicating the part of the pipeline you are currently editing.

5. Drag a Copy activity onto the design surface and open its *Source* configuration tab. Select the "ABS_CSV" dataset and enter the value "output" for its "Container" parameter. Set the *File path type* option to "Wildcard file path," and then in *Wildcard folder path*, enter a pipeline expression to return the log file path from the earlier Copy activity. Set *Wildcard file name* to "*".

Note   The log file path reported by the Copy activity includes the blob storage container – your pipeline expression must remove this prefix. One expression that achieves this is `@join(skip(split(activity('Import sales data').output.logFilePath, '/'), 1), '/')`.

---

6. Configure the Copy activity's *Sink* tab to specify the [dbo].[LoadingError] table using your new Azure SQL Database dataset.

Note   When you select an activity inside the If Condition on the design surface, no breakpoint circle is displayed. ADF Studio does not permit you to set a breakpoint on any nested activity.

Run the Pipeline

Run the pipeline again to load the Naughty but Nice sales file "NBN-202006.csv". Watch the pipeline configuration pane's *Output* tab as the pipeline runs, refreshing it regularly to monitor progress. Notice that each of the pipeline's six activity runs is added to the output list as it is queued, but that the If Condition activity's status remains *In progress* until the Copy activity it contains is queued, executes, and completes. Nested activity runs can be viewed more intuitively by switching the *Output* pane from "List" to "Container" view – Figure 6-17 shows the output of a "ImportSTFormatFile_Divert" pipeline run presented in this way.

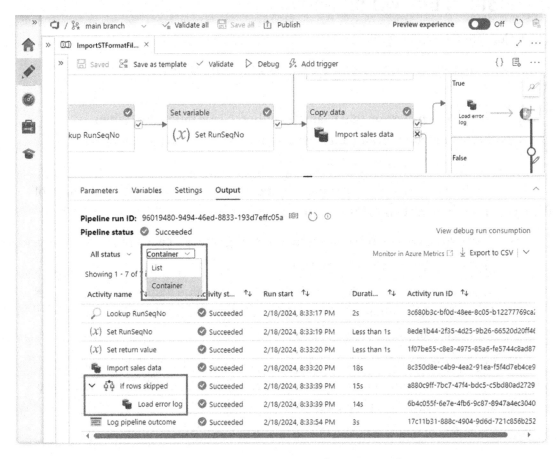

Figure 6-17. *Nested activity runs shown using "Container" view*

When the pipeline has completed successfully, verify that the database table [dbo].
[LoadingError] now contains 16 rows copied from the log file. The database log table
[dbo].[PipelineExecution] reports that 16 fewer rows were copied than were read.

Finally, run the pipeline again, loading a different Naughty but Nice sales file,
for example, "NBN-202004.csv". This file contains no formatting errors – the pipeline
configuration pane's *Output* tab shows that the If Condition activity is executed (to allow
its expression to be evaluated), but that the log file copy is not.

Understand the Switch Activity

The If Condition is made up of

- Two *cases* – *True* and *False* – each of which contains zero or more
  activities.

- A *pipeline expression* that evaluates either to true or to false. When
  the expression is evaluated at execution time, the activities in the
  corresponding case are then executed.

The *Switch activity* is ADF's other conditional activity. Switch is a generalization of
the If Condition activity to more than two cases. It consists of

- Up to 25 cases – identified by different string values – each of which
  must contain one or more activities.

- A pipeline expression that evaluates to a string value. When this
  expression is evaluated at execution time, the activities in the
  corresponding case are executed.

Additionally, the Switch activity always contains a *Default* case. If the evaluated
pipeline expression matches none of the identified cases, activities in the Default case –
of which there may be none – are executed.

Tip   ADF does not permit conditional activities to be used within other conditional activities. If you require nested-if logic, the Switch activity may help you to implement it as a series of cases. An alternative workaround is to create your "inner" If Condition or Switch in one pipeline and your "outer" conditional activity in another – you can then use the Execute Pipeline activity to call the inner pipeline from the outer conditional activity.

Figure 6-18 shows a configured Switch activity with four cases: "A," "B," "C," and *Default*. When the pipeline expression @variables('MyVariable') evaluates to "A," case A's activity is executed. The activities in cases B and C are executed when the expression evaluates to "B" or "C," respectively. If the expression evaluates to any value except "A," "B," or "C," the *Default* case's Fail activity is executed.

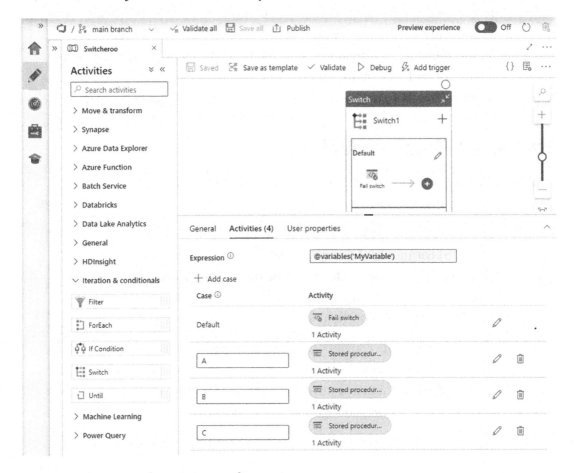

Figure 6-18. *Switch activity configuration*

Use the If Condition activity when your control flow requires only two cases – if you need more cases, use the Switch activity.

For SSIS developers   SSIS contains no control flow task directly comparable to the If Condition or Switch activities but provides similar functionality using expressions in precedence constraints. In SSIS, it is occasionally necessary to create a dummy predecessor task, to provide a precedence constraint to implement if/switch-like behavior – this is not required in Azure Data Factory because pipeline expressions and activity dependencies are decoupled.

Use Iteration Activities

The pipeline you developed in the previous section provides more sophisticated process control and error handling than those from earlier chapters but – by design – loads only a single, specified file. To load all Naughty but Nice sales files, the pipeline must be executed once for each file. In this section, you will use one of Azure Data Factory's *iteration activities* to do this automatically, iterating over a list of files to be loaded.

Use the Get Metadata Activity

Before you can iterate over a list of files, you must first obtain one – you can do this in ADF using the *Get Metadata* activity.

1. Create a new pipeline in the "Chapter6" folder and name it "ImportSTFormatFiles." Create a pipeline parameter called "FolderPath," giving it the default value of the Naughty but Nice sales data folder ("azure-data-factory-by-example-main/ SampleData/NaughtyButNice").

2. Drag a Get Metadata activity – found in the *General* section of the Activities toolbox – onto the design surface. Name it "Get file list." The Get Metadata activity returns metadata relating to an ADF dataset – on its *Settings* configuration tab, choose the "ABS_CSV" dataset.

3. The files to be loaded are those in the "NaughtyButNice" blob storage folder – you will use the Get Metadata activity to list the folder's files. Set the dataset's "Container" property to "sampledata." Populate the "Directory" property with a pipeline expression that returns the value of the pipeline's "FolderPath" parameter.

4. The "ABS_CSV" dataset requires a file parameter. If you do not specify one, ADF will use the default value ("."") that will fail to match the "NaughtyButNice" folder. To work around this, replace the period in the dataset's "File" property field with a space character, as indicated in Figure 6-19.

5. Scroll down the *Settings* configuration tab to the *Field list* section (also indicated in the figure). This is where metadata items to be returned by the activity are specified. Add three arguments: "Exists," "Item type," and "Item name."

6. Run the pipeline. If you have configured it correctly, the activity's output JSON will include three fields: exists = true, itemType = "Folder", and itemName = "NaughtyButNice". If exists is false, check your configured file path for errors.

7. Add a fourth argument to the *Field list* on the activity's *Settings* configuration tab: "Child Items." Run the pipeline again and verify that the activity's output now includes a childItems array field containing the list of files in the "NaughtyButNice" folder.

Tip   If the Get Metadata activity's "Child Items" argument is specified for a path that identifies a file instead of a folder, the Get Metadata activity will fail. Delaying adding the "Child Items" argument until step 7 allows you to check first that your configured path refers correctly to a folder.

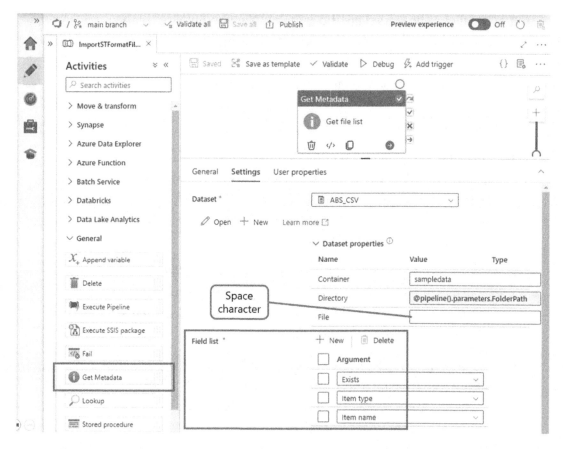

Figure 6-19. *Configuring the Get Metadata activity*

Use the ForEach Activity

The *ForEach activity* is one of Azure Data Factory's two iteration activities. It allows you to specify a set of activities to be performed repeatedly, once for every item in a given JSON array – for example, an array of child items returned by the Get Metadata activity.

1. Drag a ForEach activity onto the design surface, making it dependent on the Get Metadata activity.

2. On the ForEach activity's *Settings* configuration tab, open the pipeline expression builder in the *Items* field.

3. Choose the output of your Get Metadata activity from the pipeline expression builder's *Activity outputs* tab, then add ".childItems" to the expression in the expression pane. The final expression should be `@activity('Get file list').output.childItems`.

4. To edit the set of activities to be executed on each iteration, click the pencil icon on the ForEach activity's *Activities* configuration tab. (Alternatively, use the pencil icon displayed in the activity graphic on the design surface.)

5. Drag an Execute Pipeline activity onto the empty ForEach design surface. Open its *Settings* configuration tab and set its *Invoked pipeline* to "ImportSTFormatFile_Divert". Configure the invoked pipeline's "Directory" parameter to use the value of this pipeline's "FolderPath" parameter.

6. The invoked pipeline's "File" parameter value should be the name of the file for the current iteration of the ForEach activity. The current item in a ForEach activity's array is specified using the pipeline expression item(). In this example, item() returns an object element of the childItems array in the Get Metadata activity's output. The name of the file is located in the object's name field, so the full file expression is @item().name. The configured Execute Pipeline activity is shown in Figure 6-20.

7. Run the pipeline.

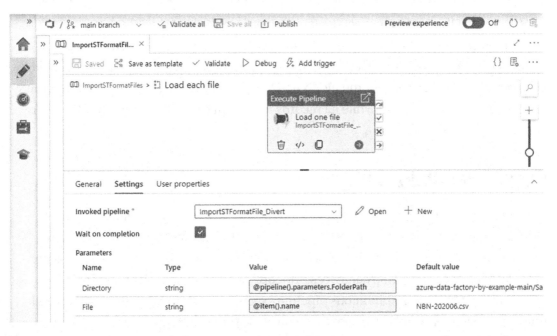

Figure 6-20. *Execute Pipeline activity using the containing ForEach activity's item() pipeline expression*

When you run the pipeline in debug mode, ADF Studio warns you that "All the activities inside the foreach loop will be run sequentially and each run pipeline activity will wait on completion for debugging purposes." This is in contrast to published pipelines, where the default behavior of the ForEach activity is to execute up to 20 iterations simultaneously, in parallel. One of the key advantages of Azure Data Factory over on-premises services is the ability to scale out in this way, briefly leveraging more resource to reduce end-to-end processing time.

When you configured the ForEach activity's *Items* array (on its *Settings* configuration tab), you will have noticed two additional options: a *Sequential* check box and a *Batch count* field. These options allow you to constrain the maximum parallelism exhibited by the activity. Ticking the *Sequential* check box eliminates parallel execution, requiring iterations to run sequentially. When the check box is unticked, *Batch count* specifies the maximum number of iterations permitted to run in parallel (up to 50).

Tip   Because ForEach activity iterations are often run sequentially in debug mode, it is not sufficient to test pipelines in ADF Studio alone. Issues with parallelization may not become apparent until pipelines are tested in a published ADF environment. Publishing pipelines is discussed in Chapter 10.

Use your SQL client to inspect the latest records in the log table [dbo]. [PipelineExecution]. The table shows six new pipeline runs, one for each month's Naughty but Nice sales data. The [Comments] column indicates which file was loaded by each pipeline run – the run for the file "NBN-202006.csv" again indicates that more rows were read than were copied, while all records read from each of the other five files were copied successfully.

Ensure Parallelizability

You first encountered issues with parallelizability at the end of Chapter 5, when it became necessary to chain two Execute Pipeline activities together to prevent them from running simultaneously. The pipelines you have built so far are not parallel-safe, because in each case the Copy activity's pre-copy script truncates the [dbo].[Sales_ LOAD] table. Multiple simultaneous pipeline executions using this pattern run the risk that any one of them could truncate the table while others are mid-copy.

The ForEach activity cannot benefit from ADF's scale-out ability unless iterations can be isolated from one another. In this section, you will modify your per-file pipeline to move loaded data into a separate table, allowing the pipeline to take responsibility for removing only its own records from [dbo].[Sales_LOAD]. This will replace the previous approach of housekeeping the table by regularly truncating it.

1. Listings 6-5 and 6-6 provide code to create a table called [dbo].
    [Sales] and a stored procedure to update the table from [dbo].
    [Sales_LOAD]. Run these two scripts in your SQL client to create
    the two database objects.

2. Edit your "ImportSTFormatFile_Divert" pipeline, adding a Stored
    procedure activity between the "Import sales data" Copy activity
    and the "If rows skipped" If Condition activity.

3. Configure the Stored procedure activity to call procedure [dbo].
    [PersistLoadedSales] from Listing 6-6, using the pipeline's
    "RunSeqNo" variable to provide the stored procedure's
    parameter value.

4. Edit the Copy activity, removing the *Pre-copy script* from the
    activity's *Sink* configuration tab.

Listing 6-5. Table [dbo].[Sales]

```
CREATE TABLE dbo.Sales (
  RowId INT NOT NULL IDENTITY(1,1)
, Retailer NVARCHAR(255) NOT NULL
, SalesMonth DATE NOT NULL
, Product NVARCHAR(255) NOT NULL
, SalesValueUSD DECIMAL(19,2) NOT NULL
, UnitsSold INT NOT NULL
, RunSeqNo INT NOT NULL
, CONSTRAINT PK__dbo_Sales PRIMARY KEY (RowId)
);
```

Listing 6-6. Procedure [dbo].[PersistLoadedSales]

```
CREATE PROCEDURE dbo.PersistLoadedSales (
  @runSeqNo INT
) AS

DELETE tgt
FROM dbo.Sales tgt
  INNER JOIN dbo.Sales_LOAD src
    ON src.Retailer = tgt.Retailer
    AND src.SalesMonth = tgt.SalesMonth
    AND src.Product = tgt.Product
WHERE src.RunSeqNo = @runSeqNo;

DELETE
FROM [dbo].[Sales_LOAD]
OUTPUT
  deleted.[Retailer]
, deleted.[SalesMonth]
, deleted.[Product]
, deleted.[SalesValueUSD]
, deleted.[UnitsSold]
, deleted.[RunSeqNo]
INTO dbo.Sales (
  [Retailer]
, [SalesMonth]
, [Product]
, [SalesValueUSD]
, [UnitsSold]
, [RunSeqNo]
)
WHERE RunSeqNo = @runSeqNo;
```

The [dbo].[Sales_LOAD] table will now be empty most of the time, except for the intervals between a pipeline loading data from a file and copying it into [dbo].[Sales]. To complete this setup, use your SQL client to truncate the [dbo].[Sales_LOAD] table, consistent with its new resting state.

Finally, rerun the pipeline "ImportSTFormatFiles" to load all six Naughty but Nice sales files. When execution is complete, verify that sales data for all six months between April and September 2020 is present in the table [dbo].[Sales] and that the table [dbo].[Sales_LOAD] is empty.

Although ADF Studio forces the pipeline's ForEach activity to load the six files sequentially during debugging, the pipeline can now safely load files in parallel when published. This is because each pipeline run removes from [dbo].[Sales_LOAD] only the data it loaded, so it will not interfere with other activities (in this or other pipelines) running at the same time.

Tip   Remember that pipeline variables are scoped at the level of the pipeline, so ADF's Set variable activity is never parallel-safe. ForEach iterations that modify variables will produce unpredictable results and must be avoided. A common workaround is to encapsulate an iteration's activities in a nested Execute Pipeline activity, just as you have done here.

Understand the Until Activity

Like the ForEach activity, ADF's *Until activity* allows you to specify a set of activities to be performed repeatedly. Instead of iterating over a fixed array of elements, the Until activity repeats indefinitely until its *terminating condition* is met (or the activity times out). Figure 6-21 shows an example of an Until activity's terminating condition pipeline expression – the activity will repeat until the value of a variable called "FilesLeft" falls to zero, or the default timeout of 12 hours is reached.

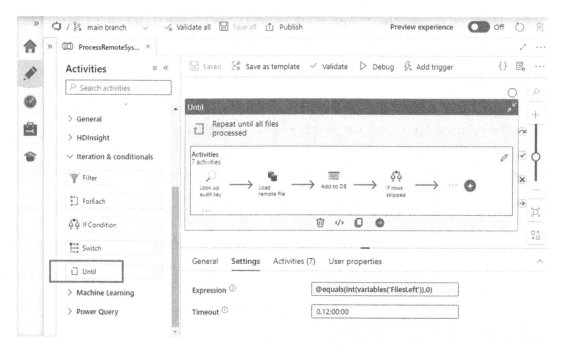

Figure 6-21. *Pipeline expression providing an Until activity's terminating condition*

Tip   ADF does not permit nesting of iteration activities, nor does it allow you to use them inside conditional activities. As before, a workaround is to use different pipelines to implement the inner and outer loops of a nested iteration.

Typical use cases for the Until activity are situations involving external dependencies – for example, to delay extracting data from a data source until the source system is ready. One or more activities inside the Until activity usually have the task of reevaluating the situation in each iteration – in the example of Figure 6-21, this might consist of recalculating the number of files remaining and then using the Set variable activity to assign the calculated value to the "FilesLeft" variable.

Because the Until activity's iterations do not correspond to array elements, the item() syntax is not supported in this context. For the same reason, parallel iterations are not possible – execution of Until activity iterations is always sequential. The Until activity's terminating condition expression is reevaluated at the end of every iteration – this means that the activities inside an Until activity are always executed at least once.

For SSIS developers   ADF's ForEach activity is directly comparable to SSIS's Foreach Loop Container, although SSIS additionally permits nested loops within a single package. The indefinite iteration pattern of ADF's Until activity is not directly supported in SSIS. An SSIS For Loop Container specifying no AssignExpression achieves a similar effect, but with the difference that EvalExpression is evaluated at the start of every iteration (so an execution with zero iterations is possible).

Chapter Review

In this chapter, you used three varieties of tool to control pipeline execution flow:

- **Activity dependency conditions:** To determine what happens after an activity's execution is complete

- **Conditional activities:** To execute separate subsets of a pipeline's activities under different conditions

- **Iteration activities:** To execute subsets of a pipeline's activities repeatedly

Used together with the Execute Pipeline activity – and where necessary nesting conditional and iteration activities in different pipelines – these tools form a comprehensive arsenal for controlling flow within pipelines and orchestrating large and complex multi-pipeline workflows.

Key Concepts

- **Dependency condition:** Characterizes an activity dependency. An activity dependent on another is only executed if the associated dependency condition is met – that is, depending on whether the prior activity succeeds, fails, or is skipped.

- **Multiple dependencies:** An activity dependent on multiple activities is only executed if each prior activity satisfies a dependency condition. If an activity specifies multiple dependency conditions on the same prior activity, only one needs to be met.

- **Leaf activity:** A leaf activity is a pipeline activity with no successors.

- **Conditional activities:** ADF has two conditional activities – the If Condition activity and the Switch activity.

- **If Condition activity:** Specifies a pipeline expression that evaluates to true or false and two corresponding contained sets of activities. When the activity runs, its expression is evaluated, and the corresponding activity set is executed.

- **Switch activity:** Specifies a pipeline expression that evaluates to a string value and up to 25 corresponding contained sets of activities. When the activity runs, the expression is evaluated, and the corresponding activity set, if any, is executed. If no matching case is found, the default activity set is executed instead.

- **Iteration activities:** ADF has two iteration activities – the ForEach activity and the Until activity.

- **ForEach activity:** Specifies a JSON array and a set of activities to be executed once for each element of the array. The current element of the array is addressed in each iteration using the `item()` pipeline expression.

- **Parallelism:** By default, ForEach activity executions take place in parallel, requiring care to ensure that activities from simultaneous iterations do not interfere with one another. Variable modification must be avoided, but the Execute Pipeline activity provides an easy way to isolate iterations. ADF Studio executes ForEach iterations sequentially in debug mode, which can make parallelism faults hard to detect at development time.

- **Until activity:** Specifies a terminating condition and a set of activities to be executed repeatedly until the terminating condition is met. Activities within an Until activity are executed at least once and never in parallel.

- **Nesting:** Iteration activities may not be nested in other iteration activities. Conditional activities may not be nested in other conditional activities, although they may be used inside iteration activities. A common workaround is to implement inner and outer activities in separate pipelines, calling the inner activity from the outer using the Execute Pipeline activity.

- **Breakpoints:** ADF Studio does not support breakpoints inside iteration or conditional activities.

- **Get Metadata activity:** Returns metadata that describes attributes of an ADF dataset. Not all metadata attributes are supported by all datasets – for example, specifying the "Child Items" argument on a nonfolder target will cause the activity to fail.

- **Fault tolerance:** The Copy activity supports enhanced error handling through its Fault tolerance settings, enabling individual error rows to be diverted into an external log file without completely abandoning a data load.

- **Raising errors:** Errors can be raised directly in a pipeline using the Fail activity. It is sometimes convenient to raise errors in external services – for example, by using SQL Server's RAISERROR or THROW statements – causing the calling ADF activity to fail.

For SSIS Developers

Azure Data Factory activity dependencies and conditions are similar to SSIS precedence constraints, but activity dependencies do not support expressions. Conditional execution is controlled separately using the If Condition or Switch activities. An activity will only be executed if a dependency condition is satisfied by every activity on which it depends – unlike SSIS, there is no alternative "Logical OR" behavior configurable for multiple dependencies.

Unlike in SSIS, error propagation cannot simply be switched on or off in ADF. Pipeline outcome is determined by the outcome of a pipeline's leaf activities – error propagation is controlled by structuring activity dependencies to produce the required behavior.

SSIS's Foreach Loop Container is similar in operation to the ADF ForEach activity, albeit without the automatic scale-out capabilities of ADF. The SSIS For Loop Container could be simulated by the ADF ForEach activity given an appropriate JSON array of numbers; the Until activity provides a more direct implementation of indefinite iteration than is available in SSIS.

CHAPTER 7

Data Flows

The Copy activity is a powerful tool for moving data between storage systems, but it has limited support for data transformation. Columns can be added to the activity's source configuration, or removed by excluding them from the source to sink mapping, but the activity does not support manipulation of individual rows or allow data sources to be combined or separated.

The Azure platform offers a number of tools based on *Apache Spark*, including Azure Databricks, Azure Synapse Analytics Spark pools, and Azure HDInsight. Apache Spark is an open source analytics engine that supports large-scale data transformation by automatically distributing data processing workloads across a cluster of computers (referred to as *nodes*) to enable highly parallelized execution. Transformation processes are implemented using code written in one of several supported languages, such as Scala, R, or Python.

ADF Studio's Activities toolbox contains a variety of activities that provide access to external Spark resources, but this requires you to implement and manage a separate Spark cluster (e.g., in a Databricks workspace or a Synapse Analytics workspace) and to code data transformations in the language of your choice. Azure Data Factory *data flows* provide an alternative, low-code route to the power of Spark. Data flows are implemented using a visual editor, converted automatically into Scala code by ADF, and executed in an ADF-managed Spark cluster. This chapter introduces you to authoring ADF data flows.

Build a Data Flow

Azure Data Factory data flows are independent, reusable ADF resources, implemented in ADF Studio using a visual *data flow canvas*. The execution of a data flow occurs in an ADF pipeline using the *Data flow activity* – in this section, you will create a data flow, create a pipeline to execute it, and run that pipeline.

© Richard Swinbank 2024
R. Swinbank, *Azure Data Factory by Example*, https://doi.org/10.1007/979-8-8688-0218-8_7

1. Open the ADF Studio authoring canvas. In the *Factory Resources* explorer, you will find the *Data flows* resource type (below the familiar *Pipelines* and *Datasets* resource types). Create a new "Chapter7" folder using the Data flows *Actions* menu.

2. On the "Chapter7" folder's *Actions* menu, click *New data flow*.

3. The data flow canvas opens. In the *Properties* flyout, change the name of the data flow to "TransformJollyGoodSales," then close the flyout in the usual way.

This data flow will be used to load ABC sales data for a UK-based confectionery vendor named "Jolly Good Ltd."

Enable Data Flow Debugging

Although triggered from a pipeline activity, the execution of Azure Data Factory data flows takes place on a Spark cluster managed by ADF. A cluster must be provisioned before a data flow can be executed, whether in a published environment or when debugging in ADF Studio. Provisioning a cluster may take a few minutes, so your first task when developing a data flow is to spin up a cluster for convenient debugging.

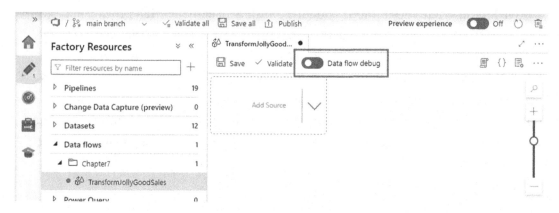

Figure 7-1. Data flow debug disabled

1. The *Data flow debug* toggle is located immediately above the data flow canvas – switch it to the "On" position. When in the "Off" position, as in Figure 7-1, the toggle's background color is gray.

2. The *Turn on data flow debug* flyout is displayed, prompting you to select an *Integration runtime* and *Debug time to live*. Leave the default values selected and click *OK*. Integration runtimes are discussed in more detail in Chapter 8.

The *Data flow debug* toggle is disabled, and to its right a spinner indicates that the cluster is starting. When the cluster is ready for use, the toggle's background color changes to blue and the spinner is replaced by a tick mark in a green circle, as shown in Figure 7-2. This means that the cluster is now available to run data flows in debug mode from ADF Studio.

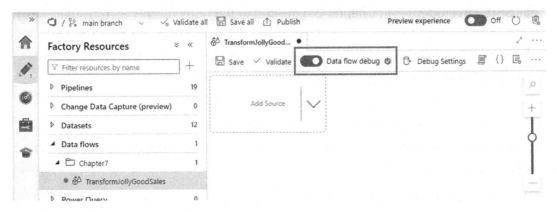

Figure 7-2. *Data flow debug enabled*

The debug cluster's default time to live (TTL) is one hour – after that time, if the cluster is not being used, it is automatically shut down. When cluster timeout is approaching, the green tick cluster status icon is replaced by a filled orange circle. If you wish to prevent the cluster from shutting down, you must run the data flow or take another action that uses the cluster.

When you have finished developing and debugging, disable the debug cluster – although it will shut down automatically when its TTL is reached, you can save yourself the cost of running the cluster for the remainder of that time.

Add a Data Flow Transformation

You are now ready to start data flow development. A data flow is made up of a sequence of connected *transformations*. Conceptually, each transformation in the sequence

- Receives a stream of data rows from the previous transformation

- Modifies rows in the stream as they pass

- Emits modified rows to the next transformation

For SSIS developers   In Chapter 3, I described the Copy activity as providing functionality like a basic SSIS Data Flow Task. ADF Data Flows are much more similar – the behavior of the data flow canvas and transformations is closely comparable to that of SSIS's data flow surface and components.

A special *Source transformation* reads data from an external source and emits it as a stream of rows to be transformed by the data flow. Every data flow contains at least one Source transformation.

1. The empty data flow canvas for your new data flow contains an *Add Source* tile with a dashed outline. Click the tile to add a source to your data flow. You must add a source before you can do anything else.

2. Like ADF activities on the pipeline authoring canvas, data flow transformations are configured using a tabbed configuration pane below the data flow canvas. Every transformation has a unique name within the data flow called its *Output stream name* – set this value appropriately on the *Source settings* tab (shown in Figure 7-3). Transformation names may only contain alphanumeric characters – spaces are not permitted – and must begin with a letter.

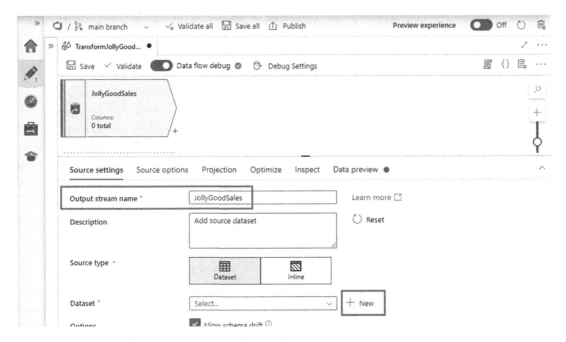

Figure 7-3. *Data flow source transformation's Source settings tab*

3. Ensure that the transformation's *Source type* is set to "Dataset,"
   and then to the right of the *Dataset* dropdown list, click the + *New*
   button (indicated in the figure).

4. The *New dataset* flyout familiar from earlier chapters opens. Select
   the *Azure Blob Storage* data store, click *Continue*, then choose
   the *Excel* file format (Jolly Good sales data is supplied in Excel
   spreadsheet files). Click *Continue*.

5. Name the dataset, then choose your original blob storage linked
   service (a linked service that defines no parameters). Browse
   to locate and select the file "Sales Apr-Sep 2020.xlsx" from the
   "sampledata" container's "JollyGood" folder. Select *Sheet name*
   "SALES" and ensure that *First row as header* is ticked. The
   completed flyout is shown in Figure 7-4 – click *OK* to create the
   dataset.

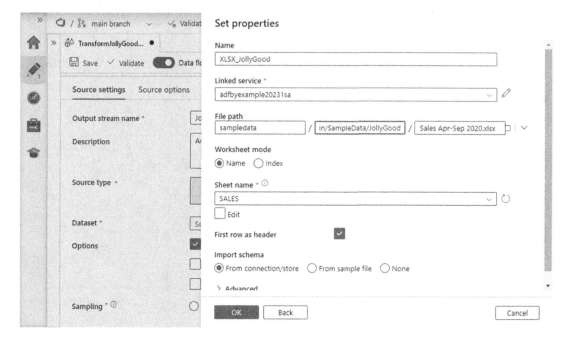

Figure 7-4. *Properties for Jolly Good Excel dataset*

6. Select the Source transformation's *Inspect* tab. This tab, available for every type of transformation, provides details of a transformation's input and/or output schema. (A Source transformation has no input schema.) The schema shown here is the one imported into the new dataset.

7. Select the Source transformation's *Data preview* tab. This tab, also shared for transformations of all types, enables you to preview data emitted by a transformation. Click *Refresh* to load the preview.

Tip   Data preview is only available with debug mode enabled – that is, when a debug cluster is running. If ADF Studio warns you that your debug cluster session is about to time out, previewing a transformation's output is a convenient way to prevent the cluster from shutting down.

---

8. From the preview (shown in Figure 7-5), notice features of Jolly Good sales data that would be difficult to handle using a Copy activity. The value of product sales is reported as a combination of units sold and unit price rather than as a single sales total. Unit price is provided in a mixture of currencies. The file includes a total row for each month that must be excluded. ADF data flows can manage all of these features and more.

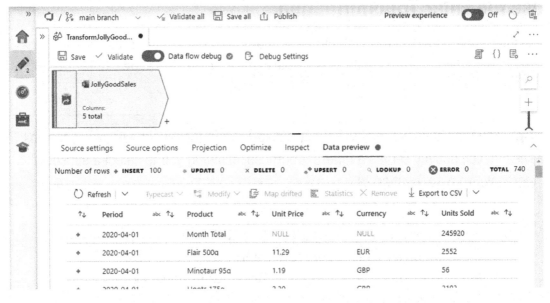

Figure 7-5. *Preview Jolly Good sales data*

9. Select the Source transformation's *Projection* tab. This tab is specific to the Source transformation and displays the five columns present in the Excel file's "SALES" sheet. The column types are all reported as "string" – use each column's *Type* dropdown to refine types. As the data values previewed in Figure 7-5 suggest, the column "Period" is of type "date," "Unit Price" is of type "double," and "Units Sold" is an "integer" column.

10. Click *Save all* in the factory header bar to save your work so far (including the new Excel dataset).

Like other factory resources, data flows are saved to your Git repository as JSON files. The sequence of data flow transformations is stored as *Data Flow Script*, embedded in the data flow JSON file's `properties.typeProperties.scriptLines` attribute. You can use the *Code* button (braces icon) to the top right of the data flow canvas to view data flow JSON and can inspect the formatted Data Flow Script directly using the *Script* button (next to the *Code* button).

Use the Filter Transformation

The Jolly Good sales data format includes monthly total rows interleaved with product-specific sales data – the first of these is visible in the data preview shown in Figure 7-5. Exclude these rows using the data flow *Filter transformation*.

Tip   You may have noticed an activity called *Filter* in the pipeline Activities toolbox. The pipeline activity serves a different purpose, allowing you to select a subset of elements from an input array.

---

1. To add a transformation to the data flow, click the small "+" button at the bottom right of the Source transformation on the data flow canvas. This button appears in the same position for every transformation except the Sink.

2. A pop-up menu of available transformations is displayed, as shown in Figure 7-6. Find and select the Filter transformation (toward the bottom of the list). When the transformation has been added to the data flow canvas, set its *Output stream name* on the *Filter settings* configuration tab.

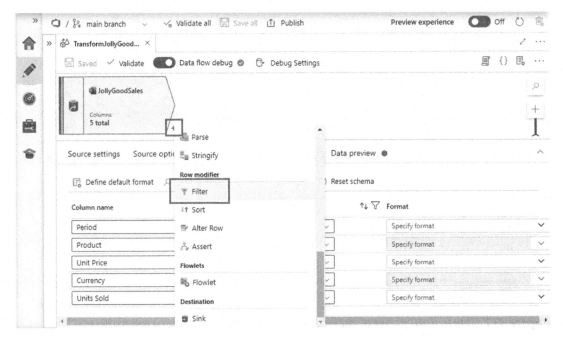

Figure 7-6. *Connect Filter transformation to Source transformation*

3. Also found on the *Filter settings* tab is a *Filter on* text area. This stores a *data flow expression* used to select rows for the transformation's output. Click into the text area to reveal an *Open expression builder* link immediately below. Click the link to open the *Dataflow expression builder*.

4. Figure 7-7 shows the dataflow expression builder for the Filter transformation, including an *Expression* pane above an operator toolbar and a list of *Expression elements*. The list of *Expression values* corresponds to the selected element type. These features – along with the collapsible *Data preview* pane at the bottom of the builder window – are always available in the expression builder.

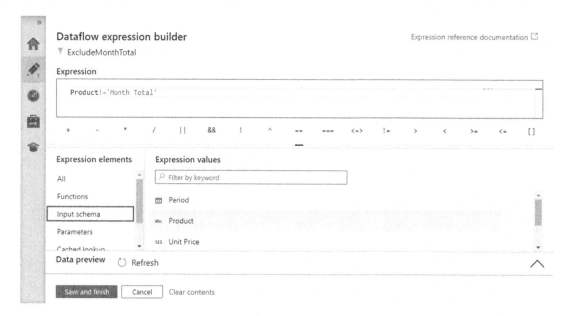

Figure 7-7. *Dataflow expression builder for the Filter transformation*

To build the expression shown in Figure 7-7, select the "Product"
column from the list of expression values in the *Input schema,*
use the operator toolbar to add the *Not equal* (!=) operator, then
add 'Month Total' to the *Expression* pane by hand. Click *Save
and finish.*

Note The data flow expression language is different to that used in ADF pipeline
expressions and is much richer. All text comparisons are case-sensitive unless you
use an explicitly case-insensitive option (like the <=> operator or its equivalent
function equalsIgnoreCase). Unlike pipeline expressions, the data flow
expression language includes a variety of infix operators, shown in the operator
toolbar in Figure 7-7.

---

5. Select the Filter transformation's *Data preview* tab and click *Refresh*
   to load the preview. Notice that the initial Month Total row no
   longer appears.

6. Save your updated data flow.

Use the Lookup Transformation

The *Lookup transformation* enables you to use values in a data stream to look up matching rows from another data stream. (This is different from ADF's Lookup activity, which loads a dataset into a pipeline, allowing you to refer to elements within it.) In this section, you will use the Lookup transformation to obtain exchange rate information for currencies in the Jolly Good sales data file.

Add a Lookup Data Stream

A second data stream containing exchange rate information is required for the Lookup activity.

1. Add another data source to your data flow by clicking the *Add Source* tile displayed below your Jolly Good sales data Source transformation. Name it "ExchangeRates."

2. In addition to ADF datasets, data flow Source transformations support a number of *inline datasets*. The set of formats supported by inline datasets is not the same as that supported by ADF dataset objects, although there is some overlap. Set the transformation's *Source type* to "Inline", then choose an *Inline dataset type* of "Excel".

3. Use the *Linked service* dropdown below the *Inline dataset type* to choose the linked service for your blob storage account.

4. Select the *Source options* tab – it will now contain options specific to blob storage datasets. Use the *Browse* button to the right of the *File path* fields to select the file "ExchangeRates.xlsx" from the "sampledata" container's "SampleData" folder. Select *Sheet name* "Sheet1" and ensure that *First row as header* is ticked.

5. Select the *Projection* tab. It is empty because no schema information has been imported yet – the inline dataset has no preexisting dataset object to refer to. Click *Import schema*. On the displayed *Import schema* flyout, click *Import* to accept the default options and proceed. Four appropriately typed columns appear, as shown in Figure 7-8.

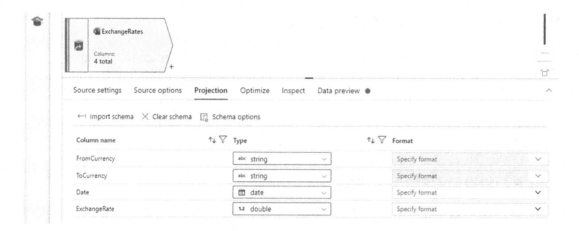

Figure 7-8. *Imported exchange rate schema on the Projection configuration tab*

6. Select the *Data preview* tab and click *Refresh* to inspect the data in the file. The data includes conversion rates between three currencies – USD, GBP, and EUR – in effect on the first day of each month in the period April to September 2020.

7. The Lookup transformation behaves in a similar way to a SQL join. To ensure that the lookup joins to the correct row, filter the exchange rate source to exclude conversions to currencies other than USD. Figure 7-9 shows a Filter transformation configured to achieve this.

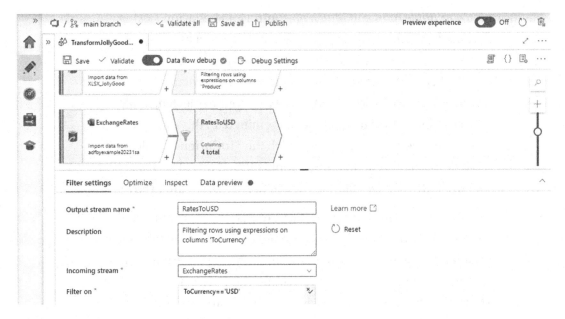

Figure 7-9. *Filter transformation excluding non-USD currency conversions*

Add the Lookup Transformation

The exchange rate stream you have prepared is now ready for use as a rate lookup.

1. Use the "+" button on the Jolly Good data stream's Filter transformation to connect a Lookup transformation. On the *Lookup settings* tab, set the *Output stream name* appropriately.

2. The *Primary stream* field is prepopulated with the name of the upstream transformation where you connected the Lookup. Set the value of *Lookup stream* to the output stream name of the exchange rate Filter transformation – take care to select the correct transformation in the exchange rate stream.

3. *Match multiple rows* and *Match on* control join behavior. Ticking the *Match multiple rows* check box creates an effect like a SQL join, in which every matching pair of records adds a row to the output stream – this may result in an output that contains more rows than either of its inputs. Without this option selected, *Match on* determines which matching pair is emitted. In this example, you require the matching pair in which the "ToCurrency" value is "USD" – this requirement is more sophisticated than *Match on* can support and is why you filtered the exchange rate stream in advance.

4. Specify two *Lookup conditions*. First, match the "Currency" field on the *Left* to the "FromCurrency" field on the *Right* of the lookup. By default, Lookup conditions contain only one criterion – add a second by clicking the "+" button to the right of the first condition. Match the "Period" field on the left to the "Date" field on the right. Both conditions should use the == equality operator for matching. Figure 7-10 shows the correctly configured lookup.

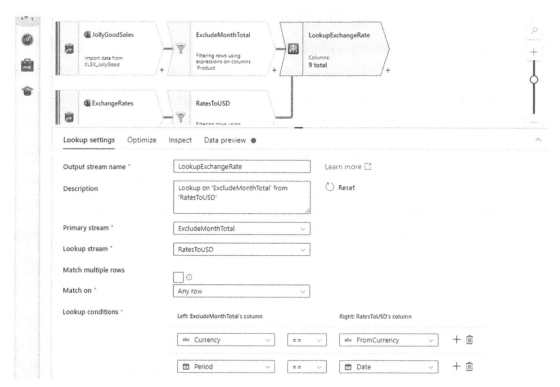

Figure 7-10. *Configured exchange rate Lookup transformation*

5. Select the *Data preview* tab and click *Refresh* to inspect the output of the transformation. Save your changes.

Use the Derived Column Transformation

The *Derived Column transformation* allows you to add new columns to the data flow. In this section, you will use the transformation to add columns necessary for the [dbo]. [Sales_LOAD] table: total sales value (in USD), retailer, and the run sequence number used for pipeline execution logging.

1. Connect a Derived Column transformation to the Lookup transformation on the data flow canvas and name it appropriately.

2. You can either add columns on the *Derived column's settings* tab directly or by using the dataflow expression builder. For now, click *Open expression builder* above the list of derived columns (indicated in Figure 7-11).

3. The dataflow expression builder for the Derived Column transformation contains transformation-specific features (in addition to those you saw for the Filter transformation) including a *Column name* field and a *Derived Columns* sidebar enumerating columns derived in this transformation. Set the column name to "SalesValueUSD."

4. The total USD sales value is the product of the unit price, the number of units sold, and the exchange rate. Use *Input schema* expression elements and the * operator to build this expression. The completed expression appears in Figure 7-11.

5. In the *Derived Columns* sidebar, click the + *Create new* menu button and select *Column* to add another column. Name the new column "Retailer" and give it the literal string value 'Jolly Good Ltd'.

6. Add a third column in the same way, this time called "RunSeqNo" – this column will contain the pipeline run sequence number. Its value will be obtained in the same way as in earlier chapters, using the ADF pipeline's Lookup activity, and will be passed to the data flow as a parameter.

221

7. You can create the "RunSeqNo" parameter right here in the expression builder by selecting *Parameters* from the *Expression elements* list. When you click *+ Create new* under *Expression values*, the *Create new parameter* blade slides over the expression builder. In the top left, name the parameter "RunSeqNo" and set its type to "integer." In the *Default value* pane, provide a value of -1. Click *Create* to create the parameter and close the blade.

8. The dataflow expression builder resumes with the new parameter displayed in the *Expression values* list. Click the parameter name to select it as the derived column expression. Click *Save and finish*.

Figure 7-11 shows the configured Derived Column transformation, including the column expressions constructed in the expression builder. If you wish to edit any one expression, you can click the expression field to reveal an *Open expression builder* link (as shown in the figure for the "Retailer" column), or you can simply edit the expression in situ.

Figure 7-11. *Configured Derived Column transformation*

The "RunSeqNo" parameter you created using the dataflow expression builder is an input parameter for the data flow itself. Click into blank space on the data flow canvas to view configuration options at the data flow level – the new parameter can be seen on the data flow's *Parameters* configuration tab.

Use the Select Transformation

The data flow *Select transformation* enables columns in the data stream to be renamed or removed. You will use it here to align the output schema with that of the sink table.

1. Connect a Select transformation to the Derived Column transformation configured in the previous section.

2. The *Select settings* tab contains a list of column mappings between the transformation's input and output schemas. To the right of each mapping is a trash can *Remove mapping* button. Use it to remove the mappings for "Unit Price," "Currency," "FromCurrency," "ToCurrency," "Date," and "ExchangeRate." This removes those columns from the transformation's output stream.

3. Use the *Name as* field (on the right of each mapping) to rename "Period" to "SalesMonth" and to remove the space character from the middle of "Units Sold."

4. Use the *Data preview* tab to verify the effect of the transformation. The value in the "RunSeqNo" column will be -1, the default value for your "RunSeqNo" parameter. This will be replaced by a real run sequence number at runtime.

Use the Sink Transformation

A *Sink transformation* is used to persist data flow outputs in external data storage. A valid data flow requires at least one Sink transformation – you can save incomplete flows as you work, but you will be unable to run them. In this section, you will add a Sink transformation to write transformed Jolly Good sales data into your [dbo].[Sales_LOAD] database table.

1. Connect a Sink transformation to the Select transformation you added in the previous section.

2. On the *Sink* tab, name the transformation, and ensure that *Sink type* is set to "Dataset." Choose the dataset "ASQL_dboSalesLoad" from the *Dataset* dropdown.

3. On the *Mapping* tab, disable auto-mapping using the *Auto mapping* toggle. This has the effect of displaying the existing set of automatically created mappings.

4. You may find that the [RunSeqNo] and [SourceFileName] output columns are missing – this is because they were absent from the [dbo].[Sales_LOAD] table when the corresponding ADF dataset was created. To remedy this, reimport the dataset's schema by opening the dataset directly – it should be in your "Chapter3" datasets folder – then using the *Import schema* button on its *Schema* configuration tab. Return to the Sink transformation's *Mapping* tab on the data flow canvas and click *Reset* to synchronize the transformation with the updated dataset.

5. Verify that all six input columns are now mapped correctly. The output columns [RowId], [ManufacturerProductCode], and [SourceFileName] have no corresponding inputs and can be left unmapped.

6. Inspect the transformation output using the *Data preview* tab, then save your changes. Data preview in the Sink transformation indicates the data that would be written to the sink at runtime, but no data is actually written.

Execute the Data Flow

With the addition of the final Sink transformation, the data flow is ready for execution. The complete flow is shown in Figure 7-12.

Figure 7-12. *Complete data flow for loading Jolly Good Ltd sales data*

Create a Pipeline to Execute the Data Flow

The data flow will be executed using an ADF pipeline similar to the pipelines you created earlier. In this case, instead of using the Copy activity, the Data flow activity will be used to move data by executing the data flow.

1. In the ADF Studio *Factory Resources* explorer, create a "Chapter7" pipelines folder, then create a new pipeline inside it. Name the new pipeline "LoadJollyGoodSales." You may also wish to move your Excel dataset into a folder named for this chapter.

2. Add a Lookup activity to the pipeline. On its *Settings* configuration tab, select *Source dataset* "ASQL_dboSalesLoad". Set *Use query* to "Stored procedure," then select the "[dbo].[LogPipelineStart]" procedure from the *Stored procedure name* dropdown. Click *Import parameter*, then provide appropriate pipeline expressions for the three stored procedure parameters.

3. Drag a Data flow activity from the Activities toolbox's *Move and transform* group onto the design surface. Connect the new activity as a dependent of the Lookup activity.

4. On the activity's *Settings* tab, select the "TransformJollyGoodSales" data flow from the *Data flow* dropdown. On the *Parameters* tab, you will find the "RunSeqNo" parameter you created for the data flow, with its default value of -1.

5. Data flow parameters can be specified using either the pipeline expression language or the data flow expression language. Click the *Value* field to edit the parameter value, then select *Pipeline expression* from the popup that appears.

6. In the pipeline expression builder, enter a pipeline expression to return the `firstRow.RunSeqNo` property from the Lookup activity's output. Be careful to wrap the expression in the `int` conversion function, to avoid type conflicts when the activity attempts to start the data flow.

7. Execute the pipeline in the usual way by clicking *Debug*. Pipelines containing Data flow activities can be executed in ADF Studio either using a data flow debug session – the default behavior when you click *Debug* – or using a *just-in-time (JIT)* cluster, provisioned automatically when pipeline execution starts. A dropdown to the right of the *Debug* button allows you to choose between these approaches – select "Use activity runtime" to use a new JIT cluster.

A JIT cluster takes a few minutes to be provisioned. Even when using an active debug session, the pipeline will take longer to start than you have been used to – there is a short delay while compute resource is acquired from the debug cluster.

Inspect Execution Output

As the pipeline executes, activity execution information is displayed in its *Output* tab as shown in Figure 7-13.

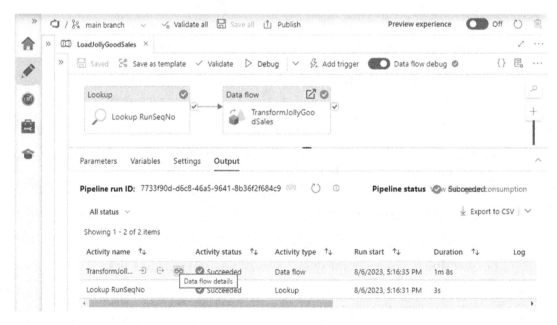

Figure 7-13. *Activity output for the pipeline using the Data flow activity*

The execution record for the Data flow activity, like that of the Copy activity, features an eyeglasses *Data flow details* button, visible in Figure 7-13 to the right of the activity's *Output* button. Click the *Data flow details* icon to open a graphical monitoring view of the data flow.

The graphical monitoring view (shown in Figure 7-14) provides detailed information about data flow performance. The *All streams* tab in the lower part of the screen reports high-level information for every transformation in the data flow. The upper part contains a simplified view of the data flow structure, similar to the layout on the data flow canvas. Clicking a node on the data flow view displays detailed execution information for that transformation in the lower part of the screen.

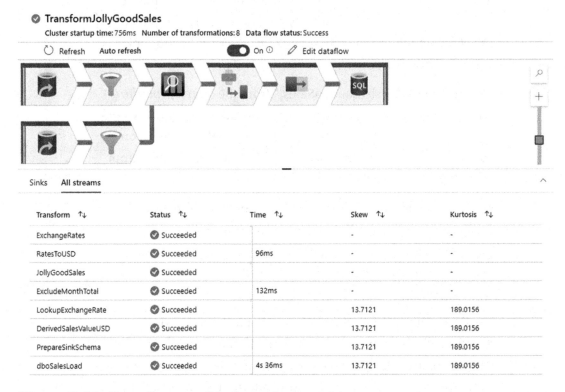

Transform	Status	Time	Skew	Kurtosis
ExchangeRates	Succeeded		-	-
RatesToUSD	Succeeded	96ms	-	-
JollyGoodSales	Succeeded		-	-
ExcludeMonthTotal	Succeeded	132ms	-	-
LookupExchangeRate	Succeeded		13.7121	189.0156
DerivedSalesValueUSD	Succeeded		13.7121	189.0156
PrepareSinkSchema	Succeeded		13.7121	189.0156
dboSalesLoad	Succeeded	4s 36ms	13.7121	189.0156

Figure 7-14. Data flow graphical monitoring view

The detailed view displayed when a node is selected often includes information about how data is partitioned during execution. Every transformation features an *Optimize* configuration tab on the data flow design canvas – you can use this to make changes to how data is partitioned, but in most situations, the default partitioning behavior is recommended.

Persist Loaded Data and Log Completion

To persist the data loaded by the Data flow activity, call the database stored procedure [dbo].[PersistLoadedSales].

1. Add a Stored procedure activity to your pipeline, configured to execute after the Data flow activity has successfully completed. On its *Settings* configuration tab, set its *Linked service* to your linked Azure SQL database.

2. Choose "[dbo].[PersistLoadedSales]" from the *Stored procedure name* dropdown, then beneath *Stored procedure parameters,* click the *Import* button. Provide an appropriate pipeline expression for the stored procedure's "RunSeqNo" parameter (using the output of the pipeline's initial Lookup activity).

3. Add a second Stored procedure activity, following the first. Configure this one to call the stored procedure "[dbo]. [LogPipelineEnd]", importing its parameters in the same way as before. Configure expressions for "RunEndDateTime," "RunSeqNo," and "RunStatus."

4. The Copy data activity's output property paths you used previously for the parameters "FilesRead," "RowsRead," and "RowsCopied" are not valid for the Data flow activity. You can either treat these fields as null or find alternative paths in the Data flow activity's output.

5. Rerun the pipeline, verifying that Jolly Good sales data has now been successfully persisted in database table [dbo].[Sales].

Maintain a Product Dimension

The data stored in table [dbo].[Sales] is not always easy to analyze, because the [Product] column combines two attributes. Each value includes the product's weight, so grouping different formats of the same product is difficult. Calculating the total weight of product sold is hard, because product weights are not stored numerically and are a mixture of ounces and grams.

Allowing individual records to be grouped and aggregated using shared characteristics is a classic application for a dimension table. In this section, you will build a data flow to maintain a product dimension to support analysis of product sales.

Note   By now, you should have accumulated sales data for several retailers in [dbo].[Sales]. If not, use the "ImportSTFormatFiles" pipeline you developed in Chapter 6 to reload data for Desserts4All and Naughty but Nice sales.

Create a Dimension Table

Listing 7-1 provides SQL code to create a dimension table called [dbo].[Product]. It has no integer key but would be suitable for use in a tabular model (supported by Power BI, Azure Analysis Services, or SQL Server Analysis Services) or for use in SQL-based analysis.

Use your SQL client to run the script and create the table in your Azure SQL Database.

Listing 7-1. Create a [dbo].[Product] table

```
CREATE TABLE dbo.Product (
  Product NVARCHAR(255) PRIMARY KEY
, ProductName NVARCHAR(255) NOT NULL
, WeightInOunces DECIMAL(19,2) NOT NULL
, WeightInGrams DECIMAL(19,2) NOT NULL
);
```

Create Supporting Datasets

If you created a parameterized Azure SQL Database dataset as suggested in Chapter 6, you can use it here in the data flow. Alternatively, create ADF datasets for each of the two tables you'll be using in this section:

1. Create a dataset to represent the existing [dbo].[Sales] table.

2. Create a second dataset to represent the new [dbo].[Product] table.

Build the Product Maintenance Data Flow

In this section, you will use a data flow to read product details out of the [dbo].[Sales] table, extract product names and weights, and then append that information to [dbo].[Product].

1. Create a new data flow in your "Chapter7" data flows folder and name it "UpdateProduct."

2. Add a Source transformation using the dataset for the [dbo].[Sales] table.

Tip   When using parameterized datasets, runtime parameter values are supplied by the executing pipeline's Data flow activity. At development time, specify values in the *Debug Settings* flyout (Figure 7-15), accessed using the button above the data flow. The button is only visible when the debug cluster is running.

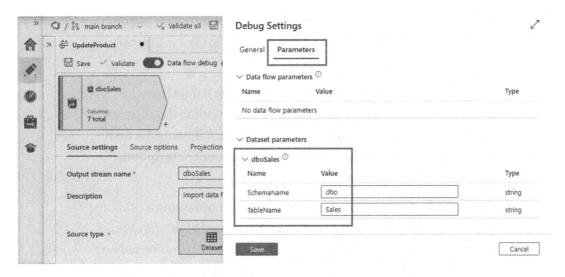

Figure 7-15. *Use Debug Settings to set development dataset parameter values*

3. If you are using a parameterized dataset, import the table schema using the *Import projection* button on the Source transformation's *Projection* tab.

4. Connect a Derived Column transformation to the output of the Source transformation, then open the dataflow expression builder.

Use Locals

In the last section, you saw how to add new columns to a data flow using the Derived Column transformation. Sometimes, it is convenient to be able to store intermediate data flow expressions for reuse in derived column definitions, without adding their results to the data flow stream. You can achieve this using *Locals*.

The value derived by a local expression can be used by other expressions within the same Derived Column transformation, but it is not included in the transformation's output. The product descriptions stored in [dbo].[Sales] contain a product name and weight, for example, "Chocolatey Nougat 3.52oz". Removing the weight string "3.52oz" from the product description yields the product name, and the same string can be reused as a simpler source of numeric weights.

1. In the *Expression elements* list of the dataflow expression builder, select the *Locals* item. Under *Expression values*, click + *Create new* to open the *Create new local* blade.

2. Name the new local "WeightString," and create a data flow expression to return only that portion of the product description. The weight string is the part of the description following the final space character – bear in mind that some product descriptions contain multiple spaces.

3. Figure 7-16 shows the *Create new local* blade containing a suitable expression. The expression uses three functions: `right`, `locate`, and `reverse`. If you hover over a function in the *Expression values* list (as shown in the figure), or over its name in the *Expression* pane, a tooltip describing the function is displayed. Click *Create* to save the new local.

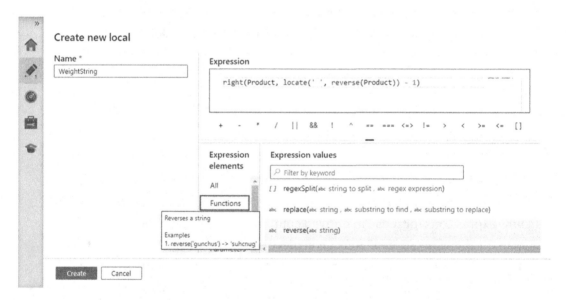

Figure 7-16. *Creating a local expression in the Derived Column transformation*

4. The new local appears in the list of *Expression values* when you select the *Locals* expression element – as shown in Figure 717 – and can be selected for use in a data flow expression just like any other expression value. Create another local, this one called

"WeightUnit," using the expression `iif(endsWith(Product, 'oz'), 'oz', 'g')`. The expression returns the unit of weight being used in the product description.

5. You're now ready to define the new column. Back in the dataflow expression builder for derived columns, name the new column "ProductName." Use the "WeightString" local in a data flow expression that returns only the name of the product. Figure 7-17 provides one such expression – the `:WeightString` element is a reference to the local.

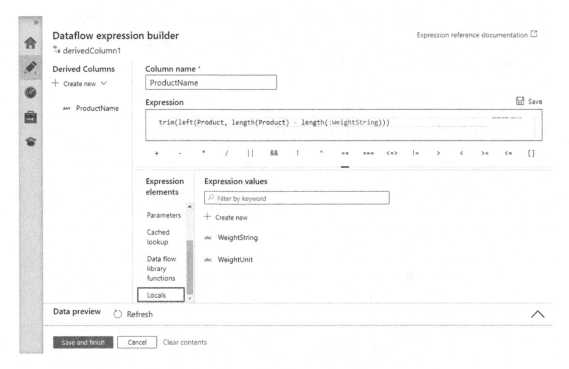

***Figure 7-17.** Using locals in a derived column data flow expression*

6. Add a second derived column called "WeightInOunces" – this should extract the numeric portion of the weight string and convert it from grams if necessary. A possible expression to achieve this is `toFloat(replace(:WeightString, :WeightUnit, ''))` / `iif(:WeightUnit=='g', 28.3495, 1.0)`.

7. Add a third derived column called "WeightInGrams." Create a data flow expression to perform a similar function to "WeightInOunces," this one converting each product's given weight to grams.

8. Click Save *and finish* to close the dataflow expression builder, then use the Derived Column transformation's *Data preview* tab to inspect the new columns – verify that your derived columns appear as expected, and notice that your local expressions do not.

Note   The numbers resulting from product weight conversions will not round tidily to a few decimal places. This is because the input values used in product descriptions have already been rounded off.

Use the Aggregate Transformation

The Derived Column transformation's output stream contains one row for each time a product appears in the [dbo].[Sales] table. To make the "Product" field unique – as required by the primary key of [dbo].[Product] – you must remove duplicates. Do this using the *Aggregate transformation*.

1. Connect an Aggregate transformation to the output of the Derived Column transformation and name it appropriately.

2. On the *Aggregate settings* tab, ensure that the toggle below *Incoming stream* is set to *Group by*, then choose "Product" from the dropdown under *Columns*.

3. Switch the toggle to *Aggregates*. Under *Column*, select "ProductName" from the dropdown. The aggregate function required in the *Expression* is `first` – you can open the dataflow expression builder to construct this or simply enter `first(ProductName)` directly.

4. In many places, the data flow canvas supports the specification of multiple columns using a *Column pattern*. Click the *+ Add* button above the Aggregates column list and select *Add column pattern*.

5. A column pattern uses a data flow expression to identify a set of columns. In *Each column that matches*, enter the expression startsWith(name, 'Weight'). You can do this directly or using the dataflow expression builder. The expression identifies the two columns whose names begin with "Weight."

6. Below the column pattern expression are fields for the aggregate column name and expression. When using a column pattern, the string $$ is a placeholder for each of the matched columns – set the column name to $$ and the expression to first($$) as shown in Figure 7-18.

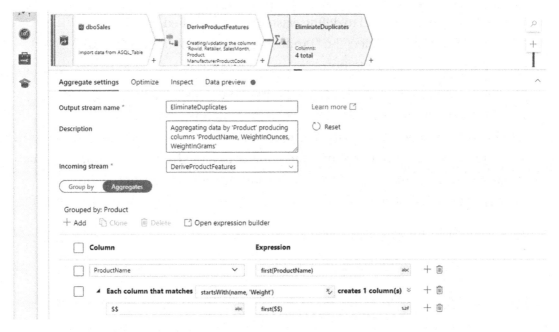

Figure 7-18. *Using a column pattern to specify multiple aggregate columns*

7. Use the *Data preview* tab to check the results of the transformation.

Use the Exists Transformation

At this moment, the [dbo].[Product] table is empty, but repeated runs of the "UpdateProduct" data flow must add new rows only – attempting to re-add existing rows will cause a primary key violation in the database table, and the data flow will fail.

The *Exists transformation* enables you to filter values in a data stream based on whether they exist – or not – in another data stream. This data flow should attempt to sink rows to the [dbo].[Product] table only if they are not already present.

1. Add a second Source transformation to the data flow, using a dataset for the [dbo].[Product] table. If you are using a parameterized dataset, remember to import the table's schema on the transformation's *Projection* tab.

2. Connect an Exists transformation to the Aggregate transformation. Set its *Right stream* to the new [dbo].[Product] Source transformation and its *Exist type* to "Doesn't exist."

3. The expressions used to define existence are specified under *Exists conditions*. Select the "Product" column on both the left and right sides on the condition.

Use the *Data preview* tab to check the results of the transformation if you wish. As the table [dbo].[Product] is currently empty, the results will look the same as those returned by the Aggregate transformation preview.

Output the transformed data with a Sink transformation that uses the [dbo].[Product] table dataset, checking that the output column auto-mapping is correct. Figure 7-19 shows the completed data flow.

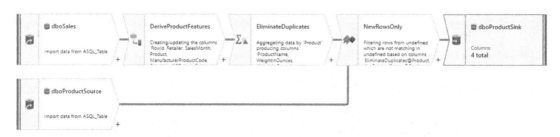

***Figure 7-19.** [dbo].[Product] maintenance data flow*

Tip   If you experience problems mapping sink columns when using a parameterized dataset, an alternative option is to configure an inline Azure SQL Database dataset in the Sink transformation.

Execute the Dimension Data Flow

The dimension maintenance data flow is now ready for execution.

1. Create a new pipeline named "UpdateProductDimension" in your "Chapter7" pipelines folder.

2. Add a Data flow activity to the design surface, selecting the new "UpdateProduct" data flow. If you are using a parameterized dataset, the activity's *Settings* configuration tab will be populated with input fields for parameter values – populate fields with the correct values to be used when the pipeline runs.

3. Run the pipeline. When execution is complete, verify that the [dbo].[Product] table has been correctly populated.

4. The data flow's Exists transformation ensures that the Sink transformation only adds new records to [dbo].[Product]. Run the pipeline again and verify that this is the case.

5. As a final test, delete some (but not all) records from [dbo].[Product]. Run the pipeline again to demonstrate that the removed records are restored.

The [dbo].[Product] table populated here is a simple dimension-style table intended to support more flexible, ad hoc analysis of data in table [dbo].[Sales]. For example, the query in Listing 7-2 returns the number, total value, and total kilogram weight of each product sold between April and September 2020 – this calculation is possible because you have used the data flow to convert the unstructured product description into structured product attributes.

Listing 7-2. Sales analysis using [dbo].[Product]

```
SELECT
  p.ProductName
, SUM(s.UnitsSold) AS UnitsSold
, SUM(s.SalesValueUSD) AS SalesValueUSD
, SUM(p.WeightInGrams * s.UnitsSold)/1000 AS KgSold
```

```
FROM dbo.Sales s
  INNER JOIN dbo.Product p ON p.Product = s.Product
GROUP BY p.ProductName
ORDER BY p.ProductName;
```

Tip   The data flow you have created here implements a basic Slowly Changing Dimension (SCD) maintenance pattern, in this case, for a type 0 SCD. ADF Studio *templates* provide reusable pipeline and data flow patterns and are available in ADF's *Template gallery.* To choose a template when creating a new pipeline, select the *Pipeline from template* option on the pipeline actions pop-up menu in the Factory Resources explorer.

Reuse Data Flow Logic

Earlier in this chapter you used a local expression, "WeightString", in a Derived Column transformation. This enabled you to use the expression in two additional columns, without repeating the same data flow expression logic. Locals permit you to define expressions for reuse within the same transformation, but when developing ADF data flows, you may find yourself repeating similar patterns in different transformations, or even in different data flows.

Azure Data Factory provides two different means of reusing data flow logic across transformations and data flows: *user-defined functions* and *flowlets*. This section explores these two features.

Create a User-Defined Function

A user-defined function (UDF) is a reusable data flow expression. A UDF may require user inputs in the form of *arguments* and like any data flow expression returns a single value. UDF definitions are stored in a *data flow library* – the first step to creating a UDF in your factory is to create a library to contain it.

Create a Data Flow Library and Function

Data flow libraries are maintained in ADF Studio's management hub.

1. Navigate to the management hub. Under *Author* in the hub sidebar, select *Data flow libraries*.

2. Click the *+ New* button at the top of the *Data flow libraries* page. The *New data flow library* flyout appears – give the new library a name.

3. A data flow library must contain at least one UDF. In the *Functions* section of the flyout, click *+ New* to create a new function. The *New data flow function* flyout appears.

4. Name the new function "ProductWeightInGrams" and use the *+ Add* button to create a new argument of type "string". Notice that no argument name is required – function arguments are referred to by position.

5. Click into the *Body* field and open the dataflow expression builder. When creating expressions in a data flow transformation, the *Expression elements* list offers columns from the transformation's *Input schema* for selection. The inputs to a user-defined function's inputs are its arguments – select the *Arguments* element to see that the argument you created in step 4 is available in the associated list of *Expression values*.

6. Unlike locals, user-defined functions may not refer to other UDFs. Create an expression to extract the weight in grams from a full product description, by combining expressions from earlier in the chapter, but using the "i1" argument in place of the "Product" column. Click *Save and finish*.

7. Figure 7-20 shows the completed *New data flow function* flyout. Click Save to return to the *New data flow library* flyout, then *Save* again to create the new data flow library and save it to the factory's Git repository.

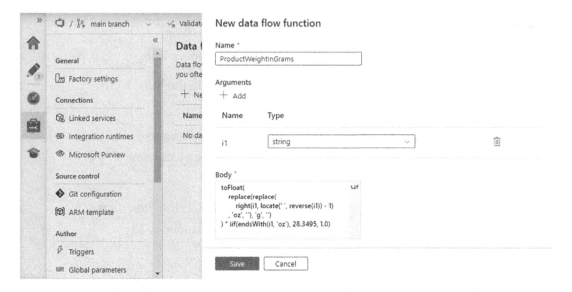

Figure 7-20. *Creating a new data flow function*

Use the Data Flow Function

User-defined functions can be used in data flow expressions in the same way as other
built-in functions you have already encountered. Test your function by modifying the
UpdateProduct data flow.

1. Return to the ADF Studio authoring canvas and open your
   "UpdateProduct" data flow. You may wish to create a backup by
   cloning the data flow and modifying the clone.

2. Select the Derived Column transformation where you previously
   defined the "WeightInGrams" column, then launch the dataflow
   expression builder.

3. Create a new derived column named "WeightInGrams2". Select
   the *Data flow library* functions expression element, then choose
   your "ProductWeightInGrams" function from the list of expression
   values. Your function takes a single argument – the full "Product"
   column (available in the *Input schema* expressions element).

4. Figure 7-21 shows the prepared expression in the dataflow
   expression builder. Click *Save and finish* to close the expression
   builder.

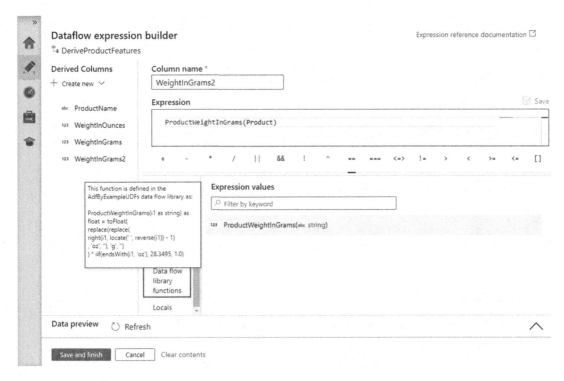

Figure 7-21. *Data flow expression using the ProductWeightInGrams UDF*

5. Use the Derived Column transformation's *Data preview* tab to inspect the results, verifying that the value in the new column matches the value in the original "WeightInGrams" column.

6. Once you are satisfied that your "ProductWeightInGrams" function operates correctly, remove the "WeightInGrams2" column and redefine "WeightInGrams" to use the UDF.

Inspect the Data Flow Library

Data flows – and data flow libraries – are stored in your factory's Git repository in the same way as other factory resources. Figure 7-22 shows the "data-factory-resources" folder in my AdfByExample repository that now contains an additional "dataflow" folder.

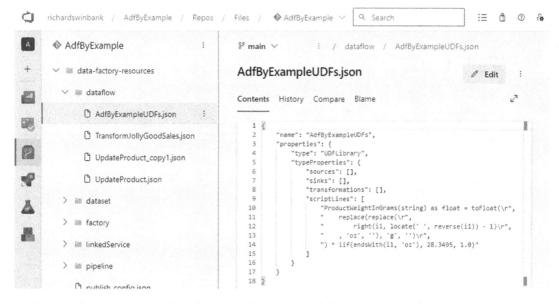

Figure 7-22. *Data flows and data flow library file structure in Git*

The folder contains four files: the two data flows created earlier in the chapter, a clone of the "UpdateProduct" data flow, and my AdfByExampleUDFs data flow library. The JSON file representing the library is shown on the right of Figure 7-22.

Note   Because data flow libraries are stored in the same folder as data flow definitions, you cannot create a data flow with the same name as a data flow library.

Create a Data Flow Flowlet

A data flow flowlet is a sequence of data flow transformations that cannot be run directly but that provides reusable sections of data flow – flowlets are composed into executable data flows using the *Flowlet transformation*. Unlike data flows, a flowlet contains no Sink transformation but contains at least one *Output transformation* – only available for use in flowlets – which emits rows for consumption by the containing data flow.

Flowlets may acquire data in two different ways: either by receiving it from the containing flow via a special *Input transformation* or by reading it from a source (in the same way as a data flow). In the following section, you will build a flowlet that reads data from a source.

Build a Flowlet

Earlier in the chapter you filtered data from a file of exchange rates to return only US dollar conversion rates. If this conversion were a regular requirement, a flowlet that provides a pre-filtered list of exchange rates might be a useful tool to have in your factory.

1. Return to ADF Studio's authoring canvas, then on the "Chapter7" folder's *Actions* menu for data flows, click *New flowlet*. Name the new flowlet "GetUSDExchangeRates". Flowlets are defined using the familiar data flow canvas, but notice that the *Add Source* tile visible when creating a data flow has been replaced by *Add Input*.

2. Click the down arrow at the right-hand edge of the tile – the pop-up menu gives you the option of adding a source or an input. Adding an input allows you to define a schema for rows to be provided by the containing data flow. For this example, click *Add Source*.

3. Configure an inline Excel source to retrieve exchange rate data, using the same settings you provided when reading the file earlier in the chapter.

4. Import its schema on the *Projection* tab – if the Import schema button is grayed out, check that your debug cluster is still running. Notice that there is no *Data preview* tab – data can only be previewed in a flowlet's Output transformation.

5. Append a Filter transformation to include only rows whose "ToCurrency" is "USD", then follow it with an Output transformation. The complete flowlet is shown in Figure 7-23.

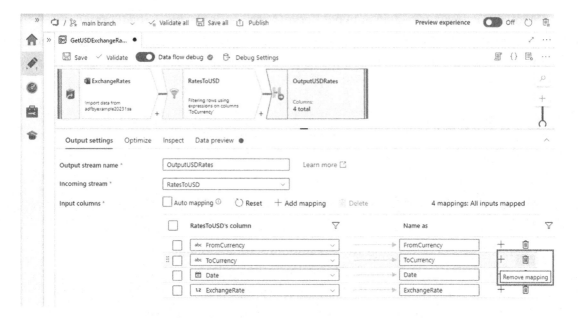

Figure 7-23. *GetUSDExchangeRates flowlet*

6. Use the Output transformation's *Data preview* tab to inspect the
    flowlet's output. The "ToCurrency" field is no longer necessary
    (because its value is always the same). Untick the *Auto mapping*
    check box on the Output settings tab to reveal field mappings, then
    delete the "ToCurrency" mapping (indicated in the figure). Save your
    changes.

Use the Flowlet

To use a data flow flowlet, you must embed it in a data flow using the Flowlet
transformation. You can use multiple Flowlet transformations to compose a data flow
from more than one flowlet, or to use the same flowlet more than once. You can replace
part of the "TransformJollyGoodSales" data flow you developed earlier in the chapter
with your new, reusable flowlet.

1. Open your "TransformJollyGoodSales" data flow. You may prefer
    to clone the data flow and to modify the clone.

2. Use the down arrow at the right-hand edge of the *Add Source* tile to choose *Add Flowlet* – a Flowlet source transformation is added to the canvas. On the *Flowlet settings* tab, use the *Flowlet* dropdown menu to choose the "GetUSDExchangeRates" flowlet.

3. The data flow's sales data stream uses a Lookup transformation to acquire exchange rates. Use the transformation's *Lookup settings* tab to replace the *Lookup stream* with your new flowlet source. Notice that the name of the lookup stream includes the name of the flowlet's output transformation – this is necessary because a flowlet may define more than one output.

4. Remove the original – now disconnected – exchange rate conversion transformations from the data flow. The amended data flow and Lookup transformation configuration appears in Figure 7-24. Save your changes and run the data flow.

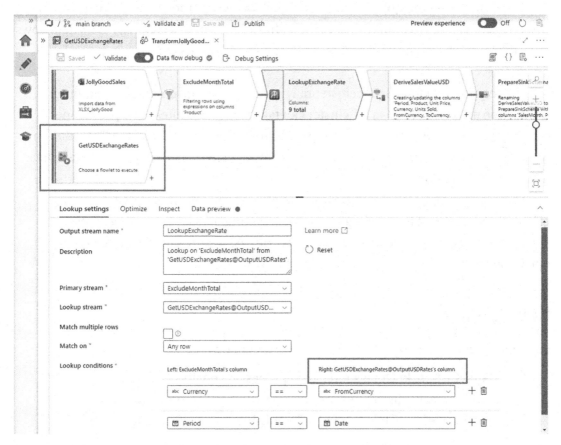

Figure 7-24. *Embed a flowlet in a data flow using a Flowlet transformation*

The flowlet you have implemented here is not complex, but it illustrates the principle of abstracting reusable sections of data flow into flowlets, allowing them to be reused and composed into multiple data flows. This example showed the use of a flowlet to simplify a data source – alternatively, the flowlet-specific Input transformation allows you to specify input stream columns that must be provided by upstream activities in the containing data flow.

At the time of writing, Input transformations do not support "passthrough" behavior – every input and output column must be specified explicitly. A reusable exchange rate *conversion* flowlet – for example – would be a more powerful tool than the simplified lookup presented here but in the absence of passthrough columns is not straightforward to achieve.

Chapter Review

Chapters 3 to 6 used the Copy activity to move data between source and sink datasets without much ability to modify data in flight. Introduced in this chapter, ADF's data flows close that gap, presenting powerful Spark capabilities in an easy-to-use graphical user interface.

The requirement for a Spark cluster may seem onerous given the time required to start one up on demand – a JIT cluster can take several minutes to be provisioned, extending the execution time of ADF pipelines that make use of Data flow activities. In the published environment, Spark clusters are always created just in time, when a Data flow activity execution begins.

The payoff is that ADF data flows can transform even extremely large datasets efficiently, saving time and scaling well by distributing dataset processing across cluster nodes. Furthermore, automatic cluster provision and teardown reduces cluster operating costs by allowing you to pay only for what you use.

Key Concepts

Concepts encountered in this chapter include the following:

- **Apache Spark:** Open source data processing engine that automatically distributes processing workloads across a cluster of servers (referred to as *nodes*) to enable highly parallelized execution.

- **Data flows:** ADF's visual data transformation tool, built on Spark.

- **Data flow debug:** Data flow debug mode provisions a Spark cluster on which you can execute data flows in ADF Studio.

- **Time to live (TTL):** The data flow debug cluster has a default TTL of one hour, after which – if it is not being used – it automatically shuts down.

- **Data flow activity:** ADF pipeline activity used to execute a data flow.

- **Parameters:** Data flow parameters are specified in Debug Settings during development and substituted for values supplied by the calling Data flow activity at runtime.

- **Data flow canvas:** Visual development environment for data flows.

- **Transformation:** A data flow is made up of a sequence of connected transformations, each of which modifies a data stream in some way.

- **Output stream name:** Name that uniquely identifies each transformation in a data flow.

- **Inspect tab:** Use a transformation's Inspect tab to view input and output schema information.

- **Data preview tab:** Use a transformation's Data preview tab to preview data emitted by the transformation. Using data preview requires data flow debug to be enabled and can be used to delay an approaching cluster timeout.

- **Optimize tab:** Use a transformation's Optimize tab to influence data partitioning in Spark when the transformation is executed.

- **Source transformation:** Reads input data from external storage. Every data flow starts with one or more Source transformations.

- **Sink transformation:** Writes transformed data to storage. Every data flow ends with one or more Sink transformations.

- **Data flow expression language:** Data flow expressions have their own language and expression builder, different from those of ADF pipeline expressions.

- **Data Flow Script:** Language in which data flow transformations are stored, embedded in a data flow's JSON file.

- **Column patterns:** Where supported, use column patterns to specify multiple columns that are to be handled in the same way. Columns are specified using data flow expressions to match column metadata.

- **Filter transformation:** Selects rows from its input data stream to be included in its output stream, on the basis of criteria specified as a data flow expression. Other rows are discarded.

- **Lookup transformation:** Conceptually similar to a SQL join between two data streams. Supports a variety of join styles and criteria.

- **Derived column transformation:** Uses data flow expressions to derive new columns for inclusion in a data flow.

- **Locals:** Named intermediate derivations in a Derived Column transformation. Used to simplify expressions and eliminate redundancy.

- **Select transformation:** Used to rename columns in a data flow or to remove them.

- **Aggregate transformation:** Aggregates one or more columns in a data flow, optionally grouping by other specified columns.

- **Exists transformation:** Selects rows from its input data stream to be included in its output stream, on the basis of the existence (or not) of matching rows in a second data stream. Other rows are discarded.

- **Templates:** Reusable implementations of common pipeline and data flow patterns.

- **Template gallery:** Source of provided templates, accessed using the pipeline actions popup menu in the Factory Resources explorer or on the *Data Factory overview* page.

- **User-defined function (UDF):** Reusable data flow expression defined outside any specific data flow.

- **Data flow library:** Factory container for user-defined functions.

- **Flowlet:** Composable, reusable sequence of data flow transformations.

- **Flowlet transformation:** Data flow transformation used to embed a flowlet in a data flow.

- **Input transformation:** Data enters a flowlet either when the flowlet reads from source (using a Source transformation) or when streamed in from the containing data flow. When streamed in, an Input transformation is used to define the schema of incoming rows. A flowlet that contains no Input transformations acts as a Source transformation in a data flow.

- **Output transformation:** A flowlet's Output transformation(s) defines the flowlet's output schema. Flowlet outputs are consumed by the containing data flow.

For SSIS Developers

Azure Data Factory data flows are similar to the implementation of an SSIS Data Flow Task on the data flow surface. ADF's Data flow activity performs the same function as a Data Flow Task – representing the data flow on the pipeline's control surface – but unlike in SSIS, the data flow implementation is a separate factory resource that can be referenced independently and reused.

Familiar notions from the SSIS data flow surface are found within a data flow. SSIS's wide variety of source and destination components is unnecessary, partly because connection details are already abstracted away using ADF datasets and linked services and partly because the single Source and Sink transformations encapsulate the detail of multiple external systems.

Most of the ADF data flow transformations encountered in this chapter have an equivalent component in SSIS, although detailed behavior may differ:

- SSIS's Conditional Split component has a direct ADF equivalent, also called Conditional Split. The *Filter* transformation's behavior is a simplified version of the Conditional Split in which rows are either retained or discarded.

- The *Lookup* ADF transformation and SSIS components provide similar functionality, although the more sophisticated join behavior of the ADF transformation makes it closer to a Merge Join component. (The Lookup transformation's functionality overlaps that of ADF's own Join transformation.)

- Both ADF and SSIS feature a *Derived Column* transformation/component, although SSIS lacks the additional flexibility of Locals.

- ADF's *Select* transformation to rename or remove columns has no equivalent in SSIS.

- Both ADF and SSIS feature an *Aggregate* transformation/component, although in general SSIS lacks the flexibility of column pattern support used in the preceding example.

- Integration Services provide no direct *Exists* transformation – existence testing in SSIS must be performed using the Lookup component and the Lookup Match/No Match outputs.

CHAPTER 8

Integration Runtimes

ADF linked services represent connections to storage or compute resource – decoupled from one another in the way described in Chapter 2 – that are *external* to Azure Data Factory. The linked services you have been using in previous chapters represent connections to external storage, and access to external compute (such as Azure Databricks or a Synapse Analytics Spark pool) is managed in the same way.

This chapter is concerned with *internal* resource – specifically compute, as ADF has no storage resource of its own. *Internal pipeline activities* such as the Copy, Lookup, Get Metadata, and Data flow activities are not executed using external compute but are executed instead using a managed compute resource, internal to ADF, called an *integration runtime* (IR).

In contrast, an *external pipeline activity* uses external compute resource (represented in ADF as a linked service) to do its work, although activity execution is still managed in ADF by an integration runtime. For example, an ADF IR *dispatches* the Stored procedure activity, but actual T-SQL execution takes place in an external database service. The detail of most external activities is outside the scope of this book, because their function is to execute processes implemented in technologies other than ADF.

Inspect the AutoResolveIntegrationRuntime

An *Azure Integration Runtime* is used to perform Copy and Data flow activities in ADF and to manage the execution of a variety of other activities. Every data factory is equipped at creation with a default Azure Integration Runtime, named *AutoResolveIntegrationRuntime* – this is the integration runtime you have been using to execute pipeline activities in earlier chapters.

Integration runtimes are defined and managed in ADF Studio's management hub. Use the management hub to locate and inspect the definition of the AutoResolveIntegrationRuntime.

© Richard Swinbank 2024
R. Swinbank, *Azure Data Factory by Example*, https://doi.org/10.1007/979-8-8688-0218-8_8

1. In ADF Studio, open the management hub and select *Integration runtimes* from the *Connections* section of the hub sidebar. The factory's integration runtimes are displayed – at this stage, only one is defined, the default AutoResolveIntegrationRuntime (shown in Figure 8-1).

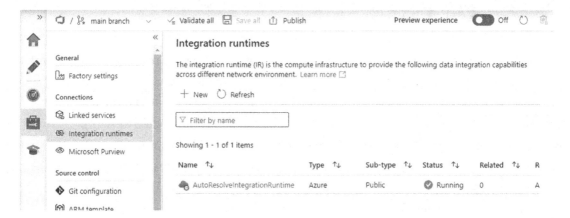

Figure 8-1. *Integration runtimes visible in the management hub*

2. Click the name of the runtime to open the *Integration runtime* flyout. You cannot edit any of the default runtime's settings, but notice particularly that the runtime's *Region* is set to "Auto Resolve."

3. Click *Close* to close the flyout.

While in the management hub, review the definitions of your blob storage and Azure SQL Database linked services. You will notice that in each case the linked service's *Connect via integration runtime* option is set to "AutoResolveIntegrationRuntime" – both linked services are using the default Azure IR.

Use Custom Azure Integration Runtimes

In some situations, you may prefer to customize your own Azure IR, instead of using the AutoResolveIntegrationRuntime. Reasons for doing this include the following:

-   You need to guarantee that data movement takes place within a given geographical region.

- You do not wish to connect to data stores over the public Internet.

- You want to control the properties of a just-in-time Spark cluster used to execute data flows.

This section explores each of these use cases in turn.

Control the Geography of Data Movement

The AutoResolveIntegrationRuntime takes its name from the "Auto Resolve" region specified in its definition. In the case of the Copy activity, "Auto Resolve" means that Azure Data Factory will attempt to use an IR located in the same region as the activity's sink data store, but this is not guaranteed. Under some circumstances, it might be possible for data to be copied by an IR in a region different from both source and sink data stores.

For certain data processing applications, you may have a legal obligation to ensure that data does not leave a given jurisdiction. In this situation, you need to be able to guarantee the location of the Copy activity's integration runtime as well as the location(s) of the source and sink data stores. Using an integration runtime in a specified region enables you to achieve this.

Identify the Integration Runtime's Auto-Resolved Region

Before configuring a new region-specific IR, run one of your existing pipelines to obtain a point of reference.

1. In ADF Studio, open the pipeline you created using the Copy Data tool in Chapter 2. Run the pipeline.

2. When complete, inspect the Copy activity's execution in the pipeline configuration's *Output* tab. The *Integration runtime* column identifies the IR used by the activity.

As Figure 8-2 illustrates, the IR used is "AutoResolveIntegrationRuntime." The runtime's region is selected automatically by the IR – in the case of Figure 8-2, it is UK South.

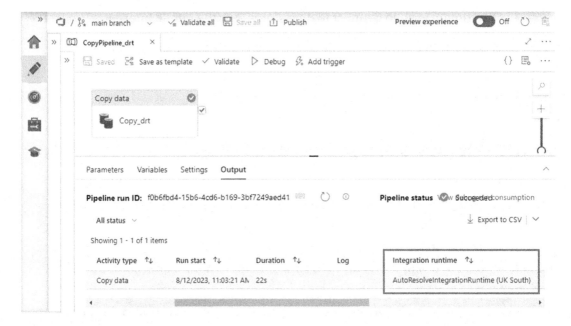

Figure 8-2. *Region selected for Copy activity execution by the AutoResolveIntegrationRuntime*

Create a Region-Specific Azure IR

Create a new Azure Integration Runtime as follows:

1. On the management hub's *Integration runtimes* page, click the + *New* button.

2. The *Integration runtime setup* flyout appears. Select the *Azure, Self-Hosted* tile and click *Continue*.

3. Under *Network environment*, select the *Azure* tile and click *Continue*.

4. You will create the integration runtime in a region geographically distant from that of your data factory and other Azure resources. On the flyout's *Settings* tab, specify a *Name* for the IR that reflects this.

5. Use the *Region* dropdown (also located on the *Settings* tab) to select a region different from your data factory instance. For the purposes of this exercise, choose a region far away from that of your data factory instance.

6. The correctly completed tab is shown in Figure 8-3 – my data factory is in the "UK South" Azure region, so I am creating an IR in "Australia Southeast." You will return to the flyout's other tabs later in the chapter – for now, click *Create* to create the IR.

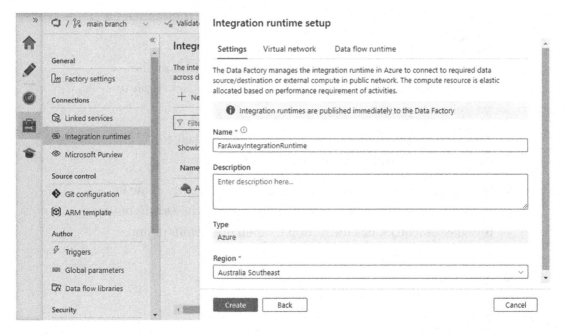

Figure 8-3. *Creating a new Azure Integration Runtime*

Configure the Copy Activity's Integration Runtime

With the exception of the Data flow activity (which specifies its IR directly), the IR used to execute an internal pipeline activity is the one specified in the activity's linked service storage connection. In the case of the Copy activity – which often uses two different linked services for source and sink – ADF uses the IR associated with the activity's sink linked service.

To use the new integration runtime in an existing pipeline, update the linked service used by the Copy activity's sink data store. You can do this directly from the activity definition on the design surface.

1. Return to the pipeline you created using the Copy Data tool in Chapter 2. Select the Copy activity on the design surface, then select its *Sink* tab. To the right of the *Sink dataset* dropdown, click the *Open* button.

2. The activity's destination dataset opens in a new authoring canvas tab. Click the *Edit* button to the right of the *Linked service* dropdown.

3. On the *Edit linked service* flyout, select your new IR from the *Connect via integration runtime* dropdown, then click *Apply* to save your changes.

4. Return to the pipeline and run it again. You are likely to experience a considerably longer runtime.

5. While the pipeline is executing, hover over the activity name in the pipeline configuration's *Output* tab to reveal the *Details* button (eyeglasses icon). Click the button to open the *Details* popup.

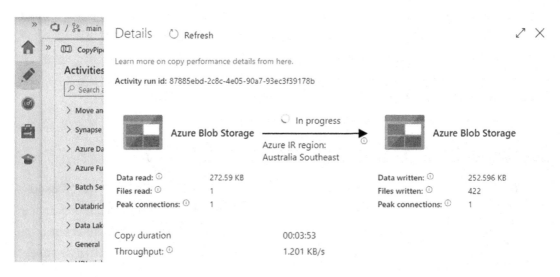

Figure 8-4. *Data copy executed by an IR distant from storage exhibits low throughput*

Figure 8-4 shows the *Details* popup for the in-progress Copy activity. The activity copies data from one container to another, in the same blob storage account. In this example, the blob storage account is in the UK South Azure region, but the copy is being performed by compute in Australia Southeast – loosely speaking, a computer in Southeast Australia is reading data from a UK blob storage location and then writing it back to a different UK blob storage location. The result is that the data throughput is very low – when I ran the pipeline using the distant IR, it took over 7 minutes to complete, compared to only 22 seconds when using the AutoResolveIntegrationRuntime.

By creating a new IR in a different region and using it in a linked service, you have relocated the Copy activity's processing away from a data center in your data factory's region and into another data center of your choice, somewhere else in the world. This has an impact on activity execution times and incurs additional processing costs in the form of a bandwidth charge (sometimes called an egress charge). In contrast, using a custom Azure IR located explicitly in the same region as your source and sink data stores guarantees that data does not leave that region during processing.

Create Secure Network Connections to Data Stores

Many Azure services offer *public endpoints* – network interfaces that can be accessed over the public Internet. The logical SQL Server you created in Chapter 3 provides a public endpoint – albeit protected by a server-level firewall – used by you to make SQL client connections and by ADF when reading and writing to database objects. The storage account you created in Chapter 2 also permits public network access, in this case without even the protection of a firewall.

Permitting access to Azure services via public endpoints is frequently unacceptable to organizations – either because it makes entry to a service possible from the public Internet or because data leaving or entering the service must travel over the public Internet. A service can be isolated from the public Internet by disabling public network access. An ADF Azure IR configured with a *Managed Virtual Network* (managed VNet) uses *private* endpoints to connect to data stores such as Azure SQL DB or blob storage, enabling ADF to interact with them even when their public endpoints have been disabled.

Disable Public Network Access to a Storage Account

To examine the effect of isolating a service from the public Internet, begin by disabling public network access to your blob storage account.

1. In the Azure portal, navigate to your storage account and select *Networking* from the portal sidebar (in the *Security + Networking* section).

2. Ensure that the *Firewalls and virtual networks* tab is selected (indicated in Figure 8-5). Under *Public network access*, select the "Disabled" option and save your changes.

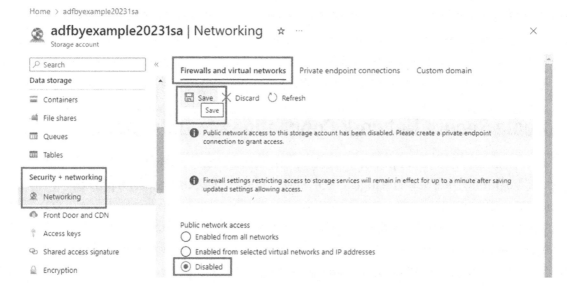

Figure 8-5. *Disable public network access to your storage account*

3. Still in the Azure portal, open the Storage browser for the storage account, then browse to your "sampledata" container. You will be denied access, with an error message like "This storage account's 'Firewalls and virtual networks' settings may be blocking access" – this is because you are trying to access the storage account's public endpoint, but public network access is no longer permitted.

4. Open ADF Studio's management hub and locate the storage
    account linked service. Select the linked service to open its *Edit
    linked service* flyout, then click *Test connection*. The connection
    test will also fail, with a similar error message.

Create an Azure Integration Runtime in a Managed Virtual Network

Now that you have disabled public network access to your storage account, your data
factory's AutoResolveIntegrationRuntime can no longer connect to the storage account
via its public endpoint. The first step to remedying this is to configure a new Azure IR
with a managed VNet (*Azure VNet IR*).

1. On the *Integration runtimes* page of ADF's management hub,
    click + *New* to create a new integration runtime. The *Integration
    runtime setup* flyout appears.

2. Select the *Azure, Self-Hosted* tile and click *Continue*. Under
    Network environment, select the *Azure* tile, then click
    Continue again.

3. Name the new IR on the flyout's *Settings* tab, then select the
    Virtual network tab and choose the "Enable" radio button (shown
    in Figure 8-6).

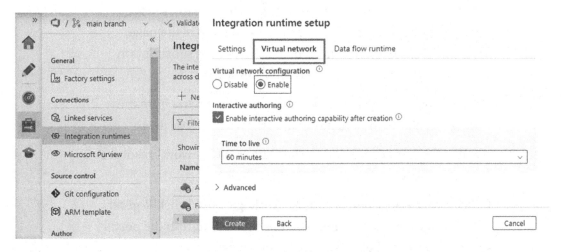

Figure 8-6. *Configure a managed VNet for an Azure IR*

4. Ensure that the *Enable interactive authoring capability after creation* check box is ticked, then click *Create* to save the IR configuration.

Compute resource for an Azure VNet IR is not pre-allocated – instead, resource is provisioned automatically at runtime when the IR is required. At development time, you must provision resource for an Azure VNet IR explicitly, by enabling interactive authoring.

Tip   If you wish to create the AutoResolveIntegrationRuntime in a managed VNet, you can do so when creating a data factory (but no later). In general, existing Azure IRs cannot be moved in or out of managed VNets after creation.

Register the Microsoft.Network Resource Provider

To work with any Azure resource, the corresponding *resource provider* must be registered to your Azure subscription. In the next section you will create a managed private endpoint – before doing so, ensure that the Microsoft.Network resource provider is registered to your Azure subscription.

1. Select "Subscriptions" from the list of Azure services displayed at the top of the Azure portal home page. (If you can't see the "Subscriptions" tile, use the search box at the top of the page to find it.) On the *Subscriptions* blade, choose the subscription containing your data factory and other resources.

2. On the Subscriptions blade, select *Resource providers* from the *Settings* section of the sidebar menu (shown in Figure 8-7).

3. Use the filter function to locate the "Microsoft.Network" resource provider, then click its entry in the list to select it.

4. If the resource provider's status is "NotRegistered," click *Register* to add it to your subscription. You may need to refresh the portal screen to see that the registration has taken effect.

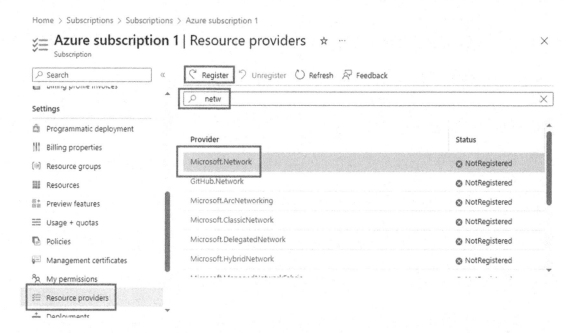

Figure 8-7. *Locate and register the Microsoft.Network resource provider*

Required resource providers are often registered automatically, for example, when creating a resource of the corresponding type in the Azure portal. This is why you have not encountered the need to register a resource provider in earlier chapters.

Create a Managed Private Endpoint

Executing an ADF Copy activity inside a managed VNet – by using an Azure VNet IR – means that connections to source and sink data stores are made from private IP addresses inside the managed VNet. A *managed private endpoint* has the effect of including a source or sink data store in the managed VNet, enabling ADF to connect to the store using a private IP address not available over the public Internet.

1. In the *Security* section of ADF Studio's management hub sidebar, select *Managed private endpoints*, then click + *New*.

2. The *New managed private endpoint* flyout appears. Choose the "Azure Blob Storage" data store and click *Continue*.

3. Provide a name for the new endpoint, then select the storage account to which you disabled public access earlier in the chapter.

261

4. Figure 8-8 shows the completed flyout. Click *Create* to request creation of the managed private endpoint and close the flyout.

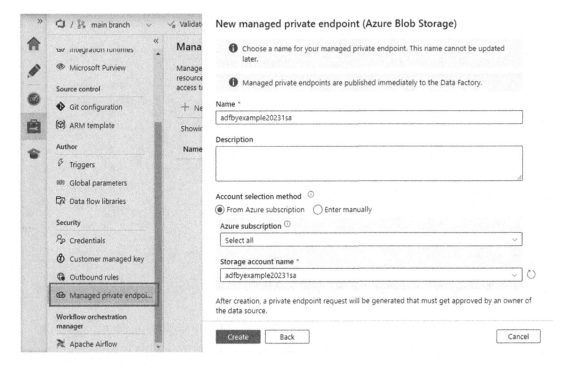

Figure 8-8. *Create new managed private endpoint*

5. The new endpoint appears in the list of managed private endpoints with a *Provisioning state* of "Provisioning" – wait a few minutes for its state to reach "Succeeded". Notice that its *Approval state* remains "Pending" – creation of a managed private endpoint must be approved by the owner of the target data store.

6. In the Azure portal, navigate to the *Networking* page of your storage account, then select the *Private endpoint connections* tab. The endpoint you requested from ADF Studio appears in the list of connections with a *Connection state* of "Pending" (as shown in Figure 8-9). Select the connection using the check box to its left, then click *Approve* and confirm.

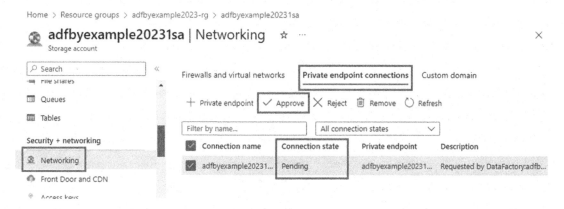

Figure 8-9. *Approve private endpoint connection request*

Update Blob Storage Linked Service

Return to ADF Studio to update your blob storage linked service to use the new Azure VNet IR.

1. Locate the blob storage linked service in ADF Studio's management hub and click its name to open the *Edit linked service* flyout.

2. Select your new Azure VNet IR from the *Connect via integration runtime* dropdown.

3. To test the connection, interactive authoring must be enabled for the Azure VNet IR. When you select the IR, if the message "Interactive authoring disabled" is displayed (as indicated in Figure 8-10), hover over the information icon to the right of the message to reveal a tooltip. Use the tooltip's "Edit interactive authoring" link to open the IR editing flyout and enable interactive authoring.

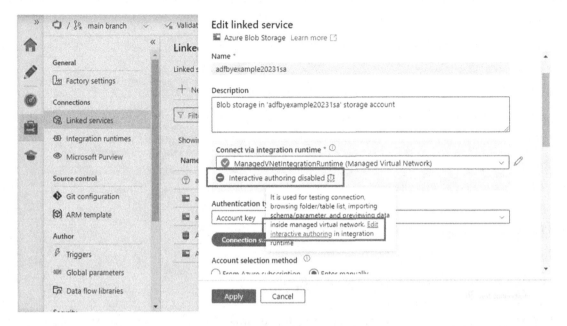

Figure 8-10. *Ensure that interactive authoring is enabled after selecting your Azure VNet IR*

4. Use the "Test connection" button on the bottom right to verify that ADF can now connect successfully to your storage account, then click *Apply* to save your changes.

5. Finally, reopen the linked service and review its configuration. Notice that in addition to the selected integration runtime, the flyout now indicates that the IR uses the managed private endpoint you created in the previous section.

   Connections made to the storage account by ADF using the Azure VNet IR take place entirely inside the IR's managed VNet – this network connection is private and neither exposes endpoints nor transfers data over the public Internet.

Copy Data Securely

The modified linked service can now be used to copy data from your storage account securely, using your Azure VNet IR to connect to blob storage via its private endpoint connection.

1. Choose an existing pipeline to test copying data from blob storage. Open the pipeline in ADF Studio and run it in the usual way.

2. ADF Studio prompts you to confirm your choice of integration runtime. Click the *Use activity runtime* button.

Note   At the time of writing, the confirmation message is somewhat misleading because it refers to data flow debug, but the intention is similar to data flow debugging options. *Continue with debug session* uses the Azure VNet IR resource already provisioned by enabling interactive authoring, while *Use activity runtime* creates it on-demand (as would take place in the published environment).

---

3. Monitor pipeline execution in the pipeline's Output configuration tab. Notice that the activity remains queued for longer than you have been used to – this is because activity execution must wait for Azure VNet IR resources to be made available.

4. Separately, you may wish to verify that you are still unable to access the storage account using the Azure portal's Storage browser – the changes you have made here enable ADF to connect securely to the storage account, without compromising general network security.

5. By default, each new Copy activity in a pipeline using an Azure VNet IR suffers its own startup delay. This results in longer overall activity duration, incurring a higher cost of execution. You can reduce this by configuring the managed VNet with a longer time to live, causing it to remain available for use by other Copy activities in the same pipeline – this option is available in the *Advanced* section of the *Edit integration runtime* flyout's *Virtual Network* tab (collapsed but visible in Figure 8-6 earlier in the chapter).

Restore Public Network Access

Before continuing, restore public network access to your storage account – this will eliminate managed VNet startup time and reduce the cost of activity execution for your learning purposes.

1. In the Azure portal, use the *Firewalls and virtual networks* tab on the storage account's *Networking* page to set *Public network access* to "Enabled from all networks".

2. In ADF Studio's management hub, restore the storage account's linked service *Connect via integration runtime* option to "AutoResolveIntegrationRuntime". Test the connection to verify that the storage account can be accessed successfully.

3. If you wish, use the management hub to delete the Azure VNet IR and remove the managed private endpoint.

In this section, you explored using an Azure VNet IR to enable ADF to make secure network connections to a well-secured storage account. You can take the same approach to secure connections to other supported data stores, including Azure Data Lake Storage Gen2 and many Azure database services. I have purposely focused the example here on connecting ADF to the data store – a real-world implementation would include additional storage account access rules to enable access from other services and client tools (such as Storage browser and Azure Storage Explorer).

Data Flow Cluster Properties

In Chapter 7, in order to run data flows in debug mode, you enabled *Data flow debug*. Enabling Data flow debug creates a Spark cluster where your data flows can be executed in pipeline debug runs. Provisioning a debug cluster may take a few minutes, but the cluster's TTL of one hour enables you to continue working in ADF Studio without interruption.

When a Data flow activity is executed by a published pipeline, the Spark cluster used to execute data flow transformations is provisioned just in time, when the activity's execution begins. The cluster's TTL is configured in the integration runtime chosen for the activity (selected using the *Run on (Azure IR)* option on the Data flow activity's *Settings* configuration tab). The AutoResolveIntegrationRuntime specifies a TTL of zero minutes, so a JIT cluster provisioned for a Data flow activity using this runtime is torn down as soon as the activity's execution is complete.

Data flow cluster properties can be modified in a custom Azure IR using the *Data flow runtime* tab on its *Edit integration runtime* flyout. The *Compute size* dropdown offers three predefined cluster configurations ("Small", "Medium", and "Large"), each with a cluster TTL of ten minutes. Alternatively, you can define a custom configuration specifying the cluster's compute type, size, and your choice of TTL. Figure 8-11 shows a custom cluster of "medium" size and type with a TTL extended to 30 minutes.

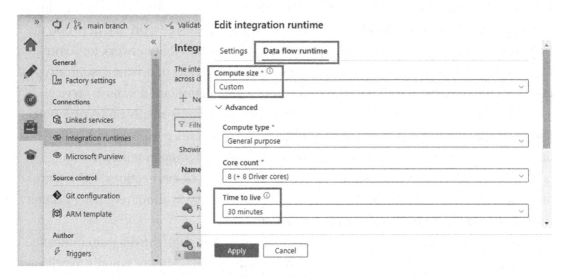

Figure 8-11. *Use a custom Azure IR to configure data flow runtime properties*

Tip   Changing the compute type and size is an advanced configuration option that should be considered with care. Microsoft's suggestion is that production workloads use a minimum cluster size of "Medium" (8 worker nodes + 8 driver nodes), but good practice for cost management is to start small and scale up as required.

The effect of a zero TTL in a pipeline containing multiple Data flow activities is that a new Spark cluster must be provisioned before each activity is executed. Extending the cluster TTL means that the cluster provisioned for the first Data flow activity may still be running when subsequent activities are queued. Using an Azure IR with a longer TTL can help to reduce overall pipeline execution duration by removing the delay associated with repeatedly provisioning clusters.

Self-Hosted Integration Runtime

The purpose of a *self-hosted integration runtime* is to provide secure access to resources in private networks, for example, on-premises source systems, or resources located in an Azure virtual network. Installed on a Windows machine inside a private network, the Integration Runtime Windows service provides a gateway into that network for Azure Data Factory. A self-hosted IR supports connections to a variety of private resource types, including file systems, SQL Server instances, and ODBC-compliant database services.

A self-hosted IR service inside a private network is linked to exactly one Azure Data Factory instance – this is insufficiently flexible in environments requiring multiple data factories. A common solution to the problem is to implement a separate data factory instance, used to encapsulate and share self-hosted IR connections. Other data factories can link to self-hosted IRs in the shared data factory, without requiring a direct relationship to the underlying gateway implementation.

Figure 8-12 illustrates this implementation pattern. Although the diagram indicates a boundary between a private network and Microsoft Azure, it applies equally to private networks implemented inside Azure – in such cases, the boundary is between the private Azure virtual network and the rest of the Azure cloud.

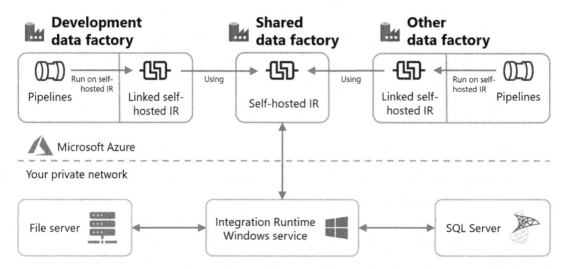

Figure 8-12. *Multiple data factories sharing a self-hosted integration runtime*

In this section, you will create a shared data factory, install a self-hosted integration runtime, and link to it from your existing development factory. If your computer is already supporting a self-hosted IR, you cannot install another one – the *"Link to a Self-Hosted Integration Runtime"* section in this chapter describes how you can link your development factory to an existing self-hosted IR.

Create a Shared Data Factory

To begin with, create a new data factory instance to contain your self-hosted IR and to share access to it.

1. In the Azure portal, use the *Create a resource* button to start the creation of a new data factory.

2. Complete the *Basics* tab, providing a unique name for the new factory and specifying other details to match your development factory.

3. On the *Git configuration* tab, tick the *Configure Git later* check box. From here, you can skip straight to *Review + create*, then click *Create* to create the new factory instance.

It is good practice to link your shared data factory to a Git repository, but for the purposes of this exercise, it is not necessary to do so.

Create a Self-Hosted Integration Runtime

You can visualize a self-hosted IR as a gateway between Azure Data Factory and your private network. The private network end of that connection consists of a Windows service installed on a nominated machine inside the private network. (At the time of writing, self-hosted IRs are only supported on Windows systems.) In this section, you will create both ends of the connection.

1. Open ADF Studio in your new shared data factory instance.

Tip   When connected to your development data factory, use the *Switch Data Factory* button in ADF Studio's navigation header bar to connect to your new shared factory.

---

2. Use the management hub's *Integration runtimes* page to create a
    new IR of the *Azure, Self-Hosted* kind. This time, choose the *Self-
    Hosted* network environment option.

3. Name the IR appropriately and click *Create*. This creates the Azure
    end of the connection into your network.

4. The *Integration runtime setup* flyout displays configuration
    tabs for the self-hosted IR. The *Settings* tab offers two options
    for setting up the self-hosted IR machine (the private network
    end of the connection). *Option 2: Manual setup* requires you to
    install the integration runtime and then to register it using one of
    the displayed authentication keys, while *Option 1: Express setup*
    downloads a customized installer that manages both installation
    and registration. Click the option 1 link *Click here to launch the
    express setup for this computer*.

5. A customized installer (.exe file) is downloaded to your
    computer – run it to install the self-hosted IR service. The installer
    steps through four stages before displaying a confirmation
    message. Click *Close* and return to ADF Studio.

6. Close the *Integration runtime setup* flyout. You can see the new
    self-hosted integration runtime displayed in the list alongside
    your Azure IRs. If its status is not shown as "Running," click the
    Refresh button to update the list.

The status of the self-hosted IR is dependent on the corresponding Windows service
running on your machine. If your machine is offline or the Windows service is stopped,
the IR will become unavailable.

Link to a Self-Hosted Integration Runtime

To link to the self-hosted runtime from your development data factory, you must first
share the runtime as follows.

1. With ADF Studio connected to your shared data factory, open
    the *Edit integration runtime* flyout for the self-hosted IR, from the
    Integration runtimes page in the management hub.

2. The *Edit integration runtime* flyout's *Sharing* tab displays the
    self-hosted IR's fully qualified Azure resource ID – click the *Copy*
    button to the right of the *Resource ID* field to copy its value to the
    clipboard.

3. Still on the *Sharing* tab, click + *Grant permission to another Data
    Factory or user-assigned managed identity*. Ensure that Resource
    type "System-assigned Managed Identity (Data Factory)" is
    selected.

4. You can search for your development factory using its name
    or system-assigned managed identity, but you will probably
    be able to see it immediately below the search box. Tick the
    corresponding check box to select the factory, then click *Add*.
    Click *Apply* to save your changes and close the flyout.

5. Use the *Switch Data Factory* function to reconnect ADF Studio to
    your development data factory, then open its management hub.

6. Use the management hub's *Integration runtimes* page to create
    a new IR, again of the *Azure, Self-Hosted* kind. This time, select
    the *Linked Self-Hosted* tile under *External Resources* (indicated in
    Figure 8-13) and click *Continue*.

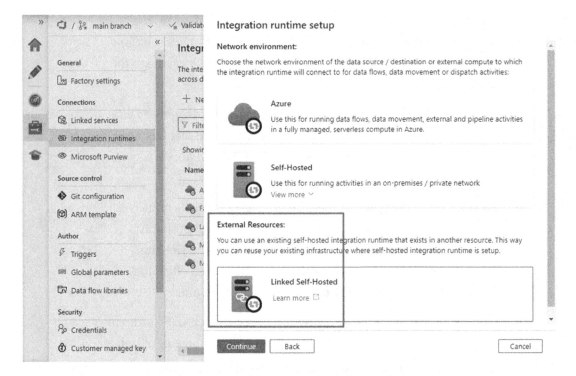

Figure 8-13. *Create a Linked Self-Hosted Integration Runtime*

7.   Name the IR appropriately, then in the *Resource ID* field, paste the self-hosted IR's fully qualified resource ID, copied to the clipboard in step 2.

8.   Ensure that *Authentication method* "System-assigned managed identity" is selected, then click *Create*.

You have now created both sides of the IR link between your two data factories – in the shared factory, you have allowed the development factory to access the self-hosted IR, and in the development factory, you have created a link to use it.

Use the Self-Hosted Integration Runtime

A major purpose of a self-hosted IR is to enable the secure transfer of data between Azure and a private network, for example, to upload data from on-premises file stores or database systems. In this section, you will use your development data factory to copy a file from your own computer into blob storage, using the linked self-hosted IR.

Enable Access to Your Local File System

Normally, the computer running the self-hosted IR Windows service is a server whose role is to provide an access route to *other* resources in the same network (such as the file server and SQL Server illustrated earlier in Figure 8-12). For this reason, access to the file system of the self-hosted IR Windows server is disabled by default.

For the purposes of this exercise, you have installed the self-hosted IR Windows service on your own computer. To copy a file from your computer into blob storage using ADF, you must first allow the Windows service to access the local file system.

1. Open a Windows command or PowerShell prompt as an administrator.

2. Change directory to the folder containing the *self-hosted integration runtime diagnostic tool,* using the command cd "C:\ Program Files\Microsoft Integration Runtime\5.0\Shared".

3. Use the diagnostic tool to enable local file system access using this command: .\dmgcmd.exe -DisableLocalFolderPathValidation.

Disabling local folder path validation disables security validation, enabling the self-hosted IR to access your local machine's file system. Figure 8-14 shows a command prompt being used to achieve this.

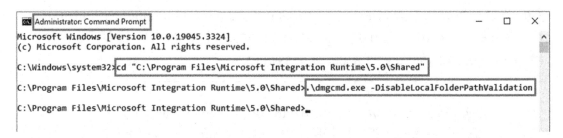

Figure 8-14. *Enable access to the self-hosted IR Windows server file system*

Tip   If you receive a timeout or other error when running dmgcmd.exe, use services.msc to make sure that the Integration Runtime Service is running.

Create a Linked Service Using the Shared Self-Hosted IR

To connect to your computer's file system from Azure Data Factory, a linked service is required.

1. With ADF Studio connected to your development data factory, use the *Linked services* page in the management hub to create a new linked service. Select the *File system* data store and click *Continue*.

2. On the next page of the flyout, name the linked service and choose the linked self-hosted IR from the *Connect via integration runtime* dropdown.

3. The *Host* field indicates the location inside your network from which you will be copying data – this could be a server UNC path if copying data from a separate file store or a location on the self-hosted IR machine itself. For now, you will copy data from your own computer – enter "C:\" (or an alternative drive letter of your choice).

4. Enter a *User name* and *Password* for ADF to use when connecting to your computer.

Tip   You may wish to create a specific user account on your computer that you can delete afterward. To avoid publishing your account credentials to ADF, create a key vault secret to store your account password.

---

5. Click *Test connection* to verify that the linked service has been correctly configured and is able to access the integration runtime. When your test connection has succeeded, click *Create* to create the new linked service.

Figure 8-15 shows the configured linked service flyout, using a key vault secret to provide the local account login password.

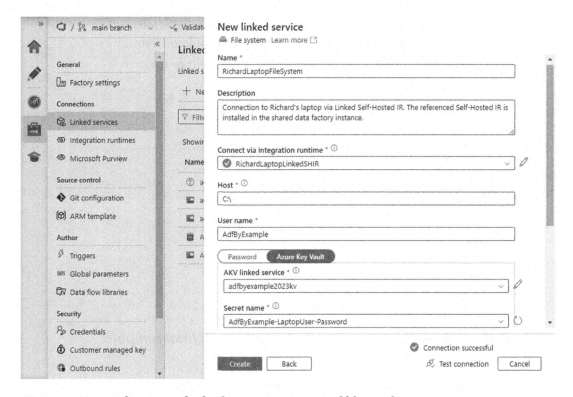

Figure 8-15. *File system linked service using a self-hosted IR*

Create a File System Dataset

The new linked service represents a connection from Azure Data Factory to your computer's file system. To represent specific files, a dataset is required.

1. In the ADF Studio authoring canvas, create a new dataset and a new "Chapter8" folder to contain it. Select the *File system* data store again, then choose the *Binary* file format. (The object of this exercise is simply to copy some files into Azure, so their internal structure is not important right now.)

2. Choose the file system linked service you created in the previous section, noticing that the first *File path* field is prepopulated with the *Host* value from the linked service.

3. Use the browse button (to the right of the *File path* fields) to
    locate a file to load from your computer. The completed flyout
    in Figure 8-16 shows a file of sample data chosen from my own
    computer.

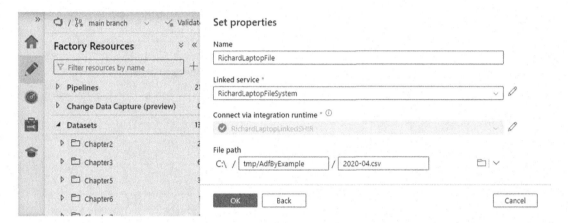

Figure 8-16. *Dataset configured to represent a file on a local computer*

4. Click *OK* to create the dataset, then save your changes.

Copy Data Using the File System Dataset

The dataset you created in the previous section can be used like any other. In this
section, you will use it as a Copy activity source to copy the file from your computer and
into Azure blob storage.

1. Create a new pipeline and drag a Copy activity onto the design
    surface. Set the activity's source dataset to the new file system
    dataset.

2. Create a sink dataset for the Copy activity using the + *New* button
    on the activity's *Sink* configuration tab. The new dataset should
    use the *Azure Blob Storage* data store and *Binary* file format. Use
    your existing Azure Blob Storage linked service and specify a file
    path in your "landing" container.

3. Run the pipeline. When it has completed successfully, use the
    Azure portal's Storage browser to verify that the file is present in
    your "landing" container.

In addition to copying data between private network and cloud data storage, the self-hosted IR can dispatch certain activities to on-premises compute services – for example, you can use the Stored procedure activity to execute a stored procedure on an on-premises SQL Server. You cannot use a self-hosted IR to perform every ADF activity – to run data flows using on-premises data, you must first copy data into Azure storage (using a self-hosted IR), after which it can be used by a Data flow activity running on an Azure IR.

In production environments, care must be taken to ensure that a self-hosted IR does not become a bottleneck or single point of failure. A self-hosted IR can be scaled out over up to four machines – referred to as *nodes* – running the Integration Runtime Windows service, allowing greater throughput and increasing availability in the event that one of them fails. Each node is registered to the same self-hosted IR in Azure Data Factory, so the abstraction of a single logical gateway into your network is maintained.

Figure 8-12 showed a self-hosted IR Windows service installed on a machine separate from the resources being exposed to ADF. While not essential, this can assist throughput by avoiding contention with other workloads. If CPU and memory usage is low but throughput remains limited, you may consider increasing the number of concurrent jobs permitted to run on the node, via the *Nodes* tab on the *Edit integration runtime* flyout.

Azure-SSIS Integration Runtime

As its name suggests, the purpose of the *Azure-SSIS Integration Runtime* is to permit the execution of SQL Server Integration Services packages in Azure Data Factory. SSIS packages running on an Azure-SSIS IR are unable to take full advantage of ADF's capabilities, but this can be a useful intermediate stage for organizations seeking to migrate legacy data processing quickly into Azure. This section assumes some familiarity with SSIS; a wider introduction is outside the scope of this book.

An Azure-SSIS IR uses an SSIS catalog database in exactly the same way as an on-premises SSIS installation, so you are required to manage some of the service infrastructure yourself. While you can generally consider ADF to be a serverless service, this makes the Azure-SSIS IR closer to an IaaS offering.

Note   At the time of writing, the Azure-SSIS IR is based on SQL Server 2017. Packages targeting older versions of SQL Server will be automatically upgraded, while packages targeting later versions will not run.

Create an Azure-SSIS Integration Runtime

In this section, you will create an Azure-SSIS Integration Runtime.

1. Use the management hub's *Integration runtimes* page to create an IR. Choose the *Azure-SSIS* tile to open the *General settings* page of the *Integration runtime setup* flyout, then provide a name for the new IR. Set its location to match that of your data factory.

2. An Azure-SSIS IR is a cluster of Azure virtual machines, managed for you by ADF. *Node size* and *Node number* settings describe the physical makeup of the cluster – how powerful each node in the cluster needs to be and how many nodes it contains. You can tune these settings to the needs of your workload – large, compute-heavy packages benefit from more powerful nodes, while a greater number of nodes may permit more packages to be processed in parallel.

   The running cost of the Azure-SSIS IR is in proportion to the size and power of its cluster, your choice of SQL Server Standard or Enterprise edition on cluster VMs, and whether or not you already own an existing SQL Server license. Choose a variety of different settings to observe the effect on the estimated running cost, displayed at the bottom of the flyout as shown in Figure 8-17.

Tip   Azure-SSIS IR cluster can execute different packages on different nodes simultaneously, but an individual package is only ever executed on a single node.

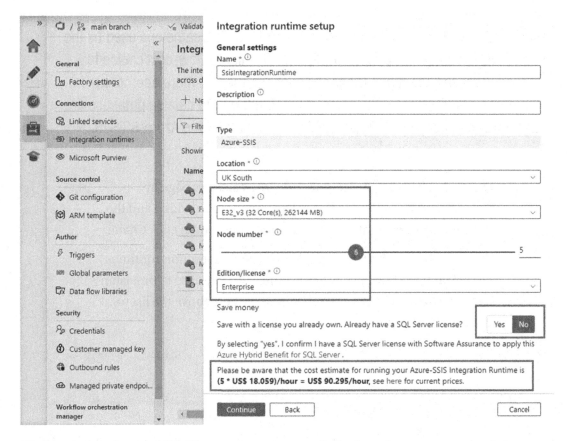

Figure 8-17. *Azure-SSIS IR running costs are linked to cluster power and size*

3. For the purposes of this exercise, choose the smallest available node size and number, and set *Edition/license* to "Standard." Click *Continue.*

4. The *Deployment settings* page relates to the SSIS catalog database. Ensure that the *Create SSIS catalog...* check box is ticked at the top of the flyout, then choose your existing Azure SQL Database server from the *Catalog database server endpoint* dropdown – this is where ADF will create the catalog database.

5. Provide your server's admin username and password, then use the *Test connection* button at the bottom of the flyout to verify that you have entered them correctly. Finally, set the *Catalog database service tier* to "GP_S_Gen5_1", then click *Continue.*

Note   "GP_S_Gen5_1" is a serverless service tier, the same one used by the
Azure SQL Database you created in Chapter 3. This is a low-cost choice for
learning purposes, but a provisioned service tier may be more appropriate in
a production environment. The costs of running the SSIS catalog database are
separate and in addition to those incurred by operating the Azure-SSIS IR.

6. Accept the default values on the *Advanced settings* page by
    clicking *Continue*. Review the settings you have provided and the
    associated cost estimate on the *Summary* page, then click *Create*.

7. The new Azure-SSIS IR appears in the list of integration runtimes
    with a Status of "Starting." A few minutes are required to provision
    and start the IR cluster – use the *Refresh* button above the list to
    monitor the IR's status (indicated in Figure 8-18).

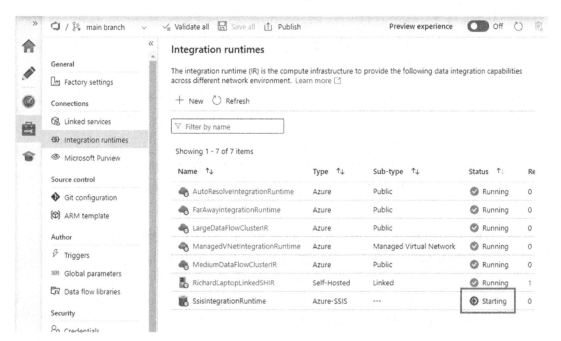

Figure 8-18. *Azure-SSIS IR starting*

8. Use the Azure portal to inspect the list of databases present
   in your Azure SQL Database server. Notice that a new SSISDB
   database has been created – this is the SQL database for the new
   integration runtime's SSIS catalog.

Deploy SSIS Packages to the Azure-SSIS IR

The GitHub repository that accompanies this book can be found at `https://github.com/Apress/Azure-Data-Factory-by-Example-Second-Edition` and includes a Visual Studio 2019 SSIS project. To build and deploy the project, you will need a Windows machine, running Visual Studio 2019, with the SQL Server Integration Services Projects extension installed.

In this section, you will deploy the SSIS project to the Azure-SSIS IR. The deployment of SSIS packages to ADF requires a running Azure-SSIS IR to enable packages to be installed in the IR's catalog database.

1. Open the solution "Azure-SSIS-IntegrationRuntimeTest.
   sln" (found in the repository's "SSIS\Azure-SSIS-
   IntegrationRuntimeTest" folder) in Visual Studio. The solution
   contains a single package called "TestPackage.dtsx" – open it.

2. The package contains two Execute SQL Tasks that call the
   database stored procedures [dbo].[LogPipelineStart] and [dbo].
   [LogPipelineEnd]. (The package has no real function other than to
   demonstrate that it can be executed within Azure Data Factory.)
   Both tasks use the "AzureSqlDatabase" connection manager defined
   in the package. Open the connection manager and update the fields
   Server name, User name, and *Password.* Use the *Select or enter a
   database name* dropdown to specify your Azure SQL Database.

3. Click *Test Connection* to verify that you have configured the
   connection manager correctly, then click *OK* to save your changes.
   Build the project.

4. Right-click the project in Visual Studio's solution explorer and
   click *Deploy* to launch the deployment wizard. Click *Next* to skip
   the introduction page (if displayed), then select the *SSIS in Azure
   Data Factory* deployment target. Click *Next.*

5. On the *Select Destination* page, check that *Authentication* is set
    to "SQL Server Authentication," then set *Server name*, *Login*,
    and *Password* to specify your Azure SQL Database server. (This
    information is used to connect to the SSIS catalog database – the
    details only match those in step 2 because both databases happen
    to be hosted in the same server.) Click *Connect* to enable the *Path*
    field, then click *Browse*.

6. In the *Browse for Folder or Project* dialog, click *New folder…* to
    create a catalog folder with a name of your choice. Click *OK* to
    create the folder, ensure that it is selected, then click *OK* to close
    the dialog.

7. Click *Next*, then review your deployment configuration. When
    you are ready, click *Deploy* to deploy the project to the Azure-
    SSIS IR. When the deployment is complete, close the deployment
    wizard dialog.

Run an SSIS Package in ADF

SSIS packages are run in ADF using the *Execute SSIS package* pipeline activity. Create a
new pipeline to run the package as follows:

1. Open the authoring canvas in ADF Studio and create a new
    pipeline. The Execute SSIS package activity is found in the
    Activities toolbox's *General* group – drag one onto the design
    surface.

2. On the activity's *Settings* configuration tab, choose your
    integration runtime from the *Azure-SSIS IR* dropdown. Click
    Refresh (to the right of the *Folder* dropdown) to load metadata
    from the catalog database. Select the *Folder* you created at
    SSIS project deployment, then choose *Project* "Azure-SSIS-
    IntegrationRuntimeTest" and *Package* "TestPackage.dtsx".
    Figure 8-19 shows the correctly configured *Settings* tab.

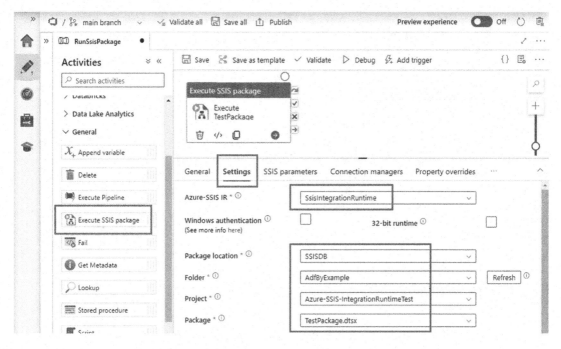

Figure 8-19. *Execute SSIS package activity settings*

3. The SSIS package specifies a "PipelineRunId" parameter value
    to pass into its call to [dbo].[LogPipelineStart]. The parameter is
    loaded automatically from package metadata and can be found
    on the *SSIS parameters* configuration tab. Replace its default value
    with a pipeline expression specifying the ADF pipeline run ID
    (indicated in Figure 8-20).

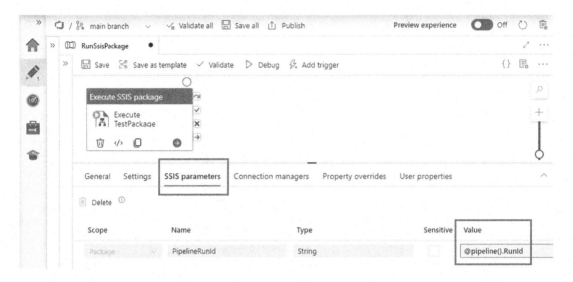

Figure 8-20. *Configure SSIS package parameters*

4. Save and run the pipeline. When execution has successfully completed, inspect the [dbo].[PipelineExecution] table for the log record created by the package – it contains the comment "Test execution from SSIS package."

While SSIS packages can be executed in ADF, doing so is less convenient and less powerful than using native ADF capabilities. Limited SSIS support for Azure-specific resources (such as blob or data lake storage) is available but requires the additional installation of the Azure Feature Pack for Integration Services in Visual Studio. Using an Azure-SSIS IR to run existing SSIS packages in ADF can be a useful stepping stone into Azure, but undertaking new development directly in ADF allows you to benefit from cloud-first design features that are simply unavailable to SSIS.

Stop the Azure-SSIS IR

Because an Azure-SSIS IR consists of a real cluster of virtual machines, it incurs costs for any time it spends running, even when not executing SSIS packages. For this reason, you should start the IR only when SSIS package execution is required and stop it afterward. Stop the IR as follows:

1. Open the management hub's *Integration runtimes* page and hover over your AzureSSIS IR in the list of integration runtimes.

2. A set of controls appears to the right of the runtime's name. The "pause" symbol (shown in Figure 8-21) in the set of controls is the IR's stop button – click it to stop the IR.

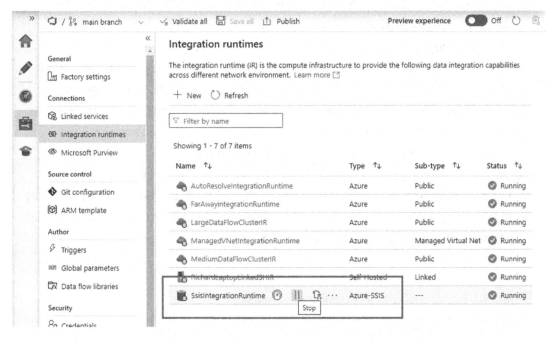

Figure 8-21. *Stop control for the Azure-SSIS Integration Runtime*

3. Click *Stop* in the confirmation dialog, then use the *Refresh* button above the list of runtimes to monitor the Azure-SSIS IR until its status is *Stopped*.

Tip   You can start and stop an Azure-SSIS IR programmatically from an ADF pipeline by using the *Web activity* to call the integration runtime's REST API endpoint – use this pattern to ensure that the IR runs only when required.

Managed Airflow in Azure Data Factory

Apache Airflow is an open source orchestration engine for batch-oriented workflows such as ETL routines. Like ADF, it orchestrates the execution of collections of smaller processes, enabling individual tasks to be composed into large, complex pipelines.

Historically, targeted support for Apache Airflow in Azure has been limited, requiring users to build their own Airflow environments from IaaS components such as Azure virtual machines, Azure SQL DB for PostgreSQL, and the Azure App Service. This process was eased with Microsoft's development of an Azure QuickStart template, but the resulting Airflow environment, using multiple IaaS services, remained the responsibility of the user – no managed service was available.

A managed Apache Airflow service in Azure entered public preview in February 2023. The managed service is available in the context of an Azure Data Factory instance – to create a managed Airflow environment, use the *Workflow orchestration manager* page in ADF Studio's management hub (Figure 8-22).

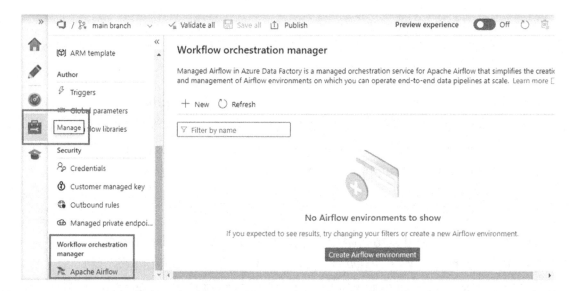

Figure 8-22. *Create a managed Airflow environment in ADF Studio's management hub*

The resulting Airflow environment is entirely separate from core ADF functions (although the managed Airflow service can orchestrate ADF pipeline execution alongside other units of work). The detail of workflow orchestration in Apache Airflow is outside the scope of this book.

> **Note**   At the time of writing, Apache Airflow also appears as a type of integration runtime on the *Integration runtime setup* flyout. Unlike other integration runtimes, an Airflow IR is not a means of executing activities in ADF – creating one has the same effect as creating an Airflow environment in the *Workflow orchestration manager* page.

Chapter Review

This chapter introduced the concept of an integration runtime (IR). Every ADF instance contains at least one Azure IR, called "AutoResolveIntegrationRuntime," which you have been using throughout the book – the chapter described other IR options and types available to support specific processing requirements.

Key Concepts

Key concepts encountered in the chapter include the following:

- **External pipeline activity:** An ADF pipeline activity executed using compute resource provided by a service outside Azure Data Factory, for example, Stored procedure, Synapse Analytics, or Databricks activities.

- **Internal pipeline activity:** An ADF pipeline activity executed using compute resource provided internally by Azure Data Factory.

- **Integration runtime:** Compute resource managed by Azure Data Factory.

- **Dispatching:** Management of ADF activity execution.

- **Azure IR:** A fully managed, serverless integration runtime that executes data movements and transformations defined by the Copy and Data flow activities. Azure IRs also manage dispatching of external activities to storage and compute environments like Azure blob storage, Azure SQL Database, and others.

- **AutoResolveIntegrationRuntime:** An Azure IR present in every data factory instance. The location of IR compute is determined automatically at runtime, and Spark clusters created for Data flow activities using this IR have a TTL of zero.

- **Custom Azure IR:** You may create your own Azure IRs to gain control over properties such as geographic location, virtual networking, and data flow cluster configuration.

- **Azure VNet IR**: A custom Azure IR that runs in a managed VNet. The decision to enable VNet configuration or not must be taken at IR creation time.

- **Resource provider**: Azure uses resource providers to create and manage resources. In order to use a resource in an Azure subscription, the corresponding resource provider must be registered to that subscription.

- **Self-hosted integration runtime:** An IR installed on one or more servers provided by you in a private network. A self-hosted IR permits you to expose private resources to ADF, for example, source systems that are hosted on-premises or for which no native ADF connector is available.

- **Linked self-hosted IR:** A self-hosted IR is connected to exactly one Azure Data Factory instance. A common pattern used to enable access in other data factories is to share a self-hosted IR, enabling other factories to create linked self-hosted IRs that refer to the shared IR.

- **Azure-SSIS IR:** A fully managed integration runtime that supports SSIS package execution in ADF. An Azure-SSIS IR consists of a VM cluster of a specified size and power – although the cluster is managed for you, its infrastructure is more visible than in serverless Azure IRs.

- **Web activity:** ADF pipeline activity supporting calls to web URLs such as REST API endpoints.

- **Airflow IR:** A managed Apache Airflow environment created in a data factory. Unlike other integration runtimes, this IR is a separate service providing Airflow workflow orchestration.

For SSIS Developers

Prior to the introduction of the Azure-SSIS IR, the usual approach to running SSIS packages in Azure was to host an instance of SQL Server Integration Services on an Azure VM. Replacing this IaaS approach with the Azure-SSIS IR in ADF removes the burden of infrastructure maintenance and provides more flexible scale-up and scale-out capabilities, by allowing you to control the size and power of the underlying VM cluster.

The existence of the Azure-SSIS IR makes it possible to expedite migration of existing ETL workloads into Azure with PaaS support, but SSIS packages are unable to exploit many of the features available to ADF. SSIS package development and maintenance for Azure requires additional tooling and cannot benefit from ADF's rich library of external system connectors or automatic on-demand resource scaling.

Power Query in ADF

ADF data flows, covered in Chapter 7, model a data integration process as a stream of data rows that undergoes a succession of transformations to produce an output dataset. This approach to conceptualizing ETL operations is long established and may be familiar from other tools, including SQL Server Integration Services. While powerful, this view of a process can be inconvenient – for example, for users new to data engineering practices, or when a new, unknown source dataset is being evaluated and understood.

Power Query is a data preparation tool that takes a *wrangling* approach to data exploration, allowing you to interact directly with your data as you design and build the transformations you need. Power Query transformations, or *mashups*, are defined using M formula language expressions, built automatically by the visual Power Query Editor. The tool is available in a variety of Microsoft products – it may be familiar to you from Microsoft Excel, Power Platform data flows, or Power BI. Azure Data Factory includes built-in support for Power Query mashups using the *Power Query activity*.

Power Query mashups implemented in ADF benefit from at-scale distributed execution on a managed Spark cluster. A mashup's M script is translated at runtime into Data Flow Script, enabling execution in the same way as the data flows you implemented directly in Chapter 7. ADF's Power Query activity does not support the full range of M functions or ADF linked service connectors but nonetheless offers an accessible route into Azure Data Factory for users already familiar with Power Query.

Create a Power Query Mashup

In this section, you will create a Power Query mashup to wrangle the Handy Candy data you saved in Parquet format in Chapter 3.

1. In ADF Studio, create a "Chapter9" folder in the *Power Query* section of the *Factory Resources* sidebar. On the new folder's *Actions* menu, click *New power query*.

2. A new authoring canvas tab opens with the *Properties* flyout displayed. Name the Power Query and dismiss the flyout.

3. The canvas displays the message "No source dataset". Expand the *Dataset* dropdown list and click + *New* to create a new one, as shown in Figure 9-1.

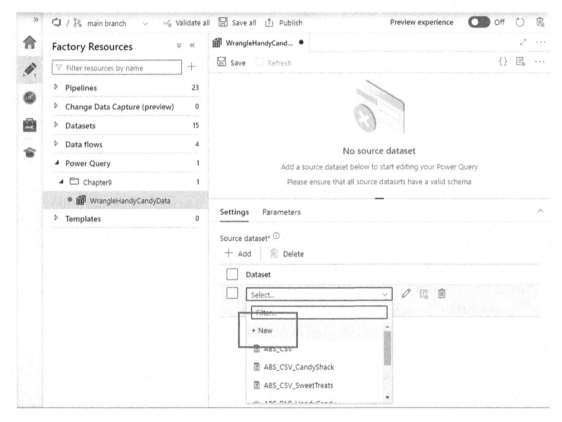

Figure 9-1. *Create a new source dataset in the Power Query Editor*

Note   You cannot use the Parquet dataset you created in Chapter 3 because it contains no schema information – source datasets for Power Query must have a valid schema.

CHAPTER 9   POWER QUERY IN ADF

4. On the *New dataset* flyout, select the *Azure Blob Storage* data store
    and click *Continue*. The *Select format* page follows – choose the
    Parquet file format, then click *Continue*.

5. Name the new dataset, then select your original blob storage
    Linked service. Note that the Power Query activity is unable to use
    linked services that access key vault secrets.

6. When you have selected your linked service, the usual *File path*
    fields are shown. Use the browse button to their right to find and
    select the "HandyCandy.parquet" folder (located in the "datalake"
    folder of the storage account's "output" container).

7. Click *OK* to close the dataset properties flyout. The Power Query
    Editor loads after a short delay, showing the first few rows of data
    from the Parquet file.

Explore the Power Query Editor

The Power Query Editor opens inside ADF Studio – the editor may be familiar to you if
you have previously used Power Query in other Microsoft products and services. Above
the Power Query Editor is an authoring canvas toolbar containing *Save*, *Refresh*, *Code*,
and *Properties* buttons.

The newly opened editor is shown in Figure 9-2. At the top of the editor is a warning
that "not all Power Query M functions are supported for data wrangling." Unsupported
functions can still be selected from the Power Query Editor and may even display
correct results in the editor's data preview pane, but they are not valid in ADF because
the required M expression translation is not available. When you select an unsupported
function, a "UserQuery : Expression.Error" warning appears, followed by a description of
the error.

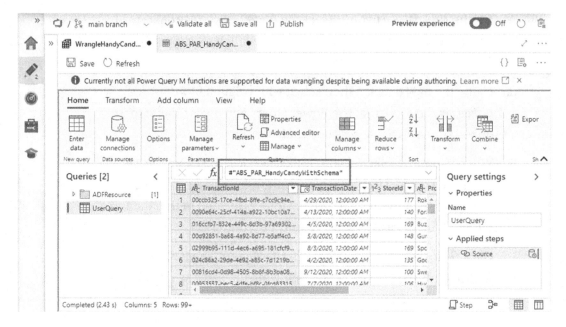

Figure 9-2. *Power Query Editor opened for data wrangling*

Immediately below the warning message (which you can close if you wish) is the command ribbon with five tabs.

- Dataset editing features on the *Home* tab include column and row removal.

- The *Transform* tab provides operations to make modifications to the dataset's existing rows and columns.

- The *Add column* tab provides operations to define additional columns.

Many column definition features appear on both the *Transform* and *Add column* tabs, differing only in their being used to modify existing columns or to define new ones.

Below the command ribbon, the data preview pane is displayed. To its right, the *Query settings* pane displays a history of modifications applied to the dataset. The detail of the modification selected in the *Query settings* pane is displayed in the step script bar at the top of the data preview pane, indicated in Figure 9-2.

To the left of the data preview, the *Queries* pane contains a query called "UserQuery" and a folder containing queries representing the mashup's source dataset(s). You are unable to interact with queries usefully here, so you may prefer to collapse this pane.

Before doing so, make sure that "UserQuery" is selected – it should be highlighted in gray, causing the name of the underlying dataset to appear in the step script bar, as Figure 9-2 illustrates.

Wrangle Data

The original Handy Candy data consists of a set of sales transaction JSON messages. Each message contains a transaction ID and the details of one or more items included in the transaction. The Handy Candy Parquet file provides a denormalized view of the same data: each row represents a single item, accompanied by the ID of the transaction to which it belongs.

Most confectionery retailer data is supplied to ABC in a pre-aggregated format. This is not the case for Handy Candy data – in this section, you will wrangle the Handy Candy data into the aggregated structure.

1. Begin by removing columns not required for the output. Right-click the "TransactionId" column header in the data preview pane and select *Remove columns* from the pop-up menu. Repeat this step for the "StoreId" column.

2. Other retailers' data identifies sales month using the date of the first day of each month. Select the "TransactionDate" column by clicking its header, then open the *Add column* ribbon tab. The data type of the column is Date, so controls that do not apply to values of that type are disabled in the ribbon.

3. In the *Date and time column* group, open the *Date* dropdown and select *Start of month* from the *Month* group, as shown in Figure 9-3. A new column called "Start of month" appears in the data preview pane, containing the first day of the month in which the corresponding transaction date appears. However, Power Query's Date.StartOfMonth function is not supported in ADF, causing an error message to be displayed as described earlier – this function cannot be used.

Note   A list of supported wrangling functions is available at `https://learn.` `microsoft.com/en-us/azure/data-factory/wrangling-functions`.

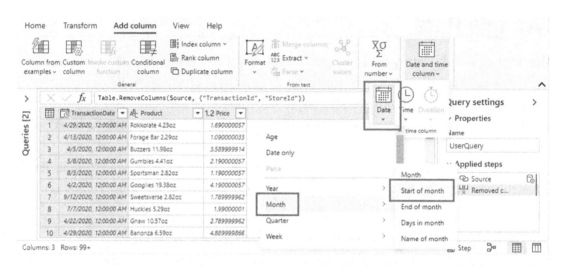

Figure 9-3. *Adding start of month based on the transaction date*

4.   Notice that the *Query settings* pane now includes three *Applied steps*. Remove the last of these – "Inserted start of month" – by selecting the step in the list, then clicking the delete button to its left (cross icon, indicated in Figure 9-4). You can remove any step except "Source" from the list in this way, but removing a step from the middle of the list may invalidate later steps.

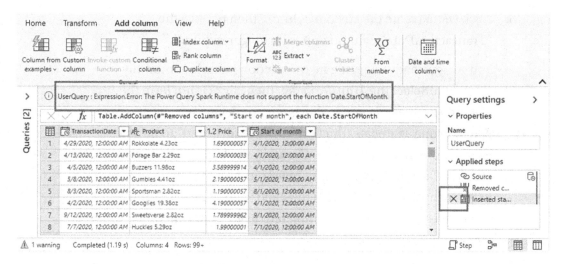

Figure 9-4. *Remove a wrangling step using its delete button*

5. On the *Add column* tab's ribbon, choose *Custom column*. In the custom column dialog, name the new column "SalesMonth" and set *Custom column formula* to `Date.AddDays([TransactionDate], 1 - Date.Day([TransactionDate]))`. The correctly configured formula is shown in Figure 9-5.

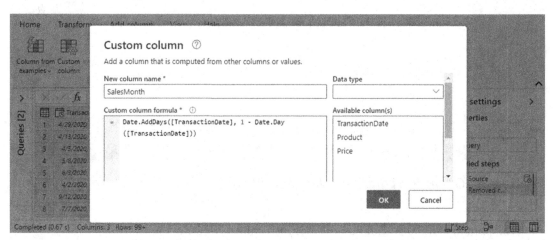

Figure 9-5. *Add a SalesMonth column*

6. Click *OK* to create the custom column, then remove the "TransactionDate" column as it is no longer required.

7. You're now ready to aggregate transaction items into monthly sales data. Select the *Transform* tab, then click *Group by* in the ribbon. The "Basic" setting allows you to specify one grouping field and one aggregate function – select "Advanced" to be able to add more than one of each. Group by the "SalesMonth" and "Product" columns, then count rows and sum the "Price" column in two new columns named "UnitsSold" and "SalesValueUSD", respectively. The correctly completed dialog is shown in Figure 9-6.

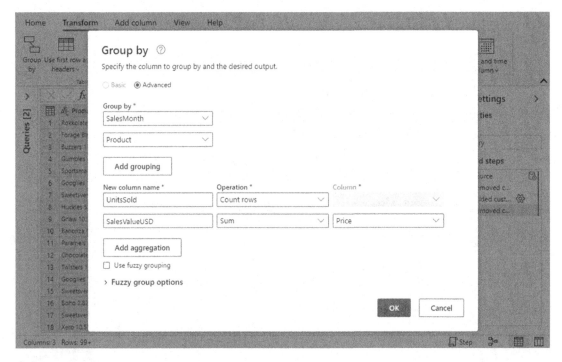

Figure 9-6. *Count rows and sum the Price column*

8. Finally, add another custom column called "Retailer," with the constant value "Handy Candy" – include the quotation marks around the retailer name in the custom column formula to indicate that this is a string literal.

Save your Power Query mashup and source dataset before proceeding. If you wish to inspect the M expression that the Power Query Editor has built for you, click the *Advanced editor* button (found in the *Query* group on the *Home* ribbon tab).

Run the Power Query Activity

Like data flows, Power Query mashups are executed inside an ADF pipeline using a dedicated pipeline activity – in this section, you will create a pipeline using the Power Query activity.

1. Create a new pipeline (in a new "Chapter9" pipelines folder) and name it appropriately.

2. Drag a Power Query activity, found in the Activities toolbox's *Power Query* group, onto the design surface. Name the activity, then use its *Settings* configuration tab to choose the Power Query you created in the previous section.

3. A Power Query mashup specifies its own data source(s), but no sink for transformation output. The sink must be specified in the Power Query activity's *Sink* tab – choose the Azure SQL DB dataset representing the database table [dbo].[Sales_LOAD].

4. Click *Debug* to run the pipeline in the usual way. If a debug cluster is not already running, you will be prompted to turn on data flow debug (provisioning a debug cluster with a minimum TTL of one hour). Alternatively, you can choose *Use activity runtime* from the *Debug* dropdown menu.

5. After pipeline execution is complete, verify that rows have been loaded into the database table [dbo].[Sales_LOAD]. In addition to [RowId], the columns [Retailer], [SalesMonth], [Product], [SalesValueUSD], and [UnitsSold] should have been populated. If this is not the case, check that the names of the columns added to your mashup exactly match those in the database table – the Power Query activity uses column names to map its output to sink columns automatically.

This example pipeline omits activities to log pipeline start and end or to manage pipeline run IDs – the reason for this is that Power Query activities do not support the injection of external values. The *Parameters* group on the Power Query Editor *Home* tab refers to Power Query parameters, which are not supported by the ADF Power Query activity.

As in the case of ADF's Data flow activity, the *Data flow details* button (eyeglasses icon) in the Power Query activity run (displayed on the *Output* tab of the pipeline's configuration pane) opens a graphical monitoring view of the activity's execution on a Spark cluster. In this case, each of the transformations corresponds to one of the steps applied in the Power Query wrangling process. Figure 9-7 shows details of the *Group by* transformation, selected in the graphic at the top, which has been given the name "Aggregate011" automatically by ADF.

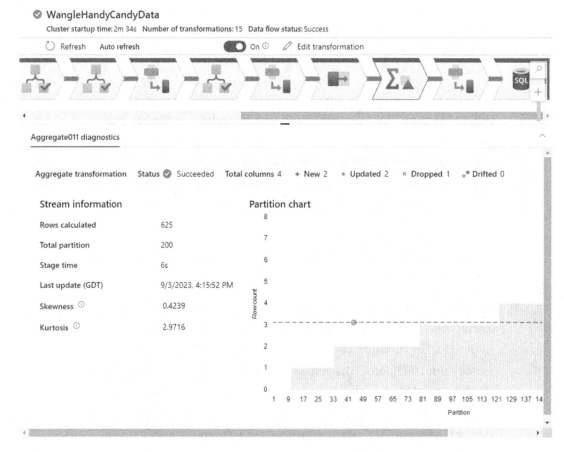

Figure 9-7. *Power Query activity execution graphical monitoring view*

Chapter Review

Power Query mashups in ADF make wrangling an attractive choice for exploratory transformation of new datasets. The approach aims to offer an intuitive, data-first alternative to implementing data preparation and transformation. This allows users from outside the field of data engineering – sometimes referred to as *citizen integrators* – to benefit simultaneously from the direct data interaction offered by the Power Query Editor and the at-scale operationalization of data pipelines running on Spark clusters.

At the time of writing, the Power Query activity lacks support for important ADF features like parameters, key vault secret–based authentication, and the full breadth of available linked service connectors. M formula language support is also incomplete, but the accessibility of the mashup editor will make Power Query an increasingly popular tool as feature support increases.

Key Concepts

Key concepts introduced in this chapter include the following:

- **Power Query:** Graphical data preparation tool available in several Microsoft products, including ADF Power Query activities, Excel, Power Platform data flows, and Power BI.

- **Data wrangling:** Interactive exploration and preparation of datasets.

- **Mashup:** Data wrangling transformation implemented in Power Query.

- **M formula language:** Language used to express transformations built in Power Query. M expressions (built using the graphical Power Query Editor) are translated into Data Flow Script at runtime by Azure Data Factory, for execution on a Spark cluster in the same way as an ADF data flow. M language support is incomplete – a list of supported functions is available at `https://learn.microsoft.com/en-us/azure/data-factory/wrangling-functions`.

- **Power Query activity:** ADF pipeline activity used to execute Power Query mashups authored in ADF Studio.

CHAPTER 10

Publishing to ADF

The relationship between ADF Studio, Git, and your development data factory, first introduced in Chapter 1, is shown in Figure 10-1. In Chapters 2 to 9, you have been authoring factory resources in ADF Studio, saving them to the Git repository linked to your development factory, and running them in debug mode using the development factory's compute (integration runtimes). Those interactions are shown in Figure 10-1 as dashed arrows.

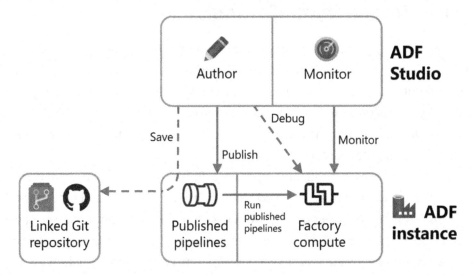

Figure 10-1. *Azure Data Factory instance, ADF Studio, and Git*

The ultimate goal of your development work is to run pipelines automatically in a production environment. The interactions indicated in Figure 10-1 by solid arrows are described here and in two later chapters:

- This chapter describes *publishing* to ADF, both from ADF Studio and from Git.

© Richard Swinbank 2024
R. Swinbank, *Azure Data Factory by Example*, https://doi.org/10.1007/979-8-8688-0218-8_10

- Chapter 11 introduces *triggers*, used to run published pipelines automatically.

- Chapter 12 addresses the topic of *monitoring*.

The first step toward execution in production is to deploy – or *publish* – factory resources. This chapter introduces a variety of approaches to doing so.

Publish to Your Factory Instance

In this section, you will publish factory resources to your development ADF instance. Published pipelines can be executed independently, outside the context of an ADF Studio session, although for the time being you will continue to execute them manually.

Trigger a Pipeline from ADF Studio

Published pipelines are typically executed automatically, either on a schedule or in response to an event such as the creation of new input files in blob storage. Patterns of automatic execution are defined and configured in ADF using *triggers*, the subject of Chapter 11. By extension, starting a pipeline execution is often referred to as "triggering" a pipeline – ADF Studio supports the manual triggering of pipelines that have been published to its connected factory instance.

As Figure 10-1 suggests, published pipeline definitions are separate from the versions stored in Git – and from unsaved changes in ADF Studio – and may differ. To illustrate this point, try to trigger one of your development pipelines that has not yet been published. (If you have already been experimenting with publishing and have no unpublished resources, create and save a new pipeline containing a single *Wait* activity, and use that one instead.)

1. Open the pipeline of your choice in the ADF Studio authoring canvas.

2. Above the design surface, to the right of the *Debug* button, find the *Add trigger* dropdown (shown in Figure 10-2). If you can't see it, look on the overflow dropdown accessed by clicking the ellipsis (...) button.

3. From the *Add trigger* dropdown, select *Trigger now*. Unlike *Debug*
    (which runs the pipeline in your ADF Studio session's debugging
    environment), *Trigger now* executes the pipeline in the factory's
    published environment.

The *Pipeline run* flyout appears, but the *OK* button at the bottom is grayed out, and
the message "Pipeline is not found, please publish first" is displayed – you are unable to
trigger a pipeline run, because the pipeline does not exist in the published environment.
The pipelines in your ADF Studio session are those loaded from your Git repository
working branch and may not match the pipelines (or versions of pipelines) already
published.

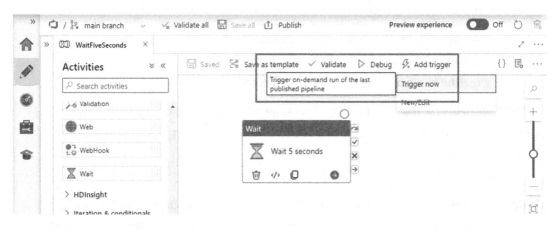

Figure 10-2. *Trigger now button*

Publish Factory Resources

Deploy resources to the factory's published environment as follows:

1. Click the *Publish* button (visible at the top of Figure 10-2, above
    the design surface's *Save as template* button). If you have unsaved
    resources, ADF Studio prompts for confirmation, warning you that
    publishing will save all pending changes.

Note   Publishing changes is only permitted from a factory's collaboration branch.
The *Publish* button is disabled when working in other branches.

---

2. The message "Gathering your new changes from collaboration branch" is displayed, before the *Pending changes* flyout opens. The flyout lists changes that will be published into the data factory and identifies the factory's *publish branch*. This is a nominated Git branch, by default `adf_publish`, specified in the factory instance's Git configuration. Click *OK* to publish the identified changes.

A series of messages is displayed as publishing proceeds, first indicating that resources have been published to the factory, then confirming that ARM templates have been saved into the factory's Git repository. The purpose of these ARM templates is described later in the chapter.

3. Use the *Trigger now* button to run your chosen pipeline again. Now that the pipeline has been published, the *OK* button on the *Pipeline run* flyout is available. Click it to run the pipeline.

As the pipeline starts, a "Running" message is displayed in the top right of the ADF Studio window, followed by a "Run Succeeded" message when pipeline execution has successfully completed.

Note   The previous section demonstrated that factory resources visible in ADF Studio may not match those in the published environment. To inspect published resources in a Git-enabled factory, expand the Git dropdown in the top left of your ADF Studio window, then select "Switch to live mode."

Inspect Published Pipeline Run Outcome

Unlike when running pipelines using *Debug*, activity execution information for published pipelines is not displayed on the pipeline's *Output* configuration tab. Execution output from published pipelines is accessed instead using ADF Studio's monitoring experience (Figure 10-3).

Chapter 12 examines the monitoring experience in greater detail. For now, open the monitoring experience by clicking the *Monitor* button (gauge icon) in the navigation sidebar. Published pipeline runs are shown on the *Triggered* tab of the *Pipeline runs* page.

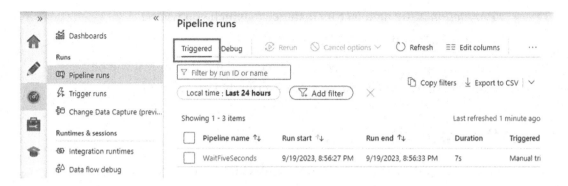

Figure 10-3. *ADF Studio monitoring experience*

Publish to Another Data Factory

A common model of ADF development and deployment is to build pipelines and other factory resources using a dedicated, Git-enabled development factory instance (as you have been doing). After development, resources are published into a separate production data factory, perhaps via one or more testing or other nonproduction environments.

A number of approaches to deploying into other environments are available. In this section, you will use the Azure portal to publish resources manually into another factory.

Prepare a Production Environment

In a real multi-environment scenario, each environment typically has one or more data factories of its own, along with corresponding external resources such as key vaults, storage accounts, SQL databases, and others. For the purpose of this exercise, your "production environment" will consist simply of a data factory instance. As would be the case in a real multi-environment situation, the production factory will gain access to shared self-hosted integration runtimes using the shared data factory you created in Chapter 8.

At the end of this section, you will have three ADF instances:

- *Development* refers to the factory you have been connected to throughout earlier chapters.

- *Production* is the data factory instance to which you will be publishing resources from development.

- *Shared* is the shared data factory you created in Chapter 8. It will be used by the two other factories, as described in that chapter.

Create the Production Factory

Start by creating the production data factory, into which you will deploy the ADF resources you have already developed. You will create the factory in the same way that you did in Chapter 1, but with one important difference: it will not be Git enabled.

1. In the Azure portal, use the *Create a resource* button to start the creation of a new data factory.

2. Complete the *Basics* tab, providing a unique name for the new factory and specifying other details to match your development factory. (This is just for convenience here – it is common practice to segregate resources belonging to different environments into separate resource groups or subscriptions.)

3. On the *Git configuration* tab, ensure that the *Configure Git later* check box is ticked. From here, skip straight to *Review + create*, then click *Create* to create the new factory instance.

The authoritative store of factory resource definitions is the Git repository attached to your development instance. The deployment process creates copies of factory resources in other ADF instances, including production. Under normal circumstances, you should treat deployed resources as read-only and avoid modifying them directly.

Grant Access to the Self-Hosted Integration Runtime

In Chapter 8, you created a self-hosted integration runtime in a shared data factory to enable it to be reused by multiple other factories. Another important reason for this approach is that – because the self-hosted IR Windows service is connected to exactly one data factory – you cannot publish self-hosted integration runtimes from one environment into another.

By creating a shared data factory, you have avoided this common deployment problem. To ensure that the development factory's link to the self-hosted IR can be published successfully, the production factory must also be granted access to the shared self-hosted IR.

1. Connect ADF Studio to your shared data factory, then navigate to the management hub. Select the *Integration runtimes* page.

2. Open the *Edit integration runtime* flyout by clicking the name of the self-hosted IR.

3. Select the *Sharing* tab, then click + *Grant permission to another Data Factory or user-assigned managed identity.* Your new production factory should be visible immediately below the search field – if not, use search to locate it.

4. Tick the check box next to the production factory, then click *Add.* Click *Apply* to save your changes and close the flyout.

Export an ARM Template from Your Development Factory

Resource definitions for publishing are described in *Azure Resource Manager (ARM) templates.* An ARM template is a set of one or more JSON files that defines Azure resources, in this case, your data factory. An Azure Data Factory ARM template describes all the resources defined inside a factory – everything from global parameters to pipelines. To obtain an ARM template that describes a data factory instance, connect to the factory and export its definition using ADF Studio.

1. Open the ADF Studio management hub in your development factory, then navigate to the *ARM template* page.

2. In the *ARM template configuration* section, indicated in Figure 10-4, tick the *Include global parameters in ARM template* check box.

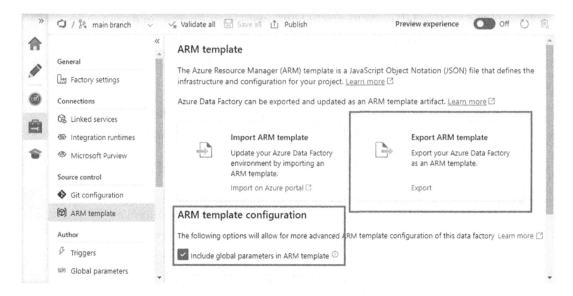

Figure 10-4. *Configure and export the factory ARM template*

3. Click the *Export ARM template* tile (also indicated in Figure 10-4) to export resource definitions from your ADF Studio session. A zip archive containing template files is downloaded to your computer.

4. Unzip the downloaded archive file.

The file `ARMTemplateForFactory.json` in the root of the zip archive describes every resource inside the ADF instance, as defined in your ADF Studio session – it reflects the state of resources in your session, saved or not. Close to the top of the file, a number of *deployment parameters* are specified, default values for which are stored in the file `ARMTemplateParametersForFactory.json`. The files in subfolders represent various subsets of resource information, useful in other situations. In this example, you will simply use the main `ARMTemplateForFactory.json` file.

Import an ARM Template into Your Production Factory

You can deploy your exported factory resource definitions into another data factory instance by importing the ARM template.

1. Connect ADF Studio to your production data factory, then open its management hub.

2. Open the *ARM template* page, then select the *Import ARM template* tile to import the ARM template you downloaded from your development data factory. This launches the Azure portal's *Custom deployment* blade in a separate browser tab.

3. On the *Custom deployment* blade's *Select a template* tab, click *Build your own template in the editor*. The ARM template editor opens.

4. Click the *Load file* button (indicated in Figure 10-5), then browse to your unzipped ARM template archive. Select the file ARMTemplateForFactory.json to open it in the template editor. Click *Save* – the portal returns you to the *Custom deployment* blade's *Basics* tab.

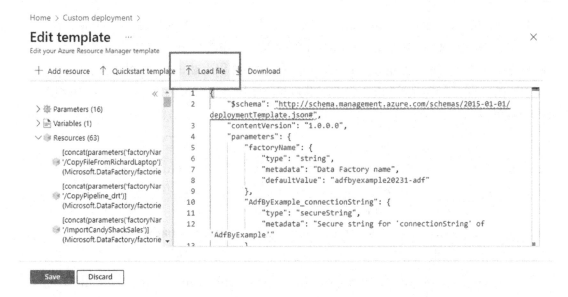

Figure 10-5. *ARM template editor during custom deployment from the Azure portal*

5. The *Basics* tab includes fields that identify the deployment target – subscription, resource group, region, and factory name – and a field for each deployment parameter. Select the resource group containing your production factory and specify its name.

6. Review the set of deployment parameters, noticing that parameterized values include your key vault URL, connection strings, and any global parameters you have created. Nonsensitive deployment parameters are prepopulated with default values from your development environment – for the purposes of this exercise, you can use these values.

7. Values for sensitive parameters are not prepopulated – these include connection strings for your storage account and SQL database, found in their respective Azure portal resource blades, and the password for the SSISDB login. Provide appropriate values, then click *Review + create*. Review your deployment settings, then click *Create* to initiate deployment.

Tip   Storage account connection strings are found on the *Access keys* page of the Storage account blade in the Azure portal. SQL database connection strings are available on the *Connection strings* page of the SQL database blade. The deployment process validates connection string formats, but connections are not tested directly.

---

8. When the deployment has successfully completed, return to ADF Studio in your production factory. Click *Refresh* in the factory header bar to load the published resource definitions – when using a factory that is not Git enabled, ADF Studio is loaded with resource definitions from the published environment.

You can make and publish changes to your production environment directly from a connected ADF Studio session, but this is not advisable. Changes made in this way are not saved to your Git repository – they will not be included in future deployments from your development environment and may be overwritten. You should consider restricting write access to nondevelopment factories, to prevent direct modification under all but exceptional circumstances (e.g., making a manual hotfix that is later also added to Git).

Tip   No standard Azure Data Factory security role provides read-only factory access – to achieve this, create an *Azure custom role* containing read permissions to data factory resources.

Understand Deployment Parameters

While importing an ADF ARM template into a data factory instance, the Azure portal prompts you to supply values for a number of deployment parameters. The purpose of these is to enable you to supply environment-specific values for particular factory resources when deploying into the corresponding environment. In the deployment example of the previous section, you reused parameter values from your development environment to specify connection information for your development key vault, storage account, and SQL database linked services. In a real multi-environment scenario, where each environment contains its own corresponding external resources, the values of such parameters must be updated to match the properties of the target environment.

The selection of factory properties to be parameterized in an ADF ARM template is determined by the factory's *parameterization template*, which can be edited in ADF Studio using the *Edit parameter configuration* tile on the management hub's *ARM template* page. A simple pattern for managing parameters in a multi-environment scenario is as follows:

- Create a separate key vault for each environment.

- Store environment-specific secrets like connection strings and access keys in the key vault.

- Implement non-secret environment-specific variables as global parameters.

Listing 10-1 shows a simplified parameterization template, suitable for use in this pattern, which specifies that only global parameters and key vault URLs are to be parameterized. Note that for global parameters to be included in an ARM template, the *Include global parameters in ARM template* check box must be ticked on the *ARM template* page.

Listing 10-1. Simplified parameterization template

```
{
    "Microsoft.DataFactory/factories/globalparameters": {
        "properties": {
            "*": {
                "value": "="
            }
        }
    },
    "Microsoft.DataFactory/factories/linkedServices": {
        "AzureKeyVault": {
            "properties": {
                "typeProperties": {
                    "baseUrl": "="
                }
            }
        }
    }
}
```

Automate Publishing to Another Factory

Publishing to your development factory instance from ADF Studio has two effects, as you saw earlier in the chapter:

- ADF pipelines are copied into the published environment and can be triggered there.

- Factory ARM templates are saved to your Git repository.

The ARM templates written to Git are named differently from those exported directly from ADF Studio, and are organized differently, but can be used in exactly the same way. Furthermore, when coupled with Git and *Azure Pipelines*, you can arrange for an ARM template to be published to a different environment whenever it is updated.

Note   The term "pipeline" is somewhat overloaded when discussing Azure Data Factory and Azure DevOps together. The remainder of this chapter deals almost exclusively with Azure Pipelines, which for clarity I refer to as Azure DevOps pipelines.

Azure Pipelines is the name of Microsoft's cloud-based CI/CD pipeline service. CI/CD – continuous integration and continuous delivery – is a development practice in which software changes are integrated into the main code base and deployed into production continuously, as they are developed. An Azure DevOps pipeline specifies a series of tasks to be performed automatically in response to events in your Git repository – for example, when a change is made in a particular location or branch. In the following sections, you will create an Azure DevOps pipeline to deploy Azure Data Factory ARM templates automatically when they are updated in Git.

Create a DevOps Service Connection

To be permitted to modify Azure resources, an Azure DevOps pipeline uses a *service connection* – a nominated Microsoft Entra ID principal with the necessary permissions. If you do not already have a pipeline service connection in your Azure DevOps project, create one as follows:

1. Open Azure DevOps and navigate to your AdfByExample project. Select *Project settings*, found in the bottom left of the browser window.

2. In the *Pipelines* section of the *Project Settings* menu, select *Service connections*. Click the *Create service connection* button that appears in the main window.

3. In the *New service connection* dialog, select "Azure Resource Manager." Click *Next*.

4. Choose the recommended authentication method "Workload Identity federation (automatic)," then click *Next*.

5. Ensure that *Scope level* is set to "Subscription" and that the correct subscription is selected in the *Subscription* dropdown. Provide a *Service connection name* of your choice.

6. Finally, ensure that the *Security* check box "Grant access permission to all pipelines" is ticked, then click *Save*.

Saving the service connection automatically creates an associated Microsoft Entra ID service principal with the necessary resource management permissions in your Azure subscription. You will now be able to use this service connection to authorize deployment pipeline actions.

Create an Azure DevOps Pipeline

Azure Data Factory's publish process writes ARM templates into a nominated publish branch in Git, by default `adf_publish` (although you can change this if you wish in the factory's Git configuration). A data factory's publish branch is not used like a conventional feature branch – it is never merged back into the collaboration branch, nor does it receive updates from the collaboration branch. Instead, it provides a stand-alone location to store published ARM templates – the branch only ever receives updates when changes are published in the development environment via ADF Studio. Azure Data Factory's use of the `adf_publish` branch specifically to contain published ARM templates means that updates to the branch can be used to trigger automated deployments.

Azure DevOps pipelines can be implemented in two different styles, either using a graphical user interface ("classic") or with a definition file written in *YAML*, a *data serialization language*. The YAML style of pipeline is preferable because, as code, a pipeline's definition can be stored under version control in your Git repository and subjected to the same review processes elsewhere in your development workflow.

Create a YAML Pipeline File

When an Azure DevOps pipeline is executed, it uses the YAML definition file stored in the Git feature branch that triggered the execution. In the case of Azure Data Factory, this means that the YAML file must be created directly within the repository's publish branch. In this section, you will create a simple pipeline YAML file.

1. In Azure DevOps, browse to the *Files* page of your Git repository. Use the branch dropdown to select the repository's `adf_publish` branch. The branch contains a folder with the name of your development ADF instance – this contains the ARM template files created by the publish process.

2. Using the vertical ellipsis button to the right of the repository name (indicated in Figure 10-6), choose + *New* and then *File*.

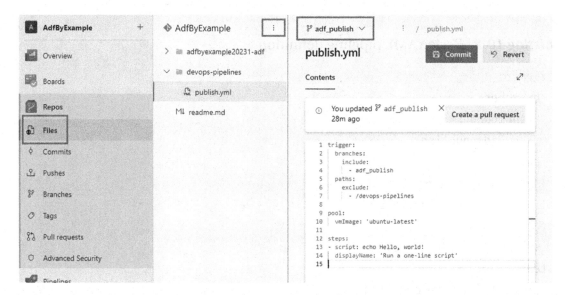

Figure 10-6. *Creating publish.yml directly in the adf_publish branch*

3. Name the new file "devops-pipelines/publish.yml", then click *Create*. An empty file editor pane opens on the right-hand side.

4. Add the text given in Listing 10-2 to the editor pane. YAML groups elements together on the basis of textual indentation, so make sure that you indent the text exactly as in the listing. A copy of the "publish.yml" file is available in the book's GitHub repository.

5. Click *Commit* to save the new file directly into the `adf_publish` branch. (You will be prompted for a commit comment – you can accept the default by clicking *Commit* again in the comment dialog.)

Note   Git requires a comment to be added to every commit. ADF Studio automatically creates commit comments when factory resources are saved, unless custom comments are enabled in the factory's Git configuration – you disabled custom comments when linking your development factory to Git in Chapter 1. This enables a smoother saving experience but does not permit meaningful commit comments – choose a Git configuration that supports your preferred behavior.

Listing 10-2. Basic YAML pipeline definition

```
trigger:
  branches:
    include:
      - adf_publish
  paths:
    exclude:
      - /devops-pipelines
pool:
  vmImage: 'ubuntu-latest'
steps:
- script: echo Hello, world!
  displayName: 'Run a one-line script'
```

Create an Azure DevOps Pipeline Using the YAML File

The YAML file you have created contains a pipeline definition but on its own is not an Azure DevOps pipeline. In this section, you will create an Azure DevOps pipeline that uses the definition stored in your YAML pipeline file.

1. In Azure DevOps, select the *Pipelines* item in the sidebar.

2. If this is your first Azure DevOps pipeline, a *Create Pipeline* button is displayed in the center of the screen – click it. (If you don't see it, use the "+" button to the right of the project name at the top of the sidebar.) A pipeline creation wizard launches.

3. On the *Connect* tab (headed *Where is your code?*), select *Azure Repos Git*. On the *Select* tab that follows, choose your factory Git repository.

4. On the *Configure* tab, select *Existing Azure Pipelines YAML file*. In the dialog box that appears, select your `adf_publish` branch, then choose "/devops-pipelines/publish.yml" from the *Path* dropdown.

5. Click *Continue*, then on the *Review your pipeline YAML* page, click *Run* to create and run the pipeline.

The Azure DevOps pipeline you have created does nothing more than print "Hello, world!" to the console, but it will now do so automatically every time that the `adf_publish` branch is updated – that is, whenever you publish changes from ADF Studio in your development environment.

Warning   If your Azure DevOps organization has not yet received a parallelism grant from Microsoft, your Azure DevOps pipeline will fail with the error "No hosted parallelism has been purchased or granted". If you have not yet made a parallelism request, review the "Looking Ahead" section at the end of Chapter 1.

Add the Factory Deployment Task

Azure DevOps pipelines are made up of *tasks*: configurable processes that perform activities required for deployment. The `script` task in your YAML pipeline is one example of a task. In this section, you will add an ARM template deployment task – the new task will make changes to resources in Azure, authorized using the service connection you created earlier.

1. Select the *Pipelines* item from the Azure DevOps sidebar again, then select your new pipeline from the list of recently run pipelines. You can edit the pipeline's YAML from here – click *Edit* to open the YAML pipeline editor.

2. Verify that the branch shown at the top of the editor pane is `adf_publish`, then add the ARM template deployment task given in Listing 10-3 to the bottom of the YAML file. (You may remove the "Hello, world!" script task from earlier if you wish.)

3. Configure the YAML task, replacing the placeholders in angle brackets with appropriate values. "<your-service-connection-name>" is the name of the service connection you created earlier in the chapter, and "<your-production-factory-location>" is the Azure region where your production data factory is deployed. Figure 10-7 shows the task configured for my development and production factory instances.

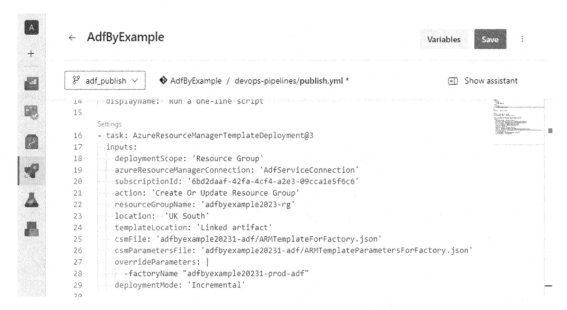

Figure 10-7. Configured ARM template deployment task in YAML

4. Save the pipeline, providing a commit message when prompted, and run it again. If you receive an error message indicating that the YAML file could not be found, make sure that you have selected the adf_publish branch.

Listing 10-3. ARM template deployment task YAML for ADF

```
- task: AzureResourceManagerTemplateDeployment@3
  inputs:
    deploymentScope: 'Resource Group'
    azureResourceManagerConnection: '<your-service-connection-name>'
    subscriptionId: '<your-azure-subscription-id>'
    action: 'Create Or Update Resource Group'
```

```
resourceGroupName: '<your-resource-group-name>'
location: '<your-production-factory-location>'
templateLocation: 'Linked artifact'
csmFile: '<your-development-factory-name>/ARMTemplateForFactory.json'
csmParametersFile: '<your-development-factory-name>/
ARMTemplateParametersForFactory.json'
overrideParameters: |
   -factoryName "<your-production-factory-name>"
deploymentMode: 'Incremental'
```

Note   The Incremental deployment mode specified in Listing 10-3 is necessary because deployment is scoped at the resource group level. Deploying a factory ARM template in Complete mode would cause other resources in the resource group – such as your storage account or SQL database – to be deleted.

The deployment task's overrideParameters argument allows you to specify values for use when the task is executed. Listing 10-3 specifies a single override parameter – the name of the deployment's target factory – but you can specify other parameters in the same way. These might include the target environment's key vault URL or values for factory global parameters.

Avoid specifying secret values directly in the overrideParameters argument, as this will cause them to be stored in your Git repository in plain text. Instead, create secret pipeline variables that can be referenced in the YAML task, for example:

```
overrideParameters: |
   -factoryName "adfbyexample-production"
   -myKeyVaultUrl "https://adfbyexample-kv.vault.azure.net/"
   -mySecretParam "$(SecretVariableName)"
```

Secret pipeline variables can be managed in a number of ways – by explicit creation in each pipeline, by storing them as secret values in an Azure Pipelines variable group, or by linking a variable group directly to an Azure Key Vault.

Trigger an Automatic Deployment

The Azure DevOps pipeline you have created deploys an ARM template automatically from the Git repository's `adf_publish` branch into your production factory, whenever you publish changes in your development factory. Test this by making a change to your development factory and publishing it.

1. Open the ADF Studio authoring canvas in your development factory, then create a "Chapter10" pipelines folder.

2. Create a new Azure Data Factory pipeline by cloning an existing one from an earlier chapter. Rename the new ADF pipeline and move it to the "Chapter10" folder.

3. Click *Save all* to save your changes to your Git collaboration branch in the usual way.

4. Click *Publish* to update the ARM templates stored in the factory's Git `adf_publish` branch, reflecting your changes. This causes your Azure DevOps pipeline to be triggered.

5. Return to Azure DevOps, then navigate to your pipeline definition in the *Pipelines* list. Click your pipeline to view the list of recent runs. Each run indicates how it was triggered – "manually triggered" runs are those that you started directly while developing your Azure DevOps pipeline, while those triggered automatically when publishing from ADF Studio are described as "Individual CI." Figure 10-8 shows a history containing both manually triggered and individual CI pipeline runs.

6. When execution of the Azure DevOps pipeline is complete, open the ADF Studio authoring canvas in your production factory and verify that the factory now also contains the ADF pipeline you created in step 2. (If you are unable to see the change, click the *Refresh* button located toward the right of the ADF Studio factory header bar.)

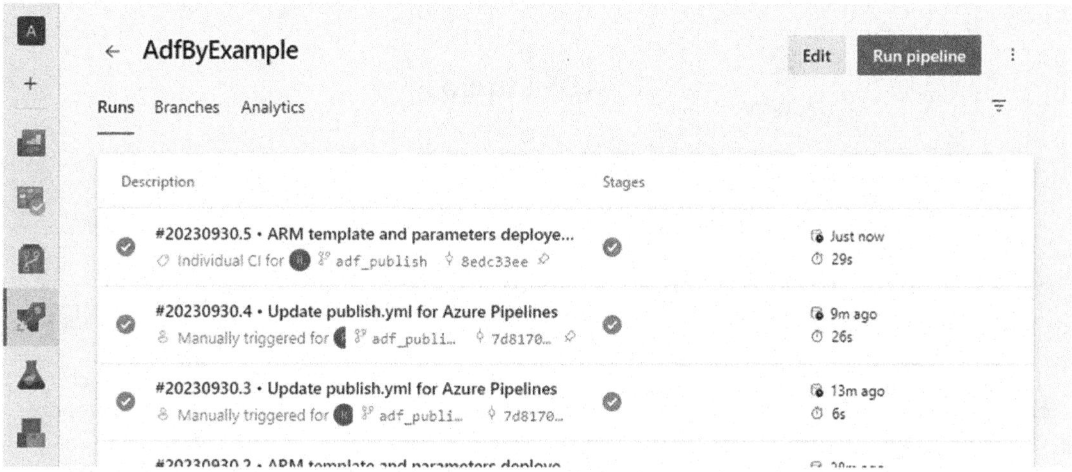

Figure 10-8. *Azure DevOps pipeline run history*

The Azure DevOps pipeline you have developed here is almost completely automatic – when development work is ready for deployment, clicking *Publish* in ADF Studio is the only additional action required to promote your work into the production environment. In this example, I referred to the target environment as "production," but DevOps pipelines are frequently used to deploy development work through a sequence of environments, enabling development work to be tested in a variety of ways before being delivered into production.

Figure 10-9 illustrates the relationship between ADF Studio, Git, and your development and production ADF instances. In this scenario, the role of ADF Studio depends on the data factory to which it is connected – in development, it is predominantly an authoring tool, while in production, its purpose is almost exclusively factory monitoring.

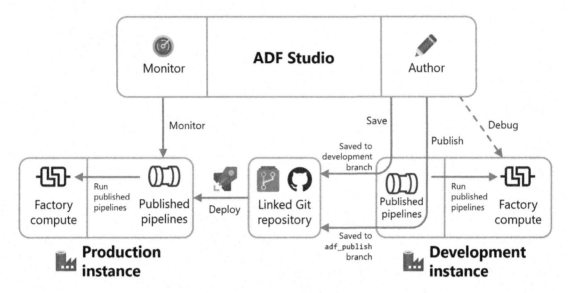

Figure 10-9. *The role of ADF Studio in different factory instances*

Clicking *Publish* in ADF Studio publishes resources to the development instance, but this is rarely of interest – publishing to the development factory at all is a relic of single-factory working practices that predate ADF's integration with Git. The primary purpose of *Publish* is to produce an ARM template for deployment to other environments – the Azure DevOps pipeline you have created is triggered when that template is saved to the Git repository's publish branch.

Feature Branch Workflow

Throughout this book, you have been working with a Git-enabled development factory, saving changes directly into the factory's collaboration branch, `main`. One of the reasons for Git's popularity as a version control system is its support for feature branches, allowing different developers to work on separate areas in isolation. Typically, a *feature branch workflow* involves creating a new branch to contain work on a specific new feature – for example, in the case of ADF, creating or modifying a data factory pipeline. ADF Studio supports feature branch workflows via the Git dropdown (shown in Figure 10-10).

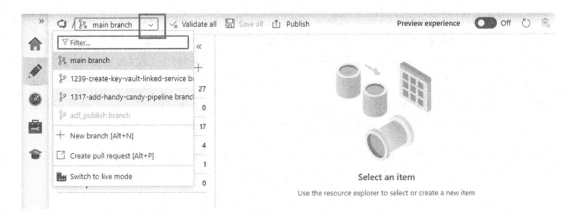

Figure 10-10. *Feature branch selection in ADF Studio*

A frequent choice when using a feature branch workflow is to prevent any direct modification of the collaboration branch. Instead, when development work in a feature branch is complete, that branch is merged into main via a *pull request*. A pull request enables other developers to review and approve the work in the feature branch, as part of wider quality assurance measures for new development. ADF Studio itself contributes to enforcing this workflow, by permitting publishing of changes from the collaboration branch alone.

In a feature branch workflow, merging changes to main on approval of a pull request is a natural trigger for automated deployment. In contrast, triggering a deployment pipeline built on the adf_publish branch requires additional manual intervention – to update ARM templates in the publish branch, you must publish resources interactively using ADF Studio. The following section reviews approaches to aligning ADF deployment and Git feature branch workflows.

Azure Data Factory Utilities

As I described in an earlier section, an effect of publishing factory resources in ADF Studio is to produce an ARM template for deployment to other environments. Microsoft's *Azure Data Factory Utilities* npm package provides a code-first route to generating an ARM template, allowing the process to be automated. In addition, the package makes ADF Studio's validation feature available for non-interactive use.

Recall that ADF resources are represented in `main` and other repository feature branches using per-resource JSON files. The Azure Data Factory Utilities npm package, available from `www.npmjs.com/package/@microsoft/azure-data-factory-utilities`, operates on these files directly – you can clone your data factory's Git repository and use the package locally, or you can download and install the package in your CI/CD pipeline.

A possible deployment workflow in this scenario is as follows:

1. A data engineer completes work on a feature branch, opening a pull request in the factory's Git repository.

2. After approval, the pull request is merged to the factory's collaboration branch, usually `main`.

3. Merging to `main` triggers an Azure DevOps pipeline.

4. The Azure DevOps pipeline downloads and installs Node.js and the Azure Data Factory Utilities npm package.

5. The Azure DevOps pipeline uses the npm package to validate factory resources and to generate an ARM template for deployment.

6. The Azure DevOps pipeline deploys the generated ARM template to the target environment, in the same way as your pipeline earlier in the chapter.

This approach eliminates the manual *Publish* step required earlier, triggering deployment from an action taken as part of the feature branch workflow instead. The removal of this step also avoids publishing resources unnecessarily to the development factory.

Publish Resources As JSON

Using ARM templates to automate Azure Data Factory CI/CD workflows is Microsoft's recommended approach but has the limitation that the factory is the only unit of deployment – you are unable to deploy subsets of factory resources. If you wish to deploy factory resources individually, you can do so by publishing resources directly from their JSON definitions. This approach integrates naturally into a feature branch workflow because no separate deployment artifact – such as an ARM template – is required.

Deploy ADF Pipelines Using PowerShell

Azure Data Factory resources can be created and deployed in a number of different ways. This book focuses on using the interactive ADF Studio environment, but in addition to supporting ARM templates, ADF provides a REST API and libraries for .NET, Python, the Azure CLI, and PowerShell. PowerShell is well supported in Azure DevOps pipelines, making it a convenient alternative tool for automated factory deployment.

In this section, you will build an Azure DevOps pipeline that deploys data factory pipelines to production when changes are made to the main branch, using PowerShell cmdlets from the Az.DataFactory module. Factory resources deployed using PowerShell, or other libraries or APIs, appear directly in the target factory's published environment – the debugging environment is a feature of ADF Studio alone.

A new, empty pipeline can be created directly using the Azure DevOps pipeline creation wizard.

1. In Azure DevOps, select the *Pipelines* item in the sidebar. Use the *New pipeline* button in the top right of the screen to create a new Azure DevOps pipeline.

2. As before, under *Where is your code?* select *Azure Repos Git,* then choose your factory's Git repository on the *Select* tab that follows.

3. On the *Configure* tab, select *Starter pipeline.* A new skeleton Azure DevOps pipeline file opens in the pipeline editor.

4. The Azure DevOps pipeline file path is displayed and can be edited immediately below the *Review your pipeline YAML* header. Change the default file name to "devops-pipelines/publish-json.yml".

5. Replace the entire contents of the pipeline editor window with the YAML code provided in Listing 10-4 (available in the book's GitHub repository).

6. The code in the listing uses the DevOps `AzurePowerShell@5` task to iterate over ADF pipeline JSON files, deploying each one using the Az.DataFactory PowerShell cmdlet `Set-AzDataFactoryV2Pipeline`. Configure the task, replacing the three placeholders in angle brackets with appropriate values as before.

7. Save the pipeline, providing an appropriate Git commit message
    and choosing the option *Commit directly to the main branch.*

8. Use ADF Studio to create or modify an ADF pipeline in your
    development factory, then verify that saving changes causes
    the Azure DevOps pipeline to run. Verify that your changes
    subsequently appear in your production data factory.

Listing 10-4. Deploy ADF pipelines using PowerShell in a DevOps pipeline

```
trigger:
  branches:
    include:
      - main
  paths:
    exclude:
      - /devops-pipelines
pool:
  vmImage: 'ubuntu-latest'
steps:
- task: AzurePowerShell@5
  inputs:
    azureSubscription: '<your-service-connection-name>'
    azurePowerShellVersion: latestVersion
    scriptType: inlineScript
    inline: |
      foreach($file in Get-ChildItem "data-factory-resources/pipeline") {
        Write-Host "Deploying $($file.Basename)"
        Set-AzDataFactoryV2Pipeline -Force `
          -ResourceGroupName "<your-resource-group-name>" `
          -DataFactoryName "<your-production-factory-name>" `
          -Name "$($file.Basename)" `
          -File "$($file.FullName)"
      }
```

Note   The purpose of this example is to illustrate that a change to main can trigger a deployment pipeline that requires no ARM templates to be generated. Deployment from main is convenient in a feature branch workflow but would be most undesirable in a workflow that allows data engineers to commit directly to the collaboration branch (in the way you have done here).

Resource Dependencies

The example of the previous section illustrates the deployment of ADF pipelines using PowerShell, but a full implementation needs also to manage the deployment of other resource types. A corresponding PowerShell Set-AzDataFactoryV2... cmdlet is available for each type of resource:

- **Set-AzDataFactoryV2IntegrationRuntime**: Deploy an integration runtime

- **Set-AzDataFactoryV2LinkedService**: Deploy a linked service

- **Set-AzDataFactoryV2Dataset**: Deploy a dataset

- **Set-AzDataFactoryV2DataFlow**: Deploy a data flow

- **Set-AzDataFactoryV2**: Deploy or update a data factory, including global parameters

Using cmdlets allows you to deploy all or a subset of factory resources as you prefer, but in either case, you must also account for dependencies between resources. For instance, attempting to deploy a dataset will fail if the linked service it uses does not already exist. The preceding Azure DevOps pipeline runs successfully because you deployed the entire factory earlier in the chapter – so resources required by each pipeline are already present.

You can avoid many dependency problems by deploying resource types in an order that respects common dependencies: linked services before datasets, for example, or datasets before pipelines. Resolving dependencies between resources of the same type is more complicated but can be achieved in a variety of different ways. A simple approach is to catch individual cmdlet failures and to retry them after other resources have been successfully deployed; a more sophisticated approach is to use the JSON `referenceName` attribute in resource definitions to identify other required resources, allowing you to deploy them in advance.

Tip   Neither the ARM template nor the JSON-based deployment approach supports deletion of removed resources. To identify resources for deletion, a comparison must be made between the set of JSON files in source control and the full list of factory resources in the published environment. Identified resources can be deleted individually using appropriate `Remove-AzDataFactoryV2...` cmdlet or REST API calls.

Chapter Review

This chapter introduced a variety of techniques for deploying developed factory resources into published factory environments, whether into the same (development) factory or into other factory instances.

- ADF resources are deployed from the development factory's collaboration branch into its published environment by clicking *Publish* in ADF Studio.

- Publishing to the development factory also generates corresponding ARM templates, saving them into the `adf_publish` branch of the factory's Git repository. These can be automatically deployed to other factories using an Azure DevOps pipeline triggered by changes to the publish branch.

- You can export ARM templates directly from ADF Studio, which allows you to create deployments from other Git branches or even from unsaved changes. ARM templates can be imported into a data factory directly, also using ADF Studio.

- The Azure Data Factory Utilities npm package can be used to create ARM templates from a factory's JSON resource definition files. This allows ARM template generation and deployment to be triggered from updates to any specified branch in the factory's Git repository.

- PowerShell cmdlets in the Az.DataFactory module enable per-resource deployment strategies to be adopted. The approach also allows deployment from any specified branch but is more complicated to manage. A range of information and open source projects supporting JSON-based deployments can be found on the Internet.

Key concepts introduced in this chapter include the following:

- **Azure Resource Manager (ARM) template:** An ARM template is a JSON file that defines components of an Azure solution, for example, the contents of an Azure Data Factory instance.

- **Publish:** To run a pipeline independently of ADF Studio, it must be deployed into a data factory's published environment. Published pipelines are executed using triggers (Chapter 11); published pipeline runs can be observed in the ADF Studio monitoring experience (Chapter 12).

- **Publish branch:** A nominated branch in a factory's Git repository, by default adf_publish. The publish branch contains ARM templates produced when publishing factory resources via ADF Studio.

- **Azure custom role:** A custom security role, built by assembling a required set of permissions, to provide security profiles not supported in the standard Azure role set.

- **Deployment parameters:** Specified in an ARM template, deployment parameters enable different values to be substituted at deployment time. In the case of ADF, this permits a single template to be used for deployments to multiple different data factories.

- **Parameterization template**: A development data factory's parameterization template specifies which factory resource properties should be made parameterizable using deployment parameters.

- **CI/CD:** Continuous integration and continuous delivery (CI/CD) is a development practice in which software changes are integrated into the main code base and deployed into production continuously.

- **Azure Pipelines:** Microsoft's cloud-based CI/CD pipeline service.

- **Data serialization language:** Human-readable language used to represent data structures in text for storage or transmission. XML, JSON, and YAML are examples of data serialization languages.

- **YAML:** Data serialization language with an indentation-based layout, used in Azure DevOps to define Azure DevOps pipelines. YAML pipeline files are stored under version control like any other code file.

- **Task:** Configurable process used in an Azure DevOps pipeline, for example, `script`, `AzureResourceManagerTemplateDeployment@3`, or `AzurePowerShell@5`.

- **Pipeline variable:** Variable defined for use in an Azure DevOps pipeline. Secret variables allow secret values to be referenced in pipeline YAML without storing them in version control.

- **Service connection:** Represents a nominated Microsoft Entra ID principal with the permissions required by an Azure DevOps pipeline.

- **Feature branch workflow:** A common Git workflow in which development work takes place in isolated feature branches.

- **Pull request:** A request to merge a feature branch back into the collaboration branch when feature development is complete.

- **Az.DataFactory:** PowerShell module providing cmdlets for interacting with Azure Data Factory.

CHAPTER 11

Triggers

In Chapter 10, you explored how to deploy Azure Data Factory resources into published factory environments. You tested running one or more published pipelines by executing them manually from ADF Studio – in this chapter, you will explore how pipelines can be executed automatically using *triggers*.

A trigger defines conditions for pipeline execution based either on defined dates and times or in response to specified external events. A trigger is associated with zero or more data factory pipelines. When the conditions for a trigger's execution are met, it runs. When the trigger runs, it starts an execution of each of its associated pipelines.

Time-Based Triggers

Azure Data Factory defines two kinds of trigger based on date and time. A *schedule trigger* runs at configured dates and times, while a *tumbling window trigger* extends the interpretation of a schedule to make use of the interval between successive scheduled executions.

Use a Schedule Trigger

In this section, you will create and use a schedule trigger to run pipelines at configured dates and times.

© Richard Swinbank 2024
R. Swinbank, *Azure Data Factory by Example*, https://doi.org/10.1007/979-8-8688-0218-8_11

Create a Schedule Trigger

Triggers can be created and linked to pipelines in the ADF Studio authoring canvas. Create a trigger for your Chapter 4 pipeline "ImportSweetTreatsSales_Audit" as follows:

1. Open the pipeline in the ADF Studio authoring canvas.

2. Expand the *Add trigger* dropdown above the design surface and select *New/Edit*. The *Add triggers* flyout appears.

3. Open the *Choose trigger...* dropdown and click + *New* to open the *New trigger* flyout.

4. Name the new trigger "RunEvery2Minutes" and ensure its *Type* is set to "Schedule." Set *Time zone* to your local time zone. *Start date* is prepopulated with the current UTC time – the default value does not change as you adjust your time zone, so amend it if necessary.

Tip   UTC times are used throughout the Azure cloud, but a schedule in your local time zone is easier to read. Applying a local time zone to a schedule causes ADF automatically to adjust trigger start times to align with daylight savings, where applicable.

---

5. Set *Recurrence* to "Every 2 Minute(s)" and ensure that the *Start trigger on creation* check box is ticked – Figure 11-1 shows the completed flyout. Click *OK* to continue.

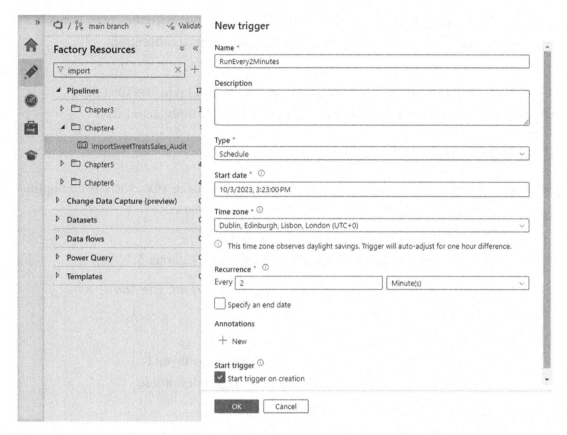

Figure 11-1. *New schedule trigger configuration*

6. The *New trigger* flyout offers you the opportunity to set pipeline
    parameter values (although this pipeline has no parameters)
    and reminds you that the trigger must be published to take
    effect. Click *Save* – this commits your changes to Git but does not
    publish them.

A schedule trigger runs for the first time at *Start date*, then again after each time
the interval specified in *Recurrence* has elapsed. If the trigger's start date is in the past
when the trigger is published, the first execution will take place at the next scheduled
recurrence. This means that *Start date* serves two purposes:

- It defines a date and time before which the trigger is not executed.
  Choosing to *Specify an end date* allows you similarly to configure a
  date and time after which the trigger will no longer run.

- It provides a base date and time that, in combination with the recurrence interval, determines the date and time of subsequent executions.

For example, to schedule a trigger to execute nightly at 11 p.m., set the time component of its start date to 11 p.m. and set its recurrence interval to 1 day.

Reuse a Trigger

Schedule triggers can be reused by multiple pipelines. In this section, you will configure another pipeline to make use of the "RunEvery2Minutes" trigger.

1. In the ADF Studio authoring canvas, open the "ImportSTFormatFolder" pipeline you created in Chapter 5.

2. Expand the *Add trigger* dropdown and click *New/Edit*. The *Add triggers* flyout appears.

3. Open the *Choose trigger...* dropdown and select "RunEvery2Minutes" from the list. The *Edit trigger* flyout is displayed. Click *OK* to accept the existing trigger definition.

4. This pipeline requires values for two parameters: "WildcardFolderPath" and "WildcardFileName." Provide the values "azure-data-factory-by-example-main/SampleData/ Desserts4All" and "*.csv", then click *Save*.

Whenever it runs, the "RunEvery2Minutes" trigger will now start two pipeline executions, one for each linked pipeline.

Inspect Trigger Definitions

You can inspect all of a factory's trigger definitions in one place using ADF Studio's management hub.

1. Open the management hub and select the *Triggers* page. The page contains a list of defined triggers, including the "RunEvery2Minutes" trigger you defined in the previous section, as shown in Figure 11-2. The number "2" in the list's *Related* column indicates that the trigger is linked to two pipelines.

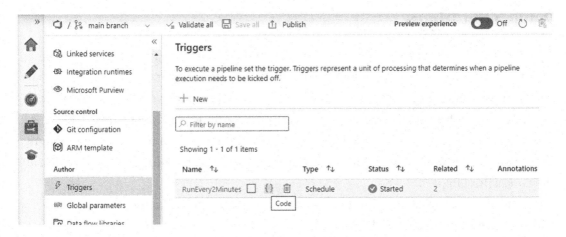

Figure 11-2. *Inspect triggers in ADF Studio's management hub*

2. Hover over the trigger name to reveal additional controls. Changes to trigger definitions made using any of the three buttons are committed to Git immediately (without you explicitly choosing to save changes). Click the central *Code* button (braces icon) to inspect the trigger's JSON definition.

3. The trigger definition includes a `pipelines` property: this is a JSON array that identifies the two pipelines linked to the trigger, including any parameter values to be used at runtime. The `runtimeState` property value is "Started" – this is because the *Start trigger on creation* check box was ticked when you created the trigger.

4. Click *Cancel* to close the code window.

As with other resources in a Git-enabled data factory, information displayed here is consistent with the contents of your working branch, not with the published factory environment. In particular, the value displayed in the *Status* column does not indicate that the trigger is running in the published environment – "Started" is simply the value of the `runtimeState` property saved in Git.

You can create new triggers directly in the management hub, using the *+ New* button at the top of the page to open the *New trigger* flyout. This approach creates a trigger in isolation, with no linked pipelines – to link a pipeline, you must add the trigger to the pipeline using the ADF Studio authoring canvas.

Publish the Trigger

To bring the "RunEvery2Minutes" trigger into effect, it must be deployed into a published factory environment. For convenience, you will publish the trigger to your development factory. If the ARM template deployment Azure DevOps pipeline you built in Chapter 10 is still active, the trigger will also be deployed to your production data factory – this will not cause a problem in this case, because triggers created by ARM template deployments are not started automatically. More information about trigger deployment is provided at the end of this chapter.

Publish the trigger in the same way that you published other factory resources, by clicking *Publish* in the factory header bar.

Monitor Trigger Runs

After publishing the trigger to your development data factory, executions begin to take place automatically. Trigger runs, like published pipeline runs, can be monitored in the ADF Studio monitoring experience.

- The *Trigger runs* page contains one record per trigger execution (irrespective of the number of pipeline executions started by the trigger).

- The *Pipeline runs* page contains records of individual pipeline runs and indicates the way in which each was triggered.

Figures 11-3 and 11-4 show the *Trigger runs* and *Pipeline runs* pages a few minutes after deploying the "RunEvery2Minutes" trigger.

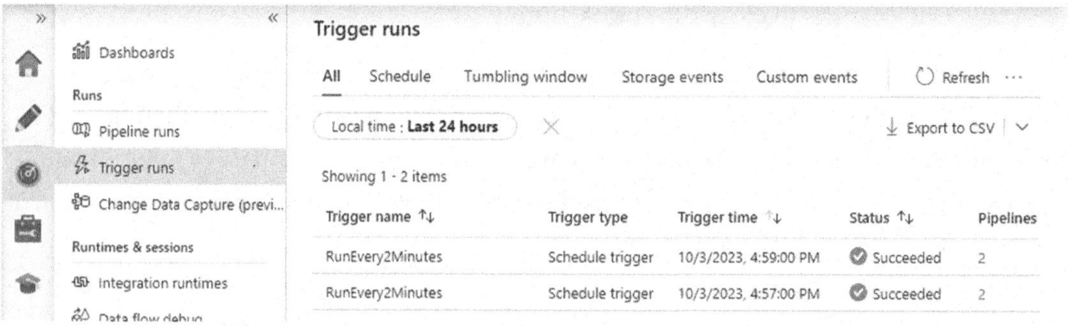

Figure 11-3. *Runs of the RunEvery2Minutes trigger*

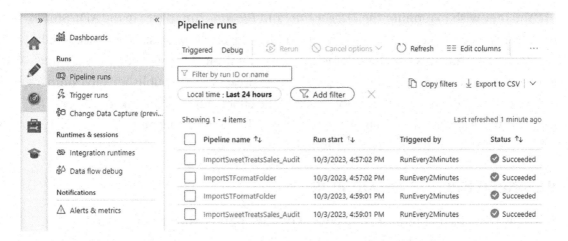

Figure 11-4. *Pipeline runs started by the RunEvery2Minutes trigger*

The trigger's configured start time and recurrence interval (as shown in Figure 11-1) define executions at 3:23 p.m., 3:25 p.m., 3:27 p.m., 3:29 p.m., and so on – its first execution at 4:57 p.m. indicates that the trigger was not published until after 4:55 p.m. Figure 11-4 shows that two pipeline runs were started by each trigger run, one for each of the trigger's two linked pipelines. The pipeline runs identify "RunEvery2Minutes" as the trigger that started each one.

Caution   When starting a pipeline run, a schedule trigger takes no account of whether or not the scheduled pipeline is currently running – it simply starts a new execution, overlapping any pipeline run still in progress.

Stop the Trigger

As the "RunEvery2Minutes" trigger has no configured end date, it will continue to run indefinitely, every two minutes. Stop the trigger to avoid incurring unnecessary pipeline execution costs.

1. Open the *Triggers* page in the ADF Studio management hub.

2. Hover over the "RunEvery2Minutes" trigger name, then click the *Stop* (square icon) button that appears. This changes the trigger's configured runtime status and saves the revised definition to Git.

3. Publish your changes to stop the published trigger.

You may wish to monitor the *Trigger runs* and *Pipeline runs* pages in the ADF Studio monitoring experience, to assure yourself that the trigger has been stopped successfully.

Remember that in a nondevelopment environment (not Git enabled), the resource definitions shown in ADF Studio are always those present in the published environment. Changes to triggers must still be published to take effect, but with no linked Git repository, the status reported in the management hub for a published trigger is its true runtime status in the published environment.

Advanced Recurrence Options

Schedule triggers offer more advanced scheduling options when the frequency of recurrence is given in days, weeks, or months. These enable you to specify execution times explicitly, instead of implying them using a recurrence pattern. Using a frequency specified in weeks or months additionally permits you to nominate specific days of the week or month, respectively. Figure 11-5 shows a schedule trigger configured to run at 9:30 a.m. and 5:30 p.m. every Monday, Wednesday, and Friday. The *Hours* and *Minutes* fields are used to specify the execution times of day, which ADF Studio then presents as an easy-to-read list of resulting *Schedule execution times*.

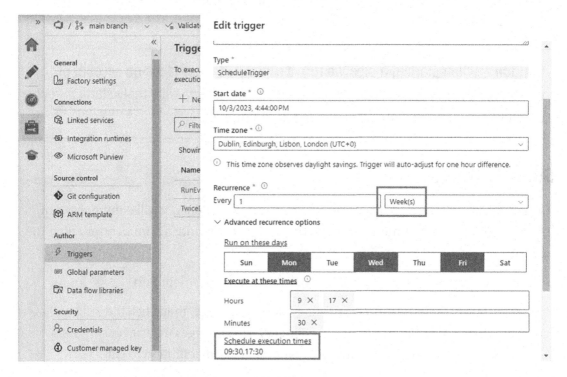

Figure 11-5. *Schedule trigger using weekly recurrence pattern*

In the same way that a single schedule trigger can be used by multiple pipelines, so a single pipeline can use multiple schedule triggers. Composing multiple triggers enables you to implement execution schedules that cannot be expressed in a single trigger. For example, no combination of hours and minutes in Figure 11-5 would cause executions at 9:15 a.m. and 5:45 p.m., but the effect can be achieved using two triggers, one for each execution start time.

For SSIS developers   In on-premises SQL Server installations, time-based scheduling of SSIS package execution is commonly achieved using the SQL Server Agent. The advanced recurrence options offered by Azure Data Factory schedule triggers offer a similar degree of scheduling flexibility.

Use a Tumbling Window Trigger

Like a schedule trigger, a *tumbling window trigger* runs at configured dates and times, but it also makes explicit the interval between successive executions. A tumbling window trigger can pass its associated interval start and end times as pipeline parameter values, allowing data processing to be time sliced.

Tumbling window triggers are based on the same simple recurrence pattern used by schedule triggers – a start date and time paired with a recurrence interval. The result is a sequence of execution times formed by adding one or more recurrence intervals to the start date and time. Using the recurrence pattern from Figure 11-1, a tumbling window series begins like this:

- 3:23 p.m. + **1** * 2 minutes = 3:25 p.m.

- 3:23 p.m. + **2** * 2 minutes = 3:27 p.m.

- 3:23 p.m. + **3** * 2 minutes = 3:29 p.m. and so on

The effect of this is to create an infinite sequence of time slices or "windows" – periods between one execution time and the next – "tumbling" over one another as each window ends and the next begins.

Prepare Data

To enable you to examine tumbling window behavior, in this section, you will create some new data files alongside existing sample data.

1. Use the Azure portal's Storage browser to access your "sampledata" container. Navigate to the "HandyCandy" subdirectory of the "SampleData" folder, used in Chapter 3.

2. The "HandyCandy" folder contains a subdirectory called "Subset1" – it contains a small subset of the Handy Candy message files and another subdirectory, called "Subset2." Open the "Subset2" folder.

3. "Subset2" also contains a few Handy Candy message files. Copy some of these into the (parent) "Subset1" folder. To copy a file using the Storage browser, select it using the check box to the left of its name – as shown in Figure 11-6 – then click *Copy* (indicated in the figure). Navigate back to the parent folder and select *Paste*.

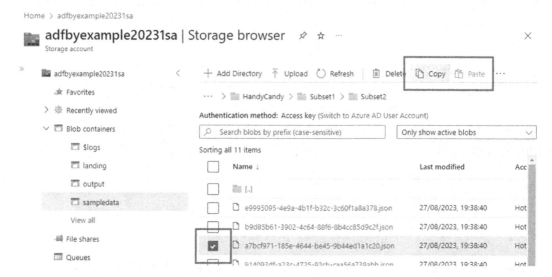

Figure 11-6. *Copying files in the Azure portal using the Storage browser*

When you have finished copying files, the folder "Subset1" will contain two groups of files:

- Files created when you loaded the sample data into your storage account, with a corresponding last modified date and time

- Files created when you copied them from the "Subset2" folder, with more recent modification times

Create a Windowed Copy Pipeline

Tumbling window triggers define a sequence of processing windows. In this section, you will create a pipeline able to use and respect window boundaries.

1. In ADF Studio, create a clone of the pipeline "IngestHandyCandyMessages" from Chapter 3. Rename it to "IngestHandyCandyWindow" and move it into a new "Chapter11" pipelines folder.

2. Define two pipeline parameters for the new pipeline, of type String, called "WindowStart" and "WindowEnd."

3. Select the pipeline's Copy activity and open its *Source* configuration tab. Edit the *Wildcard paths* folder path field, appending the "Subset1" path segment.

4. To the right of *Filter by last modified*, update the *Start time (UTC)* and *End time (UTC)* fields to use the values of pipeline parameters "WindowStart" and "WindowEnd." To avoid loading the "Subset2" files twice (the originals and the copies), untick the *Recursively* check box. Figure 11-7 shows the correctly configured *Source* tab.

5. Run the pipeline in debug mode. ADF Studio will prompt you to supply values for the two pipeline parameters – set *WindowStart* to "2021-01-01". Choose a value for *WindowEnd* that falls after the modification time of the oldest files in the "Subset1" folder, but before the modification time of the newest.

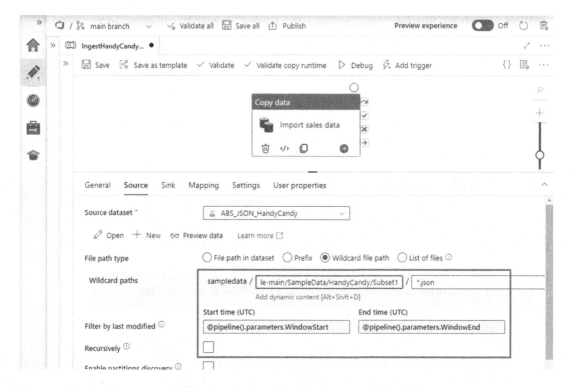

Figure 11-7. Source tab filtering input files by last modified time

6. Click *OK* to run the pipeline. When the pipeline has finished executing, use the Copy activity output to verify that the expected number of files has been copied – it should match the number of files in the folder "Subset1" having modification timestamps between the specified *WindowStart* and *WindowEnd* values.

The pipeline you have created can now be used to load arbitrary subsets of files, based on their last modified date and time.

Create a Tumbling Window Trigger

The pipeline you created in the previous section is suitable for use with a tumbling window trigger. In this section, you will create and configure that trigger.

1. Above the design surface for the "IngestHandyCandyWindow" pipeline, use the *Add trigger* dropdown to access the *Add triggers* flyout, then select the *+ New* option from the *Choose trigger…* dropdown.

2. Name the trigger "RunHandyCandyWindow" and select the value "Tumbling window" from the *Type* dropdown. Choose a *Start Date (UTC)* value that falls before the earliest file modification time in the "Subset1" folder.

3. Specify a *Recurrence* interval. For this example, try to find a value that defines several windows, but not so many that very few contain modified files. Click *OK* to continue.

4. The *New trigger* flyout now prompts for pipeline parameter values. Set *WindowStart* to "@triggerOutputs().windowStartTime" and *WindowEnd* to "@triggerOutputs().windowEndTime".

Note   `@triggerOutputs()` is an ADF pipeline expression, but pipeline parameter fields on the *New trigger* flyout are not linked to the pipeline expression builder. You can use any feature of the pipeline expression language here, but you are unable to access the clickable functions list or to benefit from expression validation.

---

5. Click *Save* to save your changes and close the flyout, then click *Publish* to deploy both the new pipeline and the trigger to the development factory's published environment.

Tumbling window triggers are associated with a single pipeline and cannot be reused. If you try to add an existing trigger to a different pipeline, you will notice that the "RunHandyCandyWindow" trigger is not available for selection.

Monitor Trigger Runs

After a tumbling window trigger is published, trigger and pipeline runs begin as follows:

-   Runs for windows whose end time has already passed begin immediately. Up to 50 trigger runs can take place concurrently – remaining runs are queued until others have finished executing.

-   Runs for future windows start automatically when their window end time is reached.

Verify that trigger runs take place as you expect – the *Tumbling window* tab of the monitoring experience's *Trigger runs* page offers a convenient view showing window start and end times. Figure 11-8 shows five runs of a trigger with the following features:

- The trigger's *Start date (UTC)* was set to 1 p.m., with a recurrence interval of one hour.

- The trigger was deployed to the published environment shortly after 4:20 p.m. on the trigger's start date.

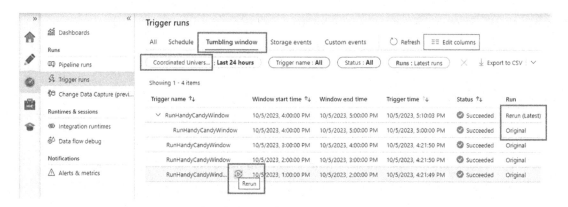

Figure 11-8. *Tumbling trigger runs*

Three trigger runs took place immediately after it was published, at the same *Trigger time,* for the finished windows 1–2 p.m., 2–3 p.m., and 3–4 p.m. A fourth run took place at 5 p.m., as scheduled, at the end of the 4–5 p.m. window.

Tip The functions @triggerOutputs().windowStartTime and @triggerOutputs(). windowEndTime return UTC times, but by default the ADF Studio monitoring hub displays times in your local time zone. You may wish to change the display time zone to UTC – as indicated in Figure 11-8 – to avoid confusion.

The latest trigger run is a rerun of the 4–5 p.m. window, invoked by clicking the *Rerun* button (indicated in the screenshot for the 1–2 p.m. window). The original run for the 4–5 p.m. window is nested beneath the rerun. This illustrates a key use case for tumbling window triggers – the ability to rerun pipelines for a specific time slice after failure, for example, or to incorporate late-arriving data.

Inspect the pipeline runs invoked by your tumbling window trigger using the monitoring experience's *Pipeline runs* page – you should observe one pipeline run corresponding to each trigger run. The *Parameters* column contains an @ symbol in square brackets – click it to inspect the parameter values passed to the pipeline by the trigger (indicated in Figure 11-9).

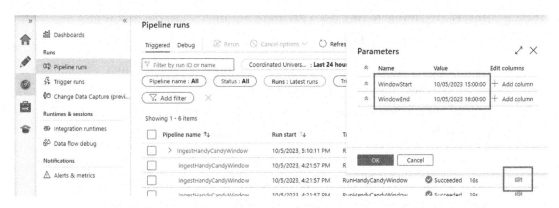

Figure 11-9. *Pipeline runs started by a tumbling window trigger, showing window start and end times passed as parameter values*

Finally, use the Copy activity output to verify that the expected files were loaded in each run. The original "Subset1" files are loaded by the pipeline run corresponding to the window during which they were created. The copied "Subset2" files fall into a later window and are loaded by the corresponding run. Any additional pipeline runs should have loaded no files. Tumbling window triggers' simple recurrence pattern means that they continue to run indefinitely until stopped – remember to stop the trigger and to publish that change.

Advanced Features

Unlike a schedule trigger, a tumbling window trigger runs for every window end time defined by its recurrence pattern, even those in the past. Combining this behavior with window start and end times – passing them as pipeline parameter values using the functions `@triggerOutputs().windowStartTime` and `@triggerOutputs().windowEndTime` – enables time-sliced processing. This provides the ability to rerun selected slices on demand or to break large legacy data loads into smaller, time-bound pieces.

Tumbling window triggers support additional advanced features such as start time offsets, retry policies, and trigger dependencies. Advanced features are configured in the *Advanced* section of the *New trigger* or *Edit trigger* flyout:

- By default, trigger runs for future windows take place at each window's end time – a nonzero *Delay* value allows you to postpone this. For example, to process a 24-hour, midnight-based window at 3 a.m., use a delay of 3 hours.

- *Max concurrency* controls the maximum number of trigger runs allowed to occur in parallel, 50 by default. You cannot increase the number above 50, but you can lower it if necessary, for example, to control the load on a source system from which multiple windows of data are being extracted.

- *Retry policy* attributes allow you to specify trigger behavior when the executed pipeline fails with a "retryable" error – for example, an intermittent error related to service conditions outside your control. You can specify the number of times a failing pipeline should be retried before abandoning it and how long ADF should wait before retrying a failed execution.

- *Trigger dependencies* permit you to link tumbling windows together, from the same or different tumbling window triggers. A dependency identifies a trigger, an offset, and a size – specifying that trigger T2 is dependent on T1 with an offset of zero means that (for example) T2's 1–2 p.m. window trigger run will not start until the pipelines executed by T1's 1–2 p.m. window have completed.

A tumbling window trigger *self-dependency* can be used to ensure that successive windows are processed in order or to prevent a new pipeline run from beginning while a prior run is in progress. If ensuring that scheduled runs do not overlap is important to you, tumbling window trigger self-dependencies may be of use.

Event-Based Triggers

Azure Event Grid is a managed publish-subscribe messaging service. Systems or services that need to notify others of events do so by *publishing* messages to an Event Grid *topic*; systems wishing to receive those messages do so by *subscribing* to the topic. Event Grid topics provided by Azure services are referred to as *system topics*; you may also create *custom topics* of your own.

Azure Data Factory event-based triggers are Event Grid topic subscribers native to ADF. *Custom event triggers* allow you to define tailored subscriptions to custom topics, managed by ADF. *Storage event triggers* provide a simplified means of subscribing to file creation and deletion events published to blob storage system topics.

Figure 11-10 illustrates this arrangement. An event-based trigger runs when it receives an event from the topic to which it subscribes. Like schedule triggers, an event-based trigger is associated with one or more ADF pipelines – when the event-based trigger runs, it executes the pipeline(s) to which it is linked.

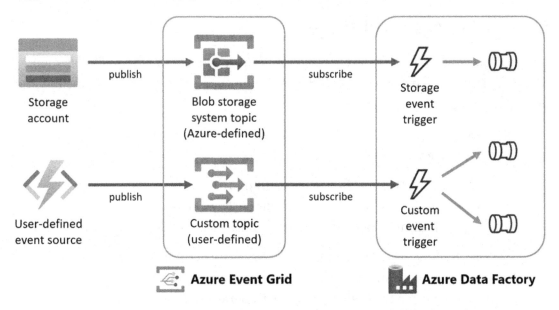

Figure 11-10. *ADF event-based triggers subscribe to Azure Event Grid topics*

Register the Event Grid Resource Provider

In order to use ADF event-based triggers, the Microsoft.EventGrid resource provider must be registered to your Azure subscription. Ensure that the provider is registered to your subscription in the Azure portal, in the same way that you registered the Microsoft.Network resource provider in Chapter 8.

Use a Storage Event Trigger

Azure Data Factory *storage event triggers* are simplified blob storage system topic subscribers. A storage event trigger specifies a storage account, a blob file path pattern, and a file creation or deletion event (or both). When a corresponding blob storage event occurs, the trigger executes the pipeline(s) to which it is linked. In this section, you will create and use a storage event trigger to run a pipeline whenever a file is created in a given blob storage location.

Create a Storage Event Trigger

A typical use case for a storage event trigger is to run a pipeline to process files as soon as they arrive in blob storage. Create a trigger for the "ImportSTFormatFile" pipeline you created in Chapter 6, as follows:

1. Open the pipeline in the ADF Studio authoring canvas and use the *Add trigger* dropdown to create a new trigger.

2. Name the new trigger "RunSTFormatImport" and set its *Type* to "Storage events." The set of fields in the flyout changes automatically to allow you to specify storage account details.

3. Use *Account selection method* "From Azure subscription," then select your blob storage account from the *Storage account name* dropdown. Use the *Container* name dropdown to choose your "sampledata" container.

4. In the *Blob path begins with* field, enter "azure-data-factory-by-example-main/SampleData/JustOneMore/SalesData/", then set *Blob path ends with* to ".txt".

Note File or folder path wildcards are not supported here – entering "*.txt" will match no files.

This sample data folder contains sales data relating to another confectionery retailer named "Just One More." This retailer also uses the Sweet Treats sales data format.

5.   Under *Event*, tick the "Blob created" check box – Figure 11-11 shows the correctly completed flyout. Click *Continue*.

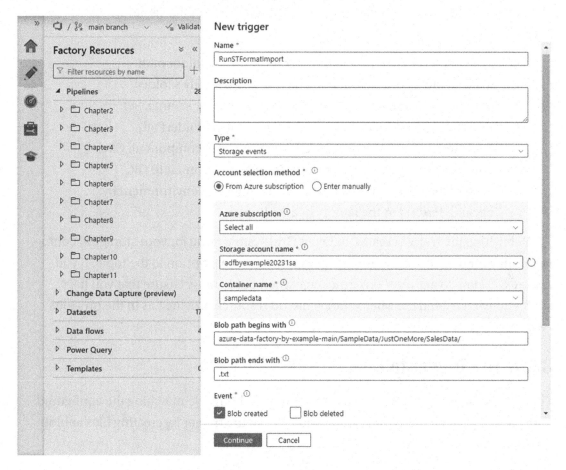

Figure 11-11. *New event-based trigger configuration*

6. The *Data preview* flyout opens, allowing you to check your blob path pattern against any existing files that match. If you have entered the path pattern correctly, a single file called "Apr-2020.txt" will be matched. Click *Continue*.

7. The *New trigger* flyout now offers you the opportunity to set pipeline parameter values. This pipeline uses two parameters: the file and folder name of the Sweet Treats format file to be loaded. The values to be used here identify the file whose creation causes the trigger to run. Enter the value "@triggerBody().fileName" in the *File* parameter value field.

8. The pipeline's *Directory* parameter represents a folder path inside a blob storage container, but the trigger body's folder path property includes the blob storage container's name. Set the parameter value to "@replace(triggerBody().folderPath, 'sampledata/', '')", removing the container name component. Click *Save* to create the new trigger definition and commit it to Git. Deploy the new trigger to the factory's published environment by clicking *Publish* in the factory header bar.

Publishing the trigger creates an Event Grid system topic for your storage account – visible in your data factory's resource group – and a subscription to the topic. If you receive a "Failed to activate" error message when publishing, ensure that you have successfully registered the Microsoft.EventGrid resource provider, as in the previous section.

Cause the Trigger to Run

The event-based trigger you have created will run when a file matching the configured path pattern is created. In this section, you will run the trigger by creating files in blob storage.

1. Open the Storage browser in the Azure portal and navigate to your "sampledata" container. Browse to the "JustOneMore" subdirectory of the "SampleData" folder.

2.   The "JustOneMore" folder contains two subdirectories: "TestData" and "SalesData." Open the "TestData" folder, then use the *Download* button to copy a few of the files to your computer.

3.   Navigate to the "SalesData" folder. It already contains one file – use the *Upload* button to upload one of the files you downloaded in step 2.

4.   Return to ADF Studio and open the monitoring experience's *Trigger runs* page. Verify that the "RunSTFormatImport" trigger has just executed (you may need to refresh the page). Notice that its *Trigger type* is "Storage events trigger."

5.   Open the *Pipeline runs* page, verifying that it reports a run of the pipeline "ImportSTFormatFile" triggered by "RunSTFormatImport." Inspect the pipeline run's parameter values to verify that the path and name of the file you uploaded were passed to the pipeline.

6.   Repeat steps 3–5 for other files if you wish.

Like a schedule trigger, a storage event trigger can be reused across multiple pipelines, and a pipeline can use a combination of multiple storage event and schedule triggers. In practice, the reuse of storage event triggers is less common, simply because files in a particular blob storage location usually require the specific processing activity implemented in an associated pipeline.

A separate event is published to a storage account's Event Grid system topic every time a file is created, so uploading multiple files causes multiple file creation events. This in turn will cause a storage event trigger to run several times, once for each file created. This behavior is exactly what is required to process each new file individually, but you must ensure that your pipelines will run safely when multiple runs are triggered simultaneously.

About Trigger-Scoped System Variables

In the same way that system variables that begin with @pipeline() can only be used in the scope of an ADF pipeline, so @trigger() system variables are available only within trigger definitions. Different trigger types support different system variables:

- Schedule triggers support `@trigger().scheduledTime` (the time at which a trigger was scheduled to run) and `@trigger().startTime` (the time at which it actually started). Dates and times returned by system variables are in UTC, irrespective of the time zone used to schedule the trigger.

- Tumbling window triggers support the same variables as schedule triggers, along with `@triggerOutputs().windowStartTime` and `@triggerOutputs().windowEndTime`. The `@triggerOutputs()` function is shorthand for `@trigger().outputs`.

- Storage event triggers also support `@trigger().startTime`, in addition to `@triggerBody().folderName` and `@triggerBody().fileName`. `@triggerBody()` is equivalent to `@trigger().outputs.body`.

Trigger-scoped system variable expressions originate from the *Workflow Definition Language* of *Azure Logic Apps*, the technology used to implement ADF triggers.

Understand Custom Event Triggers

Azure Data Factory permits you to invoke pipeline runs in response to events of your own definition, using a *custom event trigger*. A custom event trigger requires first that you implement a custom topic in Azure Event Grid, to which other services publish events – you may then create a custom event trigger that subscribes to that topic.

Azure Event Grid defines a common *event schema* to be used by event publishers, including properties such as the event's subject and type, along with other event-specific data. Figure 11-12 shows a blob storage event JSON payload received by a storage event trigger (with long lines truncated for readability). Storage event triggers are coupled to the schema of a blob storage event and automatically filter event types based on your "Blob created" and "Blob deleted" selections.

```
{
    "topic": "/subscriptions/6bd2daaf-42fa-4cf4-a2e3-5f6cale5f6c6/resourceGrou
    "subject": "/blobServices/default/containers/sampledata/blobs/azure-data-f
    "eventType": "Microsoft.Storage.BlobCreated",
    "id": "8a0649b5-501e-0022-7199-f7219306507e",
    "data": {
        "api": "PutBlob",
        "clientRequestId": "fa094454-b56a-47b2-974a-776fe7ff5033",
        "requestId": "8a0649b5-501e-0022-7199-f72193000000",
        "eTag": "0x8DBC5B087FC0559",
        "contentType": "text/plain",
        "contentLength": 7244,
        "blobType": "BlockBlob",
        "url": "https://adfbyexample20231sa.blob.core.windows.net/sampledata/a
        "sequencer": "00000000000000000000000000000C5870000000000002923d",
        "storageDiagnostics": {
            "batchId": "181d3bfb-b006-0077-0099-f73118000000"
        }
    },
    "dataVersion": "",
    "metadataVersion": "1",
    "eventTime": "2023-10-05T14:36:58.9413721Z"
}
```

Figure 11-12. *Sample blob storage event JSON payload*

As you might expect, configuration of a custom event trigger is more complex than that of a storage event trigger. When implementing a custom event trigger, you must specify your own rules for filtering events by subject, type, or other data values, to ensure that the trigger only runs in response to relevant events. Figure 11-13 shows the *New trigger* flyout during the creation of a custom event trigger.

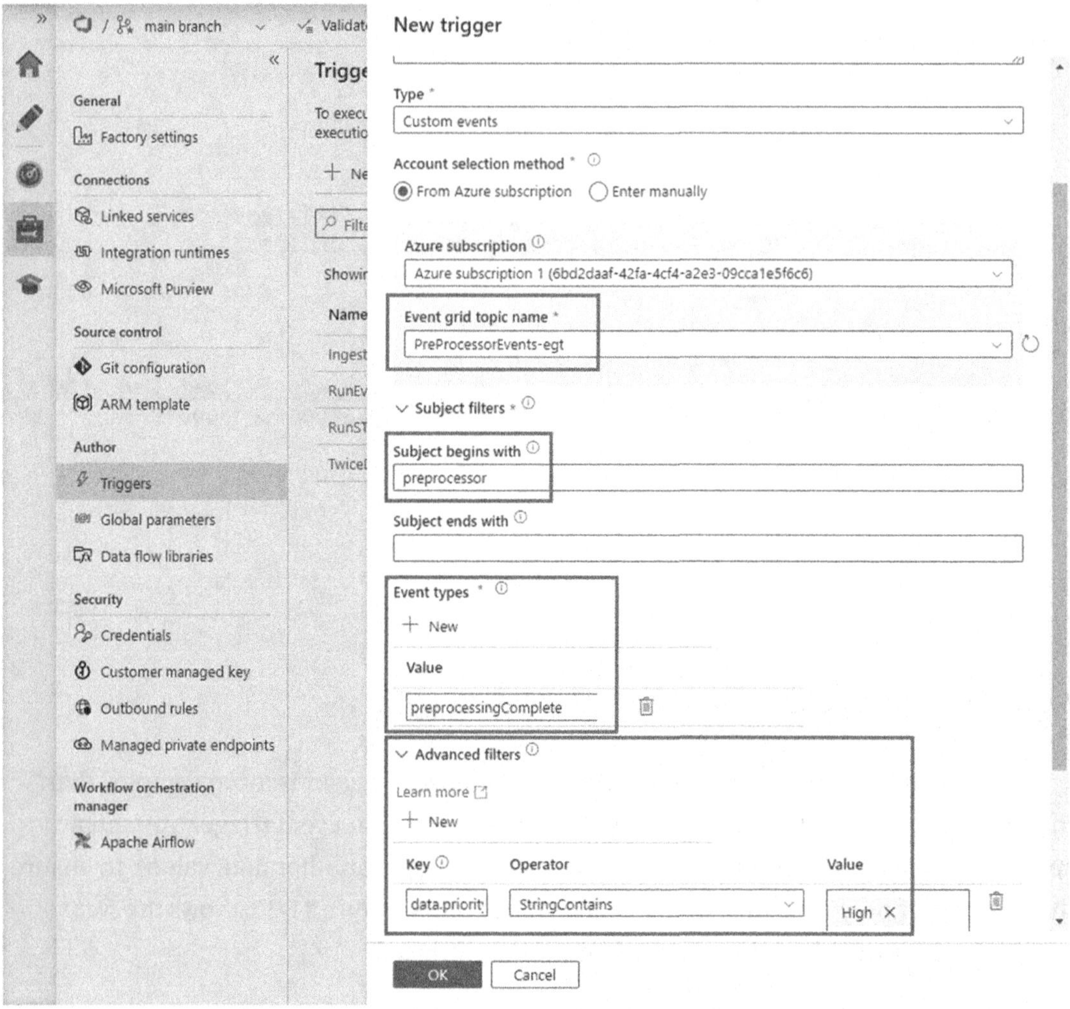

Figure 11-13. *Creation of a new custom event trigger*

After creation, the trigger will run under the following conditions:

- An event is published to the "PreProcessorEvents-egt" custom Event Grid topic.

- The event's subject begins "preprocessor".

- The event's type is "preprocessingComplete".

- The "priority" field of the event's "data" property contains the value "High".

As in the case of other triggers, when the custom event trigger runs, it will cause all associated pipelines to begin execution.

Triggering Pipelines from Outside ADF

You saw in Chapter 10 that it is possible to run a published pipeline without using an ADF trigger, by triggering a pipeline manually from ADF Studio. You can trigger pipelines in the published environment from outside the Azure Data Factory service using a variety of different technologies, for example:

- The `Invoke-AzDataFactoryV2Pipeline` cmdlet can be used to start a pipeline from PowerShell.

- The .NET API is a convenient way to start pipeline runs from a .NET application (e.g., an Azure Function).

- ADF's REST API permits you to start a pipeline run by calling an HTTP endpoint.

ADF's Execute Pipeline activity is limited to starting a fixed, named pipeline from within the same factory – using the Web activity to call the REST API enables you to parameterize pipeline names and to call pipelines in other factory instances.

Managing Triggers in Automated Deployments

Like other Azure Data Factory resources, trigger definitions are stored as JSON files in your Git repository (in the "trigger" folder of your ADF root folder) and included automatically in ARM templates for publishing. However, if the deployment process attempts to update an active trigger, the deployment may fail. To avoid this contingency during automated deployments, include tasks in your Azure DevOps pipeline to stop existing triggers prior to deployment and to restart them afterward.

This can be achieved using the Azure PowerShell task (`AzurePowerShell@5`) with three trigger-related cmdlets:

- Use `Get-AzDataFactoryV2Trigger` to list and identify active triggers in the deployment target factory.

- Use `Stop-AzDataFactoryV2Trigger` to stop active triggers prior to deployment.

- Use `Start-AzDataFactoryV2Trigger` to restart active triggers when deployment is complete.

This approach is equally applicable to deployments made using ARM templates or individual JSON resource definitions. To create or update a published trigger from its JSON definition, use the `Set-AzDataFactoryV2Trigger` cmdlet.

When an ARM template deployment creates a new trigger, its runtime state is always "Stopped," even if its JSON definition in Git indicates that it is to be started. New triggers must be started explicitly – a postdeployment step using `Start-AzDataFactoryV2Trigger` is useful in this scenario. In contrast, a deployed trigger's runtime state after a direct JSON-based deployment is always as specified in the deployed JSON definition.

Chapter Review

This chapter introduced the four types of ADF trigger resource: schedule, tumbling window, storage event, and custom event triggers.

- Schedule triggers execute pipelines on a wall clock schedule.

- Tumbling window triggers add advanced behaviors, extending the idea of recurring schedule to define a sequence of processing windows.

- Storage event triggers execute pipelines when a file is created or deleted in Azure blob storage.

- Custom event triggers execute pipelines when a configured event is published to an associated Event Grid custom topic.

In addition to using an ADF trigger resource, pipelines can be triggered directly from ADF Studio or using a variety of programmatic routes into ADF.

Key Concepts

Key concepts introduced in this chapter include the following:

- **Trigger:** A unit of processing that runs one or more ADF pipelines when certain execution conditions are met. A pipeline can be associated with – and run by – more than one trigger.

- **Trigger run:** A single execution of a trigger. If the trigger is associated with multiple pipelines, one trigger run starts multiple pipeline runs. The ADF Studio monitoring experience reports trigger and pipeline runs separately.

- **Trigger start date:** The date and time from which a trigger is active.

- **Trigger end date:** The date and time after which a trigger is no longer active.

- **Time-based trigger:** A trigger that runs according to a wall clock schedule. Schedule and tumbling window triggers are time based.

- **Recurrence pattern:** A simple scheduling model, used by time-based triggers and defined by a repeated interval after a given start date and time.

- **Schedule trigger:** A time-based trigger whose execution condition is defined by a recurrence pattern based on the trigger's start date or using a wall clock schedule.

- **Tumbling window trigger:** A time-based trigger that uses a recurrence pattern based on the trigger's start date to define a sequence of processing windows between successive executions. Tumbling window triggers also support more advanced scheduling behaviors like dependencies, concurrency limits, and retries.

- **Pipeline run overlap:** Pipeline runs may overlap if a trigger starts a new pipeline run before a previous one has finished. Use a tumbling window self-dependency with a concurrency limit of one to prevent collisions between scheduled pipeline runs.

- **Azure Event Grid:** Cloud service providing publish-subscribe messaging infrastructure for event-driven architectures. Azure blob storage uses Event Grid to publish file creation and other events; ADF subscribes to Event Grid topics to consume events and run event-based triggers.

- **Event-based trigger:** A trigger that runs on receipt of an event from Azure Event Grid. Storage event triggers and custom event triggers are event based.

- **Storage event trigger:** An event-based trigger whose execution condition is the creation or deletion of a file in Azure blob storage.

- **Custom event trigger:** An event-based trigger that runs when an event is published to an Azure Event Grid custom topic to which the trigger subscribes.

- **Event schema:** Set of properties required by Azure Event Grid in an event JSON payload.

- **Reusable triggers:** A single schedule or event-based trigger can be used by multiple pipelines. A tumbling window trigger can be used by only one pipeline.

- **Trigger-scoped system variables**: ADF system variables available for use in trigger definitions. Some trigger-scoped variables are specific to the type of ADF trigger in use.

- **Azure Logic Apps:** Cloud service for general-purpose task scheduling, orchestration, and automation. Internally, ADF triggers are implemented using Azure Logic Apps.

- **Trigger publishing:** Triggers do not operate in ADF Studio's debugging environment and must be published to a factory instance to have any effect.

For SSIS Developers

Users of SQL Server Integration Services will be used to scheduling SSIS packages for time-based execution using the SQL Server Agent. The advanced scheduling options supported by ADF's schedule trigger provide a similar experience.

When the time for a new job execution is reached, the SQL Server Agent only starts the job if it is not already running. This is not the case when using an ADF schedule trigger. To achieve the effect in Azure Data Factory, use a self-dependent tumbling window trigger with a maximum concurrency of one.

CHAPTER 12

Monitoring

The previous two chapters have been concerned principally with what happens to Azure Data Factory resources after you have finished developing them – how to get them into a production environment and how to run them automatically. This chapter completes a trio of requirements for operating a production ADF instance: monitoring the behavior of deployed factory resources, to ensure that individual resources – and the factory as a whole – continue to operate correctly.

Generate Factory Activity

To assist your exploration of factory monitoring tools, begin by generating a factory workload as described in the following:

1. Navigate to the *Triggers* page in the ADF Studio management hub and start the "RunEvery2Minutes" trigger from Chapter 11. When published, this will cause two pipelines to be executed every two minutes, until the trigger is stopped.

2. In the pipeline authoring canvas, open the pipeline "ImportSTFormatFile" from Chapter 6. Add a new schedule trigger to run the pipeline automatically.

3. Name the new trigger "RunEvery8Minutes" and set its *Recurrence* to every eight minutes. Click *OK* to set the pipeline parameter values.

363

© Richard Swinbank 2024
R. Swinbank, *Azure Data Factory by Example*, https://doi.org/10.1007/979-8-8688-0218-8_12

4. Set the value of the *Directory* parameter to "azure-data-factory-by-example-main/SampleData/NaughtyButNice" and the *File* parameter value to "NBN-202006.csv". Recall from Chapter 6 that this file contains a format error, so every triggered run of the pipeline will fail – the intention here is to simulate a mixed workload that contains occasional failures.

5. Save the new trigger, then click *Publish* to deploy your changes into the factory's published environment.

Remember to stop and republish the two triggers when you have finished exploring monitoring capabilities at the end of this chapter.

Inspect Factory Logs

The three Azure Data Factory components that "run" – triggers, pipelines, and activities – are reported in execution logs that can be inspected in the ADF Studio monitoring experience.

Inspect Trigger Runs

As you discovered in Chapter 11, trigger runs are reported separately from pipeline runs – open the ADF Studio monitoring experience and select the *Trigger runs* page.

1. The triggers you published in the previous section will not run until the first time indicated by their recurrence patterns after publishing, so the list of trigger runs may be empty. Use the *Refresh* button at the top of the page to update the list until you see new trigger runs start to appear.

2. By default, trigger runs during the last 24 hours are reported. Each trigger run includes details such as the trigger name, type, actual trigger execution time, and status. Notice that runs of both triggers are reported to succeed – this indicates that each trigger was able to start the associated pipeline runs, even if those runs subsequently failed.

3. Use the *Trigger time* column header to sort the list alternately into ascending and descending order of execution time. The pair of up/down arrows to the right of the column name – illustrated in Figure 12-1 – indicates that the list can be sorted using that column and identifies the column's current sort direction.

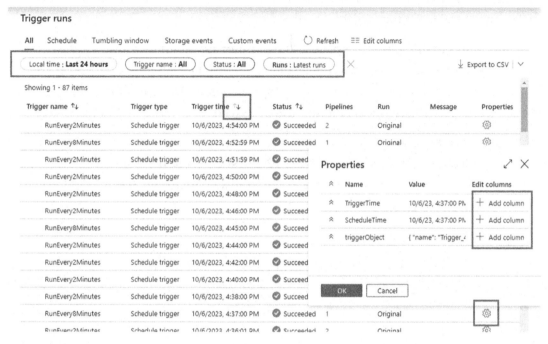

Figure 12-1. *Configure trigger runs' display order and column selection*

4. The button in the *Properties* column (gear icon) displays a dialog containing additional information specific to each trigger type. For example, in the case of a schedule trigger, this includes the run's schedule time, while for a tumbling window trigger, you can verify the associated window start and end times. You can promote these properties into list columns using the *Add column* button next to each property in the dialog (indicated in the figure).

The remaining controls at the top of the page enable you to filter the list in various different ways – for example, by trigger type, name, or status.

Inspect Pipeline Runs

The monitoring experience's *Pipeline runs* page reports runs from both the published and debugging environments. Selecting the *Debug* tab in the top left allows you to see a history of debug runs, enabling you to look at multiple prior debugging runs for a given pipeline. The *Triggered* tab lists pipeline runs that have taken place in the published environment and is the focus of this section.

1. Select the *Pipeline runs* page in the monitoring experience and ensure that the *Triggered* tab is selected. The page includes a similar set of controls to those for trigger runs, allowing you to choose which rows or columns are displayed.

2. The *Status* column reports the status of each pipeline run. For failed runs, as indicated in Figure 12-2, a speech bubble icon appears next to the status value – click the icon to inspect the associated error.

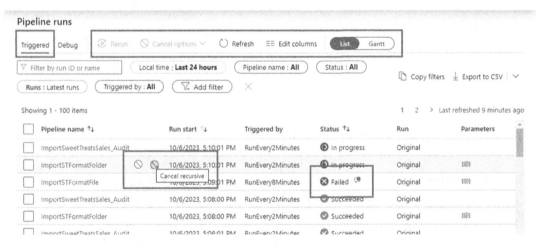

Figure 12-2. *Pipeline runs in ADF Studio's monitoring hub*

3. Hover over a pipeline's name to reveal additional controls. For pipelines still in progress – as indicated in the figure – buttons to cancel a pipeline's execution are displayed. *Cancel* stops a running pipeline, while *Cancel recursive* also stops any executions initiated by the pipeline (directly or indirectly) using the Execute Pipeline activity.

4. Hover over a completed pipeline's name to display *Rerun* and *Consumption* buttons. *Rerun* allows you to run a pipeline using the same parameter values supplied for its original run, whatever the outcome of its previous execution. (The *Run* column indicates whether a given pipeline execution was a rerun or not, with any prior runs displayed beneath the latest rerun). The *Consumption* button displays a popup summarizing resources used in the pipeline's execution.

5. Use the check boxes to the left of the *Pipeline name* column to select multiple runs. This enables you to cancel multiple running pipelines at once or to rerun several pipelines, using the *Rerun* and *Cancel* buttons at the top of the page (indicated in the figure).

6. Use the *List/Gantt* toggle at the top of the page to switch back and forth between the list of pipeline runs and a Gantt chart view. The *Edit columns* button – also available in the *Trigger runs* page – allows you to add or remove columns from the display.

7. Click a pipeline name in the list view's *Pipeline name* column to access the detail of each pipeline run's activity executions, in a layout familiar from debugging in the pipeline authoring canvas. You are unable to access nested activities using the pipeline diagram, but you can use it to select a specific activity from which to rerun a pipeline, as shown in Figure 12-3.

Figure 12-3. *Pipeline run detail*

8.   The full list of activity executions appears below the pipeline
     diagram. Use the *List/Gantt* toggle to display a Gantt chart view of
     activity runs, then click *All pipeline runs* in the top left to return to
     the list of pipeline runs.

Add Metadata to the Log

The trigger, pipeline, and activity attributes reported so far are all standard elements
of Azure Data Factory's logging functionality. Sometimes, however, it is useful to be
able to add additional metadata of your own – for example, to make it easier to identify
particular subsets of factory activity in an otherwise noisy log. The following sections
describe the use of pipeline *annotations* and activity *user properties* to achieve this.

Add a Pipeline Annotation

A pipeline annotation is a label added optionally to a pipeline's definition. Annotate your "ImportSTFormatFolder" pipeline as follows:

1. In the ADF Studio authoring canvas, open Chapter 5 pipeline "ImportSTFormatFolder," one of the two pipelines triggered by "RunEvery2Minutes."

2. Open the *Properties* flyout for the pipeline using the button at the top right of the authoring canvas. In the *Annotations* section, click the + *New* button to add a new annotation.

3. A *Name* field is displayed – enter an annotation of your choice, then save the pipeline.

Add an Activity User Property

Unlike pipeline annotations, activity user properties are name-value pairs, enabling you to specify different values for a common property across multiple activities.

1. On the pipeline design surface, select the "ImportSTFormatFolder" pipeline's Copy activity. Select the *User properties* tab in the configuration pane.

2. Click the + *New* button to add a new user property. Enter a property *Name* and *Value* of your choice.

3. Click the *Auto generate* button. This option is specific to the Copy activity and adds two copy-specific properties named "Source" and "Destination." Their values are populated with expressions that will be translated at runtime into the activity's data source and sink, then written into the pipeline run history.

4. Save the pipeline and publish your changes.

Inspect Pipeline Annotations in the Log

Annotations attached to a pipeline at the time of its execution are recorded in the log, allowing them to be used to filter and group pipeline runs. You will be able to see annotations in the log as soon as executions of the revised, annotated pipeline have taken place.

1. Open the *Pipeline runs* page in the ADF Studio monitoring experience. If the "Annotations" column is not visible, use the *Edit columns* button to add it to the display.

2. When the annotated pipeline next runs, the Annotations column will contain a luggage label icon, indicating that the run has one or more annotations. Click the icon to display the run's annotation.

3. The primary purpose of pipeline annotations is to enable you to apply custom filters to the pipeline run list. Click *Add filter*, then select "Annotations" from the dropdown list.

4. Choose your annotation value from the list, then click some empty space in the *Pipeline runs* page to apply the filter and exclude non-annotated runs from the list.

5. Remove the annotations filter, then use the *List/Gantt* toggle to switch to the Gantt chart view. By default, the Gantt chart is grouped by pipeline name – tick the *Group by annotations* check box to enable an alternative presentation. Notice that only the most recent pipeline runs appear with your annotation value – runs that took place before the annotation was created appear in the "No annotations" group.

The annotation functionality described here for pipelines and pipeline runs is also available for triggers and trigger runs. The behavior of trigger annotations is very similar and is not described separately here.

Inspect User Properties in the Log

Select one of your annotated pipeline runs to examine its activity runs in more detail. You can do this directly from the Gantt chart view by clicking the bar representing the pipeline run, then clicking the pipeline run ID value in the displayed pop-up box.

1. Locate the *User properties* column in the activity runs pane below the pipeline diagram (you may need to toggle the view back to *List* to do so). For activity runs where one or more user properties were defined, the column contains a bookmark icon – click it.

2. A *Parameters* dialog is displayed. This allows you to inspect configured user properties and their values and to promote them as columns in the activity runs list if you wish.

3. Add or remove columns using the button in the column headed *Edit columns*, then click *OK*.

4. Verify that the columns you selected for inclusion are now visible in the list of activity runs.

Inspect Factory Metrics

The structure of Azure Data Factory logs is naturally tightly coupled to the nature of factory resources, allowing concepts like triggers, pipelines, and activities to be represented in detail. In contrast, a *metric* is a simple count of a given system property, emitted and logged automatically for monitoring over time. *Azure Monitor* is a resource monitoring service used to collect data – including metrics – from all Azure resources.

Metrics emitted by ADF include factory activity levels, for example, the number of failed or successful pipeline runs. Other indicators, related to factory size and integration runtimes, contribute to an overall picture of the health of a factory instance. Inspect metrics emitted by your factory as follows:

1. Open the Azure portal, then browse to the resource blade for your data factory.

2. In the left sidebar menu, scroll down to the *Monitoring* section, then select *Metrics*.

3. The *Metrics* page displays a metric selection tool above an empty chart. (If the metric selection tool is not visible, click *Add metric* in the chart header bar.) Choose "Succeeded activity runs metrics" from the selection tool's *Metric* dropdown.

4. Click *Add metric* in the chart header bar to add another metric – this time, choose "Failed activity runs metrics."

Figure 12-4 shows these two metrics under a test workload similar to the one you created at the beginning of the chapter. In this example, the pattern is unusually regular due to the nature of the test workload.

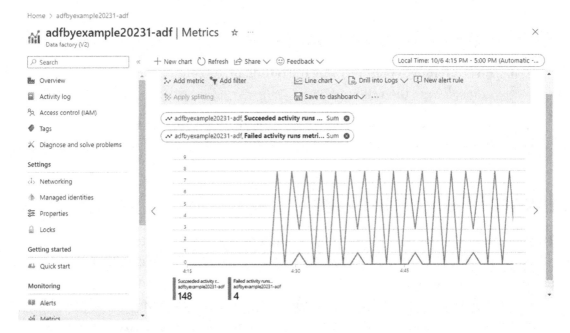

Figure 12-4. *Azure Data Factory activity runs metrics*

For SSIS developers   Metrics emitted by Azure Data Factory serve the same purpose as SSIS performance counters. They do not provide information about specific system activities but can be used in a general way to understand system health. Just as Integration Services is not the only Windows service to maintain performance counters, so many Azure resources emit resource-specific metrics that can be accessed in the same way.

Export Logs and Metrics

The log analysis capabilities offered by the ADF monitoring experience are somewhat limited, as are those for metrics in the data factory resource blade. To perform more sophisticated analysis and monitoring of the factory activity, you must export log and metric data to a service better suited to doing so. Approaches to doing this, examined in the following sections, offer the additional benefit of being able to keep diagnostic data for longer – logs generated by Azure Data Factory are purged automatically after 45 days, and metrics emitted to Azure Monitor are stored for no more than 93 days before being deleted.

Create a Log Analytics Workspace

Log Analytics is a component of Azure Monitor that supports capture and analysis of both system logs and metrics. In the next section, you will configure Azure Data Factory to send logs and metrics to Log Analytics – before doing so, you must create a Log Analytics *workspace* in which to store them.

1. In the Azure portal, create a new resource of type *Log Analytics Workspace*.

2. Select the subscription and resource group that contains your ADF instance, then under *Instance details*, enter a globally unique *Name*.

3. Ensure that *Region* matches the Azure region containing your data factory, then select *Review + Create*.

4. Review the details you have provided, then click *Create* to begin deployment.

Configure Diagnostic Settings

Every Azure resource can interact with Azure Monitor, sending logs and metrics to Log Analytics and other destinations by means of *diagnostic settings*. A diagnostic setting identifies a collection of resource logs and metrics to be sent to one or more destinations.

Diagnostic settings are not preconfigured for Azure resources. In this section, you will configure a diagnostic setting for your ADF instance, sending factory logs and metrics to blob storage and to Log Analytics.

1. Return to the resource blade for your data factory in the Azure portal, then in the *Monitoring* section of the sidebar, select *Diagnostic settings*.

2. The *Diagnostic settings* page lists settings created for the factory resource (currently none). Click + *Add diagnostic setting* to create a new one.

3. Provide a new *Diagnostic setting name*, then under *Category details,* tick check boxes to select "Pipeline activity runs log," "Pipeline runs log," and "Trigger runs log" from the *Logs* section and "AllMetrics" from the *Metrics* section.

4. Under *Destination details*, tick the "Send to Log Analytics workspace" check box to enable selection of your new workspace. Select your subscription and workspace from the respective dropdowns, and ensure that the *Destination table* toggle is set to "Resource specific."

5. Tick the "Archive to a storage account" check box to configure a storage account destination. This means that log and metric information will be streamed from your ADF instance to two separate destinations: your Log Analytics workspace and the storage account you specify here. Select your subscription and the storage account you have been using throughout from the respective dropdowns.

Note   Your existing storage account is sufficient for the purpose of this exercise, but Microsoft recommends that production logs are sent to a dedicated storage account.

---

6. Figure 12-5 shows the upper portion of the completed blade. Use the button in the top left of the blade – indicated in the figure – to save your changes.

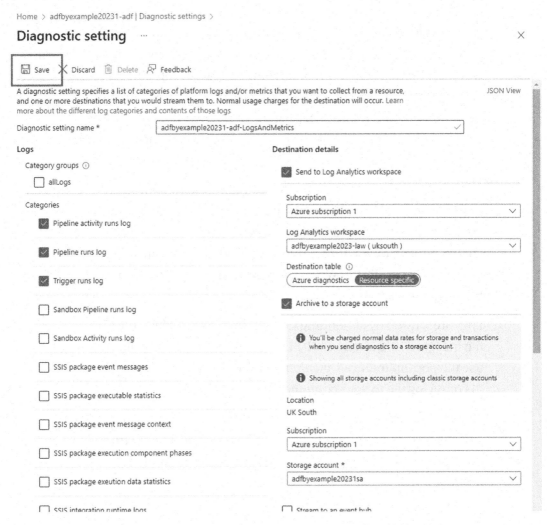

Figure 12-5. *Diagnostic setting configuration for ADF*

By default, log data sent to blob storage will remain there indefinitely, incurring ongoing storage costs. You can automatically purge older logs (or move them to a cheaper *access tier*) using a storage account *lifecycle management policy*.

Inspect Logs in Blob Storage

Blob storage is a convenient and cost-effective form of long-term storage for data of all kinds, including platform logs and metrics. It is not, however, particularly convenient for log analysis or querying, as you will see here.

1.   Open the Storage browser for your storage account in the Azure portal. As logs start to be written to your storage account – this may take around 15 minutes – new blob storage containers are created automatically to contain them. A separate container is created for metrics and another for logs from each of activity runs, pipeline runs, and trigger runs. Figure 12-6 shows the four storage account containers created by my ADF instance's diagnostic settings.

2.   Explore the activity runs container – it holds a single root folder called "resourceId=". The folder subtree corresponds to the path segments of the fully qualified Azure resource ID of the data factory, broken down further into year, month, day, hour, and minute. Keep drilling down into folders until you reach the minute folder, named something like "m=00".

3.   Logs are written by appending JSON objects to text files – the log file in Figure 12-6 is named "PT1H.json". Right-click a log file and use the pop-up menu's *Download* button (indicated in the figure) to copy a log file to your computer.

4.   Open the downloaded log file in a text editor to view its contents – you will be able to see pipeline and activity names familiar from the pipelines being triggered, along with a variety of other log information.

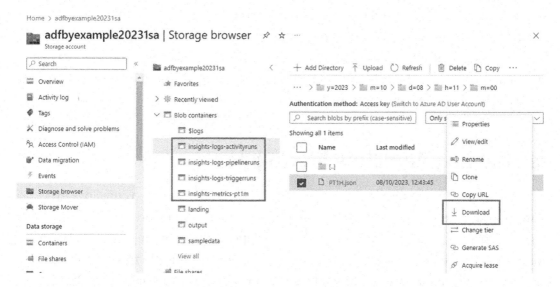

Figure 12-6. *Log and metric containers shown in Storage browser*

Alternative Diagnostic Settings Destinations

The log file you downloaded previously is not a valid JSON document – it consists of single-line JSON object definitions appended one after the other (rather than being, e.g., a true JSON array). The reason for sending log data to blob storage here was to illustrate both the possibility and some of its shortcomings – while highly cost-effective, further analysis of log data stored like this requires it to be loaded into a query engine of some kind.

Diagnostic settings for Azure Data Factory permit you to send log and metric data to up to four destinations:

- One Azure storage account

- One Log Analytics workspace

- One Azure Event Hub

- One instance of a partner solution

You have already experimented with sending logs to Azure blob storage, and in the following section, you will examine how your Azure Log Analytics workspace supports log data analysis directly.

Azure Event Hubs is a managed publish-subscribe messaging service designed for stream processing applications – unlike Azure Event Grid, it provides features to support real-time analytics such as stream partitioning and guaranteed event ordering. "Partner solutions" are supported third-party analytics and observability products such as Datadog, Elasticsearch, and Logz.io.

Use the Log Analytics Workspace

As you discovered in the previous section, using a diagnostic setting to copy logs to Azure blob storage solves only the problem of retention – further work would be required to be able to query and analyze the collected log data. As the name suggests, an Azure Monitor Log Analytics workspace can support both requirements. In this section, you will examine the tabular presentation of log data provided by Log Analytics and write queries to explore it.

1. In the Azure portal, browse to the Log Analytics workspace you created earlier in the chapter. Select *Logs* from the *General* section of the sidebar to open a new query tab.

2. If the *Queries* dialog is displayed, close it. The new query tab contains a tabbed sidebar, a query pane, and a history of recent queries.

3. Make sure that *Tables* is selected in the tabbed sidebar. The *LogManagement* section lists log tables being maintained in this workspace – as log data begins to arrive, a total of four tables appear, corresponding to the category details you selected when creating your ADF diagnostic settings. A fifth table called "Usage" reports usage data for the Log Analytics service itself.

4. Log Analytics queries are written using the *Kusto* Query Language (KQL). Kusto queries contain at least one *tabular expression statement* – a statement with table-like output. A tabular expression statement always begins with a data source, followed optionally by a sequence of transformations separated by the pipe ("|") character. The simplest query identifies a data source – one of the tables listed in the *LogManagement* section. Enter the query `ADFPipelineRun;` in the query pane and click *Run*.

5.   The query returns pipeline run details stored in Log Analytics, having been sent there by your ADF diagnostic setting – the data factory's own logs are not interrogated directly. Refine the query to return pipeline runs that have failed in the last ten minutes – the query shown in Figure 12-7 is one solution.

Figure 12-7. *Kusto query returning recent failed pipeline runs*

The tables "ADFActivityRun" and "ADFTriggerRun" report runs of pipeline activities and triggers, respectively. Run a few more queries on "ADFPipelineRun" and other tables to explore logs and metrics sent to Log Analytics by your ADF diagnostic setting. The Kusto query pane provides IntelliSense support to help you write queries more quickly.

Tip   For simple analysis of a single pipeline, it is sometimes useful to export its activity runs directly from ADF Studio. You can download a CSV file of activity runs from the monitoring experience using the *Export to CSV* dropdown (visible in Figure 12-2).

In small- to medium-sized environments, Log Analytics provides a convenient central point to gather service logs and metrics from across your Azure estate and to analyze them together. By default, data sent to a Log Analytics workspace is retained for 30 days, but you can increase this to up to 7 years.

When operating at larger scale, *Azure Data Explorer* offers the ability to query high volumes of raw log data in near real time, also using Kusto.

Receive Alerts

So far, in this chapter, you have explored how to interact with log data in the ADF Studio monitoring experience and how to do so with greater flexibility using a Log Analytics workspace. Both approaches require proactive monitoring of factory activity – a lighter-touch approach is to receive notifications automatically under prescribed conditions, requiring you to intervene only in cases of failure. The following sections introduce mechanisms available to issue *alerts* automatically in response to configured patterns of metric or log data.

Configure Metric-Based Alerts

Data factory metrics can provide useful indicators about overall system health. Configuring alerts based on metrics allows you to discover deteriorating system performance in a timely manner, before it becomes critical. In this section, you will configure an alert suitable for notifying administrators of a high pipeline failure rate.

1. Open the resource blade for your data factory in the Azure portal, then in the *Monitoring* section of the sidebar, select *Alerts*.

2. The *Alerts* page lists alerts that have been raised for the data factory – currently none. The circumstances under which an alert is raised are defined using an *alert rule*. Select the *Alert rule* option from the + *Create* dropdown at the top of the blade.

3. An alert rule has three components: its *scope, condition,* and *actions.* The scope of the new alert – the resource being monitored – is your data factory and is preselected (on the *Scope* tab). Its conditions define the circumstances under which an alert will be raised. On the *Condition* tab, select "Failed pipeline runs metrics" from the *Signal name* dropdown.

4. A chart appears automatically, displaying the signal's recent history. The *Preview* pane to the right describes in natural language when the alert will be raised – this is a summary of the conditions specified on the left under *Alert logic,* as shown in Figure 12-8.

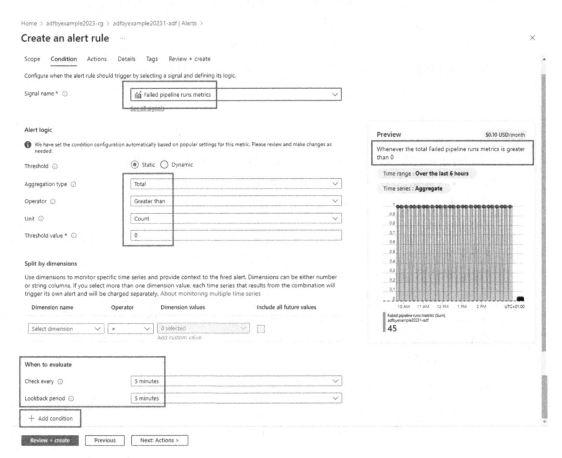

Figure 12-8. *Condition configuration during alert rule creation*

5.   Under *When to evaluate*, set the values of both *Check every* and
     Lookback period to "5 minutes." This combination of settings
     means that every five minutes, Azure Monitor will count the
     number of pipeline failures that occurred in the previous five
     minutes. If that number exceeds zero, an alert will be raised.

Tip   Together, the selected *signal*, *alert logic*, and *when to evaluate* define a single
alert condition. You can add additional conditions with the same structure using the
+ Add condition button indicated in Figure 12-8.

---

6.   Select the *Actions* tab. An alert rule's actions describe what Azure
     Monitor will do when the alert is raised. Actions are defined in an
     action group – a reusable collection of *notifications* (e.g., emails or
     SMS messages) and automated system *actions* that can be defined
     in a variety of ways (such as an Azure Function or a Logic Apps
     workflow).

7.   Open the tabbed *Create action group* blade by clicking *+ Create
     action group*. Select the subscription and resource group that
     contains your ADF instance, then under *Instance details*, enter
     the value "NotifyMe" for both the *Action group name* and
     Display name.

8.   Click *Next: Notifications* to move on to the *Notifications* tab. Select
     "Email/SMS message/Push/Voice" from the *Notification type*
     dropdown, then complete at least one option on the displayed
     flyout. In practice, your choice of notification type will be
     determined by the urgency of the alert you are creating. Click *OK*
     to close the flyout.

9.   Supply a *Name* for the new notification, then click *Review +
     create*. (For the purpose of this exercise, you need not create any
     additional notifications or actions.) Click *Create*.

10. Finally, back in the *Create an alert rule* blade, move onto the *Details* tab. Specify an *Alert rule name* of "High failure rate," select the same resource group as your data factory, and choose the *Severity* level "2 - Warning." Click *Review + create*, then *Create*.

The failure rate being detected here may not resemble a production workload but is chosen to illustrate the approach – you will now start to receive alert messages whenever the "High failure rate" alert condition is met. The "RunEvery8Minutes" trigger calling the failing pipeline does not run in every five-minute window, so this may not be immediate. Additionally, new metric-based alerts take a few minutes to come into effect in Azure.

The approach taken here to configuring alerts uses the Azure portal. Metric-based alerts for Azure Data Factory can also be created and managed from the *Alerts & metrics* page of the monitoring experience in ADF Studio.

Configure Log-Based Alerts

Receiving alerts in response to overall system health is useful from the general perspective of managing your Azure Data Factory service, but you may also have more specific notification requirements. For example, if a certain pipeline performs a particularly important data transformation process, you may wish to find out as soon as possible if it fails. In this section, you will construct an alert using a custom log query to detect failures of a specific pipeline.

1. Open your Log Analytics workspace in the Azure portal, then in the *Monitoring* section of the sidebar, select *Alerts*. As before, select the *Alert rule* option from the + *Create* dropdown.

2. Accept the default *Scope* identifying the Log Analytics workspace, then create a new alert condition using the "Custom log search" signal. Notice that the set of signals available in the *Signal name* dropdown differs from previously, because you are defining an alert in your Log Analytics resource instead of in your data factory.

3. As the name suggests, "Custom log search" enables you to create alerts based on the results of custom log queries. Selecting this option launches the Kusto query editor – enter the query given in Listing 12-1, then click *Continue Editing Alert*. (You may need to run the query in the editor to enable the *Continue Editing Alert* button.)

> **Tip**   Notice that Listing 12-1 has no terminating semicolon. Custom log search
> reduces its query result set to a count of matching rows by piping the query into
> Kusto's `count` operator. If the input query is explicitly terminated, appending "|
> count" results in an invalid expression.

4. In the *Measurement section,* set *Aggregation granularity* to "10
    minutes". Under *Alert logic,* set *Threshold value* to zero and specify
    a *Frequency of evaluation* of "5 minutes". This means that every
    five minutes, the custom log query will be executed over rows with
    a "TimeGenerated" value within the prior ten minutes.

5. Use the *Actions* tab to select the "NotifyMe" action group you
    created earlier, then on the *Details* tab, set a severity of "1 – Error".
    Provide an *Alert rule name,* click *Review + create,* then click *Create.*

Listing 12-1. Kusto query returning recent failed runs of a specific pipeline

```
ADFPipelineRun
  | where PipelineName == "ImportSTFormatFile"
  | where Status == "Failed"
```

The new rule reports an error on more specific conditions: whenever the named
pipeline fails. Windowed queries like this cannot be guaranteed to catch every error,
because there is a delay between events occurring in ADF and their being received by
the Log Analytics service. The alert frequency is intended to allow detection of failures
occurring in the previous five minutes. Its period of ten minutes allows more time for
late-arriving errors, but failure records that take more than ten minutes to arrive will not
cause an alert.

The alerts you configured in the preceding sections were based on metrics emitted
directly by your data factory and on logs sent to Log Analytics. Your ADF diagnostic
setting also sends data factory metrics to Log Analytics, so you could choose to build
ADF metric alerts there instead. The disadvantage of doing this is that it subjects metrics
to the same latency effects as other log records. Note also that ADF metrics sent to Log
Analytics appear as *log* records (in the AzureMetrics log table) – metrics reported in Log
Analytics are those emitted by that service and not by Azure Data Factory.

A more direct approach to raising alerts is to build an Azure Logic App that sends emails. While creating Logic Apps is outside the scope of this book, doing this would allow you to issue notifications from within an ADF pipeline by calling the Logic App's workflow URL (using ADF's Web activity after a prior activity has failed).

Stop ADF Triggers and Disable Alert Rules

When you have finished exploring monitoring features, stop the two triggers you started at the beginning of this chapter. Remember to publish your changes to stop the triggers in the published environment.

You should also disable the alert rules you created in the chapter. After your schedule triggers are stopped, ADF will no longer create conditions requiring notifications, but active alert rules will continue to check for them, incurring costs.

Chapter Review

In this chapter, you used factory resources developed in earlier chapters to generate a workload and then monitored it using a variety of measures and tools:

- Logs and metrics as indicators and measures of system activity and health

- The ADF Studio monitoring experience and Log Analytics to inspect and analyze logs and metrics

- Azure Monitor's alerting support to receive notifications of potential issues indicated by log and metric analyses

These tools enable you to gain insight into the workload and health of your Azure Data Factory instance, allowing you to detect and resolve issues as they arise.

Key Concepts

Key concepts introduced in this chapter include the following:

- **Pipeline annotation:** A label, added to a pipeline, that appears in the log of subsequent pipeline runs and can be used to filter or group log data. Multiple annotations can be added to a pipeline.

- **Trigger annotation:** A label, added to a trigger, providing functionality analogous to a pipeline annotation.

- **Activity user property:** A name-value pair, added to a pipeline activity, that appears in the log of subsequent pipeline runs. Multiple user properties can be added to an activity. The Copy activity supports two auto-generated properties that identify its runtime source and sink.

- **Azure Monitor:** Monitoring service used to collect, analyze, and respond to data from Azure resources.

- **Metric:** Count of a given system property, emitted automatically and logged by Azure Monitor for monitoring over time.

- **Log Analytics:** Azure Monitor component that enables sophisticated analysis of system logs and metrics.

- **Log Analytics workspace:** Identified Log Analytics provision, to which Azure resource logs and metrics can be sent for analysis and longer-term storage.

- **Diagnostic setting:** Per-resource configuration information identifying log data and metrics to be sent to other storage services, for example, a Log Analytics workspace.

- **Access tier:** Categorization of blob storage based on required frequency of access. Four tiers are available: hot, cool, cold, and archive. Warmer tiers have higher storage but lower access costs.

- **Lifecycle management policy:** Collection of user-defined rules to automate file deletion or movement to cooler access tiers.

- **Azure Event Hubs:** Managed publish-subscribe messaging service designed for stream processing applications.

- **Kusto:** Query language used to interrogate data stored in Log Analytics and Azure Data Explorer.

- **KQL:** Kusto Query Language.

- **Tabular expression statement:** Kusto query expression that returns a result set. Every Kusto query must contain a tabular expression statement.

- **Azure Data Explorer:** Analytics service for near real-time, large-scale analysis of raw data. Like Log Analytics, the service accepts read-only queries written in Kusto.

- **Alerts:** Azure Monitor supports the raising of alerts in response to configured metric or custom query output thresholds.

- **Alert rule:** Information that defines an alert – its scope (what to monitor), its conditions (when an alert should be raised), and its actions (who to notify and/or what to do when an alert is raised).

- **Signal:** Measure used to evaluate an alert condition.

- **Action group:** Defines a collection of notifications and actions, used to specify the action component of an alert rule.

- **Azure Logic Apps:** Azure service for the implementation and execution of low code automation workflows.

For SSIS Developers

Many of the logging and metric concepts presented here will be familiar to SSIS developers. Azure resource metrics are very similar to the notion of Windows performance counters and serve a comparable purpose. Just as SSIS emits performance counters specific to Integration Services, so Azure Data Factory emits ADF-specific metrics.

Automatic logging of activity will be familiar, particularly to users of the SSIS catalog, and automated log truncation may be a welcome change. Conversely, if long-term storage is required, ADF requires additional functionality in the form of Log Analytics or blob storage for indefinite retention. Users of the SSIS catalog used to being able to query and analyze SSIS logs will find comparable functionality offered by Log Analytics queries.

CHAPTER 13

Tools and Other Services

In earlier chapters of this book, you learned about the various components of Azure Data Factory and how to use them. ADF additionally provides dedicated tools for implementing standard patterns and processes quickly – armed with your understanding of the underlying technology, you will explore these tools during the first part of this chapter.

As I described in the book's introduction, its intention is to provide you with a firm grounding in Azure Data Factory, but it is impossible to ignore the existence of other services that owe much of their development to ADF. The second part of the chapter provides a brief introduction to integration pipelines in Azure Synapse Analytics and to the Data Factory experience in Microsoft Fabric.

Azure Data Factory Tools

Many of the processes built and managed by data engineers are repetitive, particularly when it comes to ingestion of data from external sources. In earlier chapters, you copied data from Azure Blob Storage and Azure SQL DB, in each case using similar information – its source system, location, schema, and so on. ETL processes commonly also consider which records to copy from a specific data source, choosing either all records, or a subset containing only records with recent updates. Another frequent question is how changes are to be integrated into a sink dataset – are existing records to be updated in situ, or is a copy of each new update to a record required?

ADF allows you to manage each of these patterns as you wish, using the components you encountered in earlier chapters. By recognizing the behaviors commonly required of ETL patterns, ADF also provides tools to automate their implementation for you.

© Richard Swinbank 2024
R. Swinbank, *Azure Data Factory by Example*, https://doi.org/10.1007/979-8-8688-0218-8_13

Prepare a Source Database

To assist your exploration of ADF tools in this chapter, in this section, you will create and populate a new Azure SQL Database. This will be used to simulate a data source to be integrated into your existing database.

Use the approach you took in Chapter 3 to create a new instance of Azure SQL DB, with the following changes:

- On the *Basics* tab, name the database "AdventureWorksLT" and select the logical SQL server you created in Chapter 3.

- In the *Data source* section of the *Additional settings* tab, set *Use existing data* to "Sample". Accept the warning message about compute and storage. Figure 13-1 shows the completed tab – when you have configured it correctly, continue to create the new database.

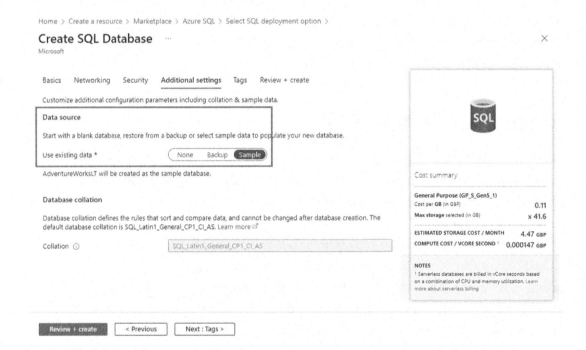

Figure 13-1. *Create SQL database using sample data source*

Metadata-Driven Data Copy

The various distinguishing features of an ETL copy process – where source data is located, the choice of records to extract, how to integrate updates – are sometimes referred to as the copy process's *metadata*. Metadata-driven data copy describes a generic implementation pattern in which process metadata is stored separately (e.g., as a *control table* in a database). In this pattern, process metadata provides a source of parameter values for a generic copy operation.

In Chapter 5, you saw how parameters for ADF pipelines, datasets, and linked services can be used to create generic pipelines. Stored pipeline parameter values can be retrieved at runtime using ADF's Lookup activity and used in pipeline expressions, providing the basis of a metadata-driven process. Rather than building such a metadata-driven data copy yourself, in this section, you will make use of a Copy Data tool wizard that collects metadata and builds the process for you.

Generate Data Copy Objects

You used the Copy Data tool's *Built-in copy task* wizard in Chapter 2. In this section, you will use its *metadata-driven copy task* wizard to build a metadata-driven process that copies data from your new [AdventureWorksLT] database. The wizard gathers the information required to build resources for a copy process – you will configure a process to copy data from multiple tables, using different patterns, into your existing database.

1. Launch the Copy Data tool as you did in Chapter 2, using the *Ingest* tile on ADF Studio's home page. (Alternatively, navigate to the authoring canvas and select the *Copy Data tool* option from the "+" dropdown at the top of the *Factory Resources* explorer).

2. On the *Properties* page, select the *Task type* "Metadata-driven copy task".

3. The *Control table data store* dropdown lists database linked services present in your data factory instance. Select the database linked service you created in Chapter 3 – this is where your control table will be stored.

4. Provide a name for the control table when prompted, ensuring that the *New table* check box is ticked. Set *Task cadence or task schedule* to "Run once now". Figure 13-2 shows the completed page – click *Next*.

Figure 13-2. *Control table configuration for metadata-driven copy task*

5. On the *Source data store* page, click + *New connection*. Choose the linked service type *Azure SQL Database* and click *Continue*. Use the *New connection* flyout to create a connection to the new "AdventureWorksLT" database.

6. When the new database linked service has been created and selected, a list appears of available tables from which to copy data (as shown in Figure 13-3). Tick the *Select all* check box, then click *Next*.

Figure 13-3. *Selecting tables from which to copy data*

7. The source configuration page allows you to specify loading behavior for each table. Select "Configure for each table individually" then notice that the default for each table is "Full load".

8. Select table [SalesLT].[Customer] and change its loading behavior to "Delta load". Set its *Watermark column name* to "ModifiedDate" and *Watermark column value start* to "1/1/2000, 12:00:00 AM". Figure 13-4 shows the configured loading behavior for [SalesLT]. [Customer]. Click *Next*.

Tip   The tool accepts a limited number of date formats for *Watermark column value start*. If you receive the error message "Delta load for table SalesLT.Customer requires a watermark column name and watermark start value", ensure that your input format is acceptable by selecting the date using the pop-up calendar.

393

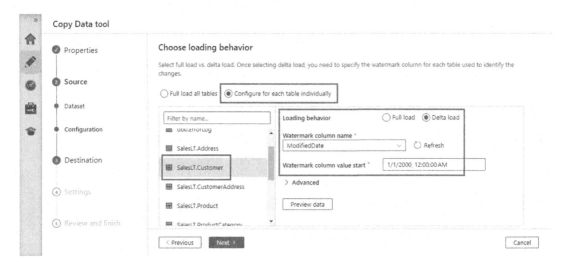

Figure 13-4. *Loading behavior for [SalesLT].[Customer]*

9. On the *Destination data store* page, select "Azure SQL Database"
    from the *Destination type* dropdown – the wizard refers to sinks
    as "destinations" – then choose the database linked service you
    created in Chapter 3. By default, each source table is mapped
    to a destination table of the same name that will be created
    automatically. Change the schema for each destination table to
    "stg", then click *Next*.

10. The tool generates default column mappings for each table by
    selecting every source column and mapping it to a target column
    of the same name. Select table [SalesLT].[CustomerAddress] to
    inspect its column mappings and to set additional sink properties.

11. In the *Azure SQL Database sink properties* pane for [SalesLT].
    [CustomerAddress] (shown in Figure 13-5), expand the *Advanced*
    section and change *Write behavior* to "Upsert". Use the *Key
    columns + New* button to add the "rowguid" column as the table's
    upsert key. Click *Next*.

Note   The term *upsert* refers to a combined update and insert operation – records with rowguid values not present in the destination table will be inserted, while existing destination records will be updated with the latest source values.

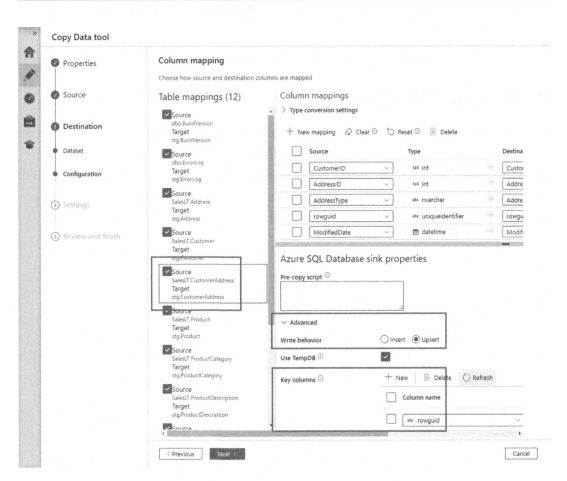

Figure 13-5. *[SalesLT].[CustomerAddress] configured for upsert*

12. On the *Settings* page, set *Task prefix name* to "Chapter13", then click *Next*. Review your summarized settings, then click *Next* again to start deployment.

13. The deployment process creates ADF datasets and pipelines but no SQL database objects. When deployment is complete, the confirmation screen displays two SQL scripts. The first script is to

create and populate the control table – copy it to your SQL client of choice, connected to your configured control table data store, and execute the query.

14. The second script creates a maintenance stored procedure for use by one of the deployed pipelines – copy this script to your SQL client and execute it.

15. Finally, return to the Copy Data tool and click *Finish*.

Run the Extract Pipeline

The deployment process you ran in the previous section created three datasets and three pipelines. Each of these resources has a name that begins with the task prefix you set in step 12, followed by a random three-character string. Resources are collected into folders named with the same prefix. Figure 13-6 illustrates a set of factory resources created by the Copy Data tool for a metadata-driven copy task.

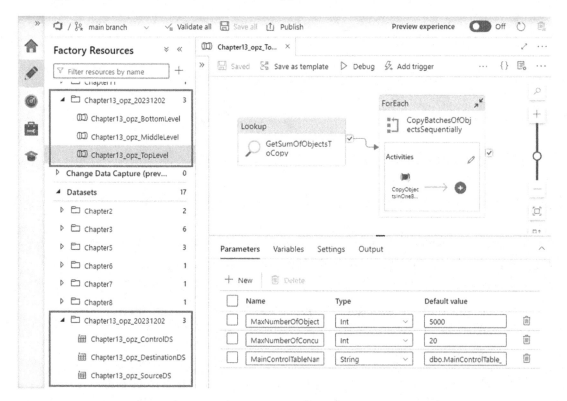

Figure 13-6. *Resources created for a metadata-driven copy task*

In the example shown in the figure, the folders and resources have the prefix "Chapter13_opz_...". The pipeline open on the design surface is "Chapter13_opz_ TopLevel".

Of the three pipelines, only the top level pipeline is intended to be called directly – it makes calls to the middle level pipeline which in turn executes the bottom level pipeline. The bottom level pipeline does the actual work of copying data; the middle and top level pipelines are concerned with splitting a large number of tables into smaller groups. This makes it possible to use these pipelines to copy thousands of data tables from the same source.

Tip   The Copy Data tool creates pipelines and datasets required to implement the copy operation. If you select a "Schedule" or "Tumbling window" task cadence when using the tool, a corresponding trigger will also be created.

Execute your top level pipeline and inspect the results as follows:

1. Run the pipeline using ADF Studio's debug mode. ADF Studio prompts for parameter values. Accept the default values, noticing the value of 20 provided for parameter "MaxNumberOfConcurrentTasks".

2. When execution has completed, use the *Output* pane below the design surface – or the *Debug* tab on the *Pipeline runs* page of the monitoring experience – to inspect pipeline executions. Notice that only one run of each pipeline is reported, because the 12 tables you copied are accommodated within the maximum number of concurrent tasks.

3. Using your SQL client for the sink database, observe that the [stg] schema has been created. Verify that it contains 12 tables and that each table contains the same number of rows as its counterpart in the AdventureWorksLT database.

4. Listing 13-1 provides a SQL query to update a subset of rows in the AdventureWorksLT database. Connect to that database and run the query.

Listing 13-1. Update a subset of source rows.

```
UPDATE [SalesLT].[Customer]
SET ModifiedDate = GETUTCDATE()
WHERE CustomerID % 10 = 0;

UPDATE [SalesLT].[CustomerAddress]
SET ModifiedDate = GETUTCDATE()
WHERE CustomerID % 10 = 0;
```

5. Run the top level pipeline a second time, wait for it to complete, then check the number of rows in each of the sink tables again.

When checking sink table row counts a second time, you will notice that most tables now contain twice as many rows as previously, with two exceptions: [stg].[Customer] contains only a few more rows, and [stg].[CustomerAddress] contains no new rows at all. This is explained by the settings you configured in the previous section:

- Most tables are configured with a *Loading behavior* of "Full load" and the default *Write behavior* of "Insert". For these tables, all rows are extracted from source every time the pipeline runs. Every extracted record is inserted into the sink table, so running the pipeline twice means that those tables now contain two complete copies of their source data.

- [stg].[Customer] has a *Loading behavior* of "Delta load". At each run, the pipeline records the highest value of [ModifiedDate] in the control table, and in the next run, only rows with a higher value are extracted. The UPDATE statement in Listing 13-1 for [stg].[Customer] updated this field for a subset of rows – these rows have been extracted again and inserted into the sink table.

- [stg].[CustomerAddress] has a *Loading behavior* of "Full load" but a *Write behavior* of "Upsert". This means that every record is extracted from the source table at each extract (even though you updated only a subset of records' [ModifiedDate] values). However, the upsert write behavior means that only new records are added to the sink table – existing records are updated in place.

You can verify these observations by inspecting the contents of the sink tables. Most tables have two copies of every row, [stg].[Customer] has two copies of a few records (one member of each pair having a recent [ModifiedDate] value), and [stg].[CustomerAddress] contains one copy of every row, some of which have a more recent value for [ModifiedDate].

Inspect the Control Table

The control table (whose name you specified when using the Copy Data tool) contains metadata used to control the behavior of pipeline runs. The top, middle, and bottom level pipelines obtain metadata from the control table at runtime to determine how pipeline execution is to proceed. Among other things, the control table indicates

- Which source tables to copy – the control table contains one row for each source table

- Which source columns to extract and to which target columns they are to be mapped

- Which source rows to extract, based on specified watermark fields and values

- Whether to integrate re-extracted data into sink tables by updating rows that already exist or by inserting new copies

Use your SQL client to connect to the sink database and inspect the control table. Notice that most columns are of type NVARCHAR and contain data in JSON format. To make changes to your metadata configuration, do not edit the table directly – instead, use the *Edit control table* feature, accessed by right-clicking the top level pipeline in the *Factory Resources* explorer (indicated in Figure 13-7).

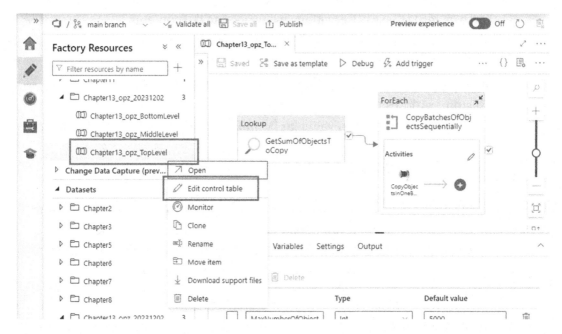

Figure 13-7. *Use the Edit control table feature to modify existing metadata-driven pipeline behavior*

Change Data Capture

As you saw in the previous section, the Copy Data tool collects and stores process metadata for use by ADF resources, creating those resources as required, along with the metadata store (control table). You have encountered each of these ADF resources – linked services, datasets, pipelines, and triggers – in earlier chapters; the novelty of the Copy data tool's metadata-driven copy task wizard is that it automatically creates them for you.

Change Data Capture (CDC) – still in preview at the time of writing – encapsulates this functionality in a single new resource type. As the name suggests, the resource is designed specifically for delta loads but otherwise uses metadata of the same kind you configured using the Copy Data tool. The difference is that when complete, your CDC resource will contain all the information required to trigger and run data extracts, without creating additional ADF resources.

Create a Change Data Capture Resource

In this section, you will create a CDC resource that copies data from your new [AdventureWorksLT] database. As in the case of the Copy Data tool, creation of a CDC resource collects metadata required to manage routine copying of multiple data sources, maintaining and using it internally within the resource.

Like other factory resources, CDC resources are created in the ADF Studio authoring canvas. Create a new CDC resource as follows:

1. In the authoring canvas, create a "Chapter13" folder in the *Change Data Capture (preview)* section of the *Factory Resources* explorer. On the new folder's *Actions* menu, click *New CDC (preview)*.

2. A flyout displaying *Choose Your Sources* options appears. Name the new CDC resource "AdventureWorksLT" and select *Source type* "Azure SQL Database". A *Source linked service* dropdown appears – select the AdventureWorksLT linked service you created using the Copy Data tool earlier in the chapter.

3. Selecting the linked service causes a list of database tables to appear, alongside *Incremental column* dropdowns that enable selection of each table's watermark column. Select tables [SalesLT].[Customer] and [SalesLT].[CustomerAddress], specifying each table's [ModifiedDate] column as *Incremental column* – this is mandatory for selected tables, because every CDC data extract is by definition a delta load. Figure 13-8 shows the upper part of the completed flyout. Click *Continue*.

Tip   When SQL Server's native CDC feature is enabled in source database tables, ADF identifies changed records using associated SQL Server CDC metadata. In such cases you are not required to specify an *Incremental column* and the dropdown is replaced by the label "SQL Server CDC".

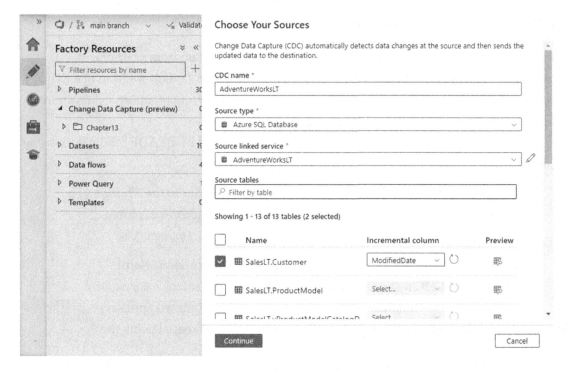

Figure 13-8. *Source configuration for ADF change data capture*

4. The flyout's *Choose Your Targets* options are displayed – the flyout refers to sinks as "targets." Select a *Target type* of "Azure SQL Database", this time specifying the linked service of your original Azure SQL DB instance.

5. The flyout's configuration defaults to the creation of new tables (referred to as entities), although if you wish you can choose tables that already exist. Click *Edit new tables* to change each target table's schema name to "chg". Figure 13-9 illustrates the result of doing this.

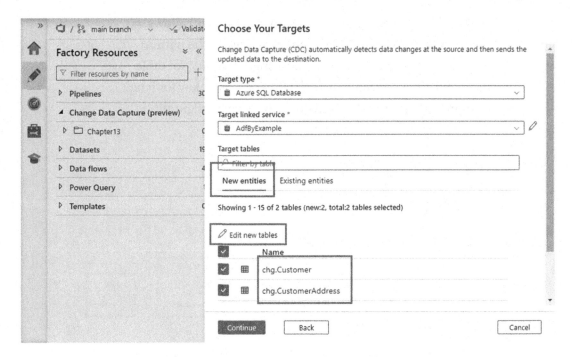

Figure 13-9. *Target (sink) configuration for ADF change data capture*

6. Click *Continue* to close the flyout. A new authoring canvas tab opens containing the details you have configured so far.

7. Like ADF data flows, execution of CDC resources takes place on a Spark cluster managed by ADF – further configuration requires an active data flow debug session. If a session has not already started, enable data flow debug as in Chapter 7, using the *Data flow debug* toggle above the design surface. Wait for the cluster to become ready before proceeding further.

8. So far, you have specified source and target tables and identified watermark columns for delta loading behavior. Column mappings and write behavior may now be configured on the design surface – although the user experience differs, this process gathers the same information as the metadata-driven copy task. For the purposes of this exercise, leave *Columns mapped* set to "Auto map", as indicated in Figure 13-10.

9. The *Keys* link (to the right of the "Auto map" toggle) allows you to specify upsert keys for each table. Repeat the pattern you used earlier in the chapter, choosing "rowguid" for table [chg].[CustomerAddress] and selecting no upsert key for [chg].[Customer]. Figure 13-10 shows the resulting configuration.

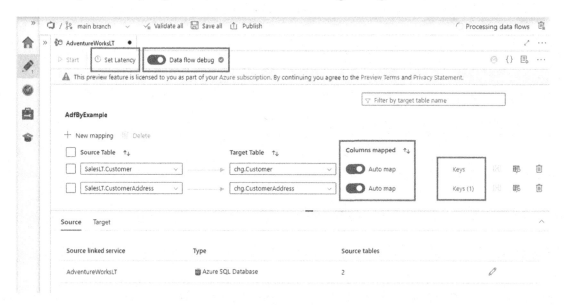

Figure 13-10. *CDC resource configured for two tables*

10. The *Set Latency* button (indicated in Figure 13-10) allows you to specify the frequency with which the CDC resource will check for changes. Latency settings produce behavior similar to a schedule trigger (introduced in Chapter 11), but no separate trigger resource is required. Use the button to set the CDC resource's latency to "Real-time", then save your changes.

11. To operate, a CDC resource must be published and started. A CDC resource's status indicates whether the *published* resource is running or not – unlike schedule triggers, a CDC resource has no `runtimeState` property, and a new CDC resource must be published before it can be started. Publish your changes to enable the *Start* button (to the left of *Set Latency*), then start the published resource.

The published CDC resource takes a few minutes to start – wait for
it to do so before moving onto the next section.

Monitor Change Data Capture

CDC resources are monitored on a dedicated page in ADF Studio's monitoring
experience.

1. In the monitoring experience, navigate to the *Change Data
    Capture (preview)* page, then select your CDC resource from the
    list. Figure 13-11 shows the activity of a CDC resource, newly
    created as described previously.

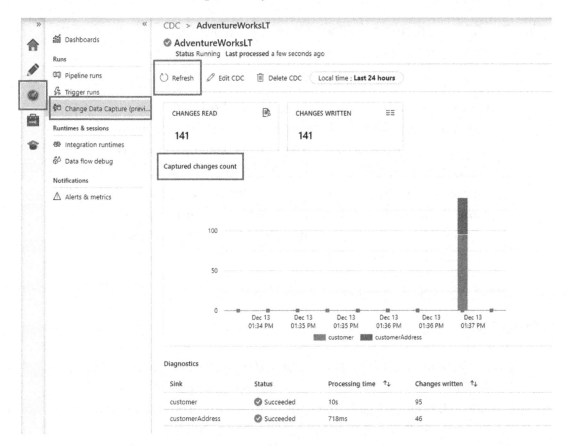

Figure 13-11. *Change Data Capture resource monitoring*

2. The *Captured changes count* chart provides detailed information
    about resource behavior. Each colored square on the chart's
    horizontal axis reports the result of checking – or *polling* – for new
    data. Notice that polling takes place several times a minute – this
    is the effect of the real-time latency setting.

3. The first few squares in Figure 13-11 are green, indicating that the
    activity succeeded, but report zero changes. A CDC resource only
    gathers changes made since it started running – if required, older
    records must be extracted separately. Use the code in Listing 13-1
    to update a few records in the two source tables.

Tip   The CDC monitoring page does not refresh automatically. Use the *Refresh*
button (indicated in the figure) to see the latest resource activity.

---

4. A red square on the *Captured changes count* horizontal axis
    indicates a failed poll – click the square for detailed information.
    At the time of writing, a CDC resource can create new tables as
    required but expects their schema already to exist. The errors
    reported in Figure 13-11 occurred when the CDC resource found
    changed records at source but was unable to create a target table
    to contain them. Use the code in Listing 13-2 to create the missing
    schema in the target database.

Listing 13-2. Create [chg] schema

```
CREATE SCHEMA [chg];
```

5. The stacked bar in the figure's *Captured changes count* chart
    shows the result of the first successful poll to return data. Use the
    code in Listing 13-1 again to cause more records to be extracted at
    the next poll. You may wish to repeat this step a few times.

6. Inspect the contents of the target tables in your Azure SQL
    Database instance. Notice that [chg].[Customer] includes
    duplicate copies of source records, but [chg].[CustomerAddress]
    does not – you specified no upsert key for [chg].[Customer], so its
    write behavior is to insert new copies of incoming records.

7. Finally, when you have finished investigating the behavior of your
    CDC resource, disable it to avoid incurring unnecessary execution
    costs. Do this using the *Stop* button found in the authoring
    workspace.

When creating your CDC resources, you may have noticed that CDC supports fewer
source types than ADF pipelines. At the time of writing, the CDC resource remains in
public preview, and support for other sources is likely to be added both before and after
the feature becomes generally available.

Related Services

Azure Data Factory is a mature, well-established service in the suite of Azure data
platform services. Azure Synapse Analytics and Microsoft Fabric are more recent
additions to that suite – each of these attempts to provide a complete data engineering
stack in one place. As such, both require services for data ingestion, low-code data
transformation, and process orchestration and both achieve this using technology
closely related to Azure Data Factory.

Azure Synapse Analytics

Azure Synapse Analytics brings together, in one place, much of the infrastructure
commonly used by an enterprise data platform. A *Synapse Analytics workspace* is
linked to a data lake (provided separately by an Azure storage account) and enables
data processing and analysis using SQL Server, Spark, and Azure Data Explorer (ADX)
analytic pools.

Movement of data into and around the data lake and orchestration of SQL, Spark, and
ADX processes can be achieved using *Synapse pipelines*. Synapse pipelines are similar
to ADF pipelines and have a familiar, low-code authoring experience, located within the
Synapse Studio online IDE's *Integrate hub* (shown in Figure 13-12; the different parts of
Synapse Studio accessed from the navigation sidebar are referred to as *hubs*).

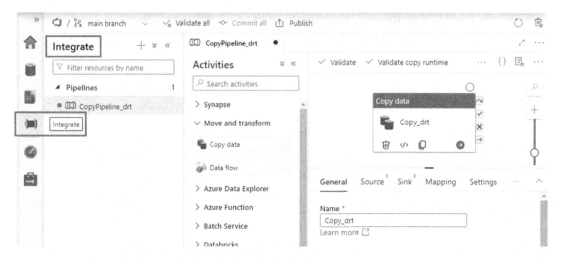

Figure 13-12. *Synapse Studio Integrate hub*

With a few cosmetic differences – such as those indicated in the figure – the pipeline creation experience is very like that of ADF Studio. Pipelines continue to interact with data and services using the abstractions of datasets and linked services, but resource types visible in ADF Studio's authoring experience are frequently located elsewhere in Synapse Studio:

- Datasets – in Synapse referred to as *integration datasets* – are found in Synapse Studio's *Data hub*.

- As in ADF, linked services can be edited in the *Manage hub*, but also in the Synapse Studio data hub. A linked service to the Synapse workspace's data lake is provisioned automatically at workspace creation.

- Data flows are managed in the *Develop hub* but as in ADF are executed in pipelines using the Data flow activity.

Internal compute resource for pipelines is provided via integration runtimes, in the same way as in ADF, with some small differences. A Synapse workspace can be configured at creation to use a *managed workspace virtual network* – Azure IRs created in such a workspace automatically use the workspace's VNet. Managed Apache Airflow is not available.

At the time of writing, neither Power Query data wrangling nor CDC resources are supported. Pipelines are invoked using triggers, just as in ADF, and both pipeline and trigger runs can be observed in the same way using the *Monitor hub*.

Microsoft Fabric

Microsoft Fabric became generally available in November 2023. Like Synapse Analytics, Fabric supports data engineering workloads based on Spark, SQL, and ADX and uses data pipelines to ingest data and orchestrate processing activities. Fabric data pipelines – located in Fabric's *Data Factory experience* – are evolved from Azure Data Factory pipelines and contain many features familiar to users of ADF. Figure 13-13 shows a Fabric data pipeline illustrating that, although the user experience is somewhat different, a familiar set of pipeline activities is supported.

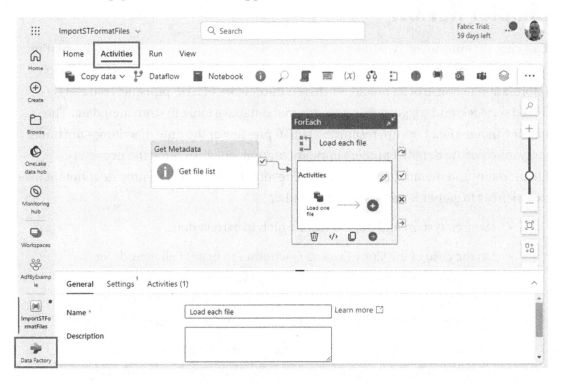

Figure 13-13.   *Data pipeline in Microsoft Fabric*

The advantages of Microsoft Fabric over Azure Synapse Analytics are outside the scope of this book, but a general improvement is that many more elements of infrastructure are managed for you – a Fabric tenant includes a single managed data lake, called *OneLake*, and all compute resources are provided as serverless services. This means that – unlike in ADF and Synapse – the notion of an integration runtime is redundant. *Connections* take the place of linked services for external storage, and internal (OneLake) storage connections are provisioned automatically. Low-code support for data transformation is available in the form of *Dataflow Gen2*, a data wrangling experience using Power Query – ADF-style data flows are not supported.

At the time of writing, many enterprise-level features – such as Git integration or VNet support – are unavailable or incomplete, but the service is evolving rapidly. Microsoft's published product roadmap, including changes related to the Data Factory experience, is available at `https://aka.ms/FabricRoadmap`.

Chapter Review

This chapter introduced two tools in Azure Data Factory that assist the implementation of data ingestion processes. The Copy Data tool's metadata-driven copy task collects information to construct a metadata-driven framework of ADF pipelines, datasets, linked services, and triggers, using an external database table to store metadata. The newer Change Data Capture resource – still in preview at the time of writing – abstracts away much of the detail of process implementation, encapsulating the necessary functionality and metadata in a single ADF resource. The two tools provide different user experiences to gather broadly similar metadata:

- Source system and objects from which to extract data.

- In the case of the Copy Data tool, whether to extract all records, or only those identified as having been updated since the previous extract. (The CDC resource only supports the latter, delta load approach.) The tool describes this as the process's *loading behavior*.

- The frequency with which new extracts are to be attempted. The Copy Data tool describes frequency with the terms "cadence" and "schedule," while the CDC resource refers to extract "latency."

- Sink system and objects into which to load data. The language used in ADF Studio to describe sinks is not always consistent – the Copy Data tool uses the term "destination," while the CDC resource specifies "target" data objects.

- Source and sink object and column mappings.

- Whether to load each extracted row as a new record, or to update the copy already in existence. (The Copy Data tool describes this as the process's *write behavior*.)

The second part of the chapter provides brief introductions to comparable data pipeline functionality in two other Microsoft services: Azure Synapse Analytics and Microsoft Fabric. The origin of pipeline implementations in both services can be traced back to Azure Data Factory, and users of ADF will find many similarities when developing data copying, transformation, and orchestration processes in those environments.

Key Concepts

- **Metadata-driven data copy:** A pattern for structuring data copy operations using generic resources which accept object-specific configuration information as parameters. Parameter values are stored separately as operation metadata.

- **Metadata-driven copy task:** Wizard provided by ADF Studio's Copy Data tool to guide the implementation of metadata-driven data copy using ADF pipelines, storing metadata in a database table.

- **Cadence:** The metadata-driven copy task describes extract frequency using the term "cadence" or "schedule."

- **Control table:** Refers to the database table created by the metadata-driven copy task to store metadata in JSON format. Do not modify this table directly – use the "Edit control table" feature to make changes to process metadata.

- **Loading behavior:** Term used by the metadata-driven copy task to describe whether a process extracts all data or only a subset of rows.

- **Delta load:** Refers to a process that extracts a subset of rows, usually those identified as having changed since the previous extract.

- **Watermark:** Value used by a delta load process to determine whether a record falls into the subset to be extracted from a source system. Values such as source record modification timestamps are frequently used as watermarks.

- **Destination:** The metadata-driven copy task frequently describes copy operation sinks as "destinations."

- **Upsert:** An operation that integrates incoming data into a sink dataset by updating existing records and inserting new ones.

- **Write behavior:** Term used by the metadata-driven copy task to describe whether a process integrates data by upserting it or simply by appending (inserting) incoming records.

- **Change Data Capture (CDC):** ADF resource that encapsulates a metadata-driven delta loading process.

- **Target:** ADF CDC resources describe copy operation sinks as "targets."

- **Latency:** ADF CDC resources describe extract frequency using the term "latency."

- **SQL Server CDC:** Native SQL Server feature that enables the database engine to track and record changes to table rows. When extracting from a CDC-enabled SQL Server table, ADF CDC resources use SQL Server CDC metadata for watermarking.

- **Monitoring:** CDC resources can be monitored using a dedicated page in ADF Studio's monitoring experience. Metadata-driven processes built using the Copy Data tool are implemented using pipelines and triggers, so they can be monitored as described in Chapter 12.

- **Azure Synapse Analytics:** Integrated data and analytics IaaS service in Microsoft Azure.

- **Synapse Analytics workspace:** Instance of Azure Synapse Analytics.

- **Synapse pipelines:** Sometimes referred to as integration pipelines, an ADF-like tool for copying data, transforming data, and orchestrating processes in Azure Synapse Analytics.

- **Synapse Studio:** Web-based IDE for development in Azure Synapse Analytics workspaces.

- **Integrate hub:** Synapse Studio functionality is organized in "hubs"; pipeline implementation takes place in the Integrate hub.

- **Integration dataset:** As in ADF, data objects are abstracted as datasets in Azure Synapse Analytics but are referred to as *integration* datasets.

- **Microsoft Fabric:** Integrated data and analytics SaaS service that supersedes Azure Synapse Analytics.

- **Data Factory experience:** Microsoft Fabric functionality is organized in "experiences"; pipeline implementation takes place in the Data Factory experience.

- **Dataflow Gen2:** Low-code data transformation tool in Microsoft Fabric, similar to Power Query in Azure Data Factory and elsewhere.

For SSIS Developers

Column metadata is tightly coupled to SSIS data transformations at development time, making the implementation of metadata-driven solutions difficult to achieve natively.

In contrast, Azure Data Factory's requirement for metadata is frequently delayed until runtime. This means that ADF pipelines are tolerant of schema evolution and that it is possible to inject parameterized schema information at runtime, as in the case of pipelines created by the metadata-driven copy task.

Index

A

ABS_CSV_CandyShack dataset, 83, 141–142

ABS_CSV_SweetTreats dataset, 71, 75, 78, 142, 155

Access policy, 132

Access tier, 375

Acme Boxed Confectionery (ABC), 37

Action group, 382

Activities toolbox, 46, 47, 96, 107, 121, 156, 188, 207, 282, 299

Activity dependency, 107, 108, 158, *See also* Dependency conditions

Activity user properties, 369

adf_publish branch, 21, 306, 316, 317, 319, 320, 322

ADF Studio

  Factory Resources explorer, 78

  Git branch dropdown, 51

  home page, 13

  IDE, 12

  linked service connection, 42, 44

    (*see also* Linked services)

  management hub, 20

  navigation header bar, 13–15

  navigation sidebar, 15–16

  storage key, 39

  web-based IDE, 23–25

ADF tools

  CDC (*see* Change Data Capture (CDC))

  copy process's metadata, 391

  create, SQL database, 390

  ETL patterns, 389

and services

  Azure Synapse Analytics, 407–408

  Microsoft Fabric, 409–410

Airflow environment, 286–288

Airflow IR, 287

Alert rule, 380–385

Alerts, 380–385

Amazon Web Services (AWS), 33

Apache Airflow, 286, 408

Apache Spark, 207

Append variable activity, 121

Array variables, 124

Authoring canvas, 15, 29, 44, 45, 52, 67, 95, 96, 208, 210, 240, 275, 282, 322, 334, 350, 367, 391, 401

AutoResolveIntegrationRuntime, 48, 251, 253, 254, 259, 266

Az.DataFactory module, 327

Azure account creation, 2

Azure Active Directory (AAD), 3, 4

Azure Blob Storage (ABS), 39, 43, 70, 90, 151, 276, 378

Azure custom role, 313

Azure Data Explorer (ADX), 380, 387, 407

Azure Data Factory (ADF)

  deployment blade, 11

  description, 1

  external compute, 47

  internal compute, 47 (*see also* Integration runtime)

  vs. SSIS, 56

Printed in the United States
by Baker & Taylor Publisher Services